The Quiz Show

TV Genres

Series Editors
Deborah Jermyn (Roehampton University)
Su Holmes (University of East Anglia)

Titles in the series include:

The Quiz and Game Show
by Su Holmes
978 0 7486 2752 3 (hardback)
978 0 7486 2753 0 (paperback)

Forthcoming titles include:

Reality TV
by Misha Kavka

The Sitcom
by Brett Mills

The Quiz Show

Su Holmes

Edinburgh University Press

© Su Holmes, 2008

Edinburgh University Press Ltd
22 George Square, Edinburgh

Typeset in Janson and Neue Helvetica
by Servis Filmsetting Ltd, Stockport, Cheshire and
printed and bound in Great Britain by
CPI Antony Rowe, Chippenham, Wilts

A CIP record for this book is available from the British Library

ISBN 978 0 7486 2752 3 (hardback)
ISBN 978 0 7486 2753 0 (paperback)

Contents

List of Figures   vi
Acknowledgements   vii

Introduction: Game On   1
1   Genre and the Quiz Show   11
2   Quiz Show Histories   32
3   Quiz Show Theory: Approaching the Programme Text   58
4   Knowledge in the Quiz Show   86
5   The Quiz Show and 'Ordinary' People as Television
    Performers   118
6   'Asking the Audience': Quiz Shows and Their Viewers   140
Conclusion: 'Not the Final Answer . . .'   162

Bibliography   166
Index   175

List of Figures

Figure 3.1   The *Mastermind* chair: 'I suddenly had a vision
             of the Inquisition'. Credit: Rex Features   64
Figure 3.2   Dale Winton goes 'wild in the aisles' with
             Supermarket Sweep. Credit: Rex Features   79
Figure 4.1   The first UK millionaire winner, Judith Keppel
             (2000). Credit: Rex Features   102

Acknowledgements

Thanks go to staff at the BBC Written Archive Centre (especially Els Boonen) for making the historical research in this book both possible and pleasurable. Thanks also go to the University of Kent for funding initial research trips to the archives, and to the University of East Anglia for allowing me to transfer my research leave when I took up my position there in 2007. Thanks also go to Sarah Edwards at EUP for commissioning the book (and the 'TV Genres' series as a whole), and for providing editorial advice and support. Thanks go – as always – to Deborah Jermyn for valuable intellectual and personal support, as well as to Nick Rumens and Aylish Wood. Lastly, thanks go to the 'Real TV' class (University of Kent, Autumn, 2006) for fully embracing the study of quiz shows, and for demonstrating why the idea behind this book was worthwhile.

Introduction:
Game On

In the summer of 2005, *Big Brother* was enjoying its sixth series in the UK. In one edition, the voice-over explains how the time is '3:21 pm, and the housemates are playing a quiz game in the garden'. Housemate Derek beams 'Welcome to "Quizmaster" on a sunny afternoon' (addressing both his fellow contestants and the home audience). Having elected himself as host and question-master, Derek promptly splits the remaining housemates into two teams, and then explains the rules of the game. Questions will cover a range of subjects and 'on certain questions, there will be no conferring'. With the 'contestants' arranged in two teams on the grass, Derek presents the first question to Team One ('Which attack caused America to go to war with Germany?'). At this point Kemal – a highly vociferous and flamboyant housemate – starts to laugh and chat, already impatient with the game. Derek swiftly interjects: 'If you're going to talk you can go back [inside] . . . do you understand?' Following Kemal's interruption, Team One asks to hear the question again. 'The rules are that the question will not be repeated,' Derek insists, and then bolsters his decision by explaining: 'The secret of learning is to shut up'. Kemal retorts: 'Well, nobody would tune into this [quiz] show, as it's all about *you*. [Viewers] . . . want the "drama" of winning, not a boring history class' (2 June 2005).

Contemporary educational theorists would no doubt find Derek's conception of learning problematic, but this sequence is fascinating for dramatising some of the cultural and generic rules which structure the television quiz show. In *Big Brother*, the housemates talk incessantly and self-reflexively about what will make 'good TV' – as based on their own previous experience of viewing the show. But in the scenario above, the housemates above refer less to the past of *Big Brother* than to another popular television form, the quiz show. The housemates' decision to play 'Quizmaster' as a way of alleviating their boredom indicates how quizzes and games are a cultural practice which exist beyond the boundaries of the television screen. But the sequence also recognises that quizzes are a *television* genre, which must work to engage an audience in particular ways. Kemal is insistent that the quiz show is less about education than watching 'ordinary' people compete under pressure (viewers 'want the "drama" of winning, not a boring history class'). The sequence then goes on to dramatise, or playfully exaggerate, some of the generic conventions of the quiz show, and their relationship with knowledge, power and control. As the quizmaster and host, Derek occupies the highest position of power. The title of the show, 'Quizmaster', also states this dominance. The contestants are permitted to answer questions when asked, but they are not permitted to answer back, or to interject at moments when their participation is not required. Derek relishes his role as quizmaster, and as the questions get progressively harder, he delights in chastising the 'contestants' for their lack of intelligence, while seizing the opportunity to display his own knowledge of the quiz show categories. Derek, a cravat-wearing, Tory political speechwriter with a decidedly upper-class accent, had often complained throughout the series about the dearth of intellect in the house (frequently calling the other housemates 'peasants'). In this regard, his suggestion that the other contestants are his intellectual inferiors consolidated his persona in the house.

As the interruptions from Kemal clearly suggest, the contestants may occupy a subordinate role, but this does not mean they are passive. 'Real' or 'ordinary' people are important for what Kemal refers to as 'the drama of winning', but they also pose challenges for hosts and producers when 'the very qualities that make them "real" make them more difficult to manage in routine ways' (Grindstaff, cited in Macdonald 2003: 80). In terms of the performances offered by the contestants, there are also notable differences in how the housemates respond to the game. It is the male housemates who drive the scenario, and despite the highly confident and outspoken personalities usually displayed by the female housemates, they look on in this instance with a mixture of boredom and disdain – more interested in sunbathing and sleeping than playing quizzes with the boys. But while Derek may approach the game with gusto, and apparently occupy the key position of authority, he also offers what (in the Western context) is a rare image of a quiz show host. Derek may be decidedly upper-class, but he is also black and gay, and his image functions as an uneasy reminder that, in the television world beyond the *Big Brother* house, the collective cultural experience of quiz shows has historically been 'shared' in particular ways.

This otherwise relatively forgettable scene from a summer's *Big Brother* viewing is fascinating in the context of this book. It dramatises, in a microcosm, a number of generic rules and cultural discourses which have worked to shape the past and present of the television quiz show. The issues at stake here, and how we might approach them, are the focus of this book.

'If you are rubbish you work in quiz or game shows': questions of cultural value

In the scene above, the *Big Brother* contestants acknowledge the ubiquity of the television quiz or game show, and we need only note how quickly quiz show catchphrases enter the linguistic bloodstream (from 'Come on down!', 'I've started so I'll finish . . .', 'Is that your final answer?', to 'You are the weakest link – goodbye!'). But the same recognition could not be attributed to scholarship on popular television. Impressive work on quiz shows does exist, and the writing of this book would not have been possible without it, but Morris B. Holbrook rightly notes how 'it is almost universally acknowledged that quiz and game shows have received less than their fair share of attention' (1993: 32). Quiz and game shows are rarely perceived as prestigious forms of national television (Moran 1998), and aside from first editions, they are rarely reviewed. Yet critics have always had plenty to say about their popularity, values and perceived cultural 'effects'. Whether described as 'sick-making programmes'[1] or 'an affront to human dignity and intelligence',[2] it is clear that a number of themes have historically shaped the cultural reception of the genre. As the *Sunday Express* neatly summarises when discussing the British version of *The Price is Right* in 1986: '[Quiz and game shows are] rubbish, chewing gum for the eyes. They encourage greed. They whip us hysteria. They offer something for nothing – contradicting the Victorian work ethic that hard work is the path to reward'.[3]

The critic expresses distaste for the valorisation of consumerism – something which apparently reflects the worst excesses of modern capitalist societies. At the same time, concern also circles around the genre's endorsement of a 'get-rich-quick mentality', the circumventing of the protestant work ethic, and the undermining of the mythical trajectory of the American Dream (in which monetary success is meant to follow hard work). In the context of television and cultural studies, quiz and game shows have only benefitted from the expanding academic interest in popular television in limited ways. David Lusted observes the 'critical sniping' which has circled around the academic discussion of the form (1998: 180), and academics have expressed a mixture of fascination and despair at 'the extraordinary event of an entire studio audience applauding a rotary iron' (Lewis 1984: 43).

This book draws upon interviews with a limited number of industry personnel who are linked to companies which produce, or schedule (Challenge TV), quiz and game shows (and the particular programmes in question are referred to later in the book). The interviews were undertaken with Mike Beale, deputy managing director of 12yard Productions; Colman Hutchinson, one of the executive producers of the UK *Who Wants to Be a Millionaire*; Danny Greenstone, executive producer of Talkback Thames; and Celia Taylor, deputy controller of Challenge TV. The idea that the quiz/game show makes little claim to be 'art' (representing a cheap form of television with several editions often filmed in one sitting) was often acknowledged by the industry personnel. As Mike Beale explains:

> There's this hierarchy, . . . I think, where if you're really the best you work in movies, if you are OK you work in TV drama or documentary, if you're not really that good you work in sitcom, and basically if you are rubbish you work in reality [TV] and quiz or game [shows]. (Beale 2006)

Perceptions of cultural value are returned to throughout this book, and it is clear that Beale nods toward a media, as well as generic, hierarchy here (film 'above' television). But while Beale positions quiz and game shows at the bottom of the generic pile, Jason Mittell observes how the quiz show

> [R]esides in a liminal space within cultural hierarchies, fluidly crossing the boundaries between highbrow and lowbrow, legitimation and condemnation . . . [Q]uiz shows have alternately been hailed as cultural enrichment and educational, or as corrupting influences encouraging gambling, . . . and dumbed down intellects . . . (Mittell 2007)

Thus, in the construction of the genre's low cultural value, it seems that particular generic examples are foregrounded over others, and these examples then come to stand in for the genre 'as a whole'. The intellectual and cultural distaste angled at *The Price is Right* is a case in point (and this antipathy has in turn been shaped by negative attitudes toward consumerism).

Television has recently extended its relationship with games and everyday life. The growth of reality TV and make-over TV has demonstrated the flexibility and appeal of game structures, with communal living, surveillance (*Big Brother*), food rationing (*Survivor, I'm a Celebrity . . . Get Me Out of Here!*), sleep deprivation (*Shattered*), homedecorating (*Changing Rooms*), house-buying (*To Buy or Not To Buy*), antique hunting (*Bargain Hunt*) and job interviewing (*The Apprentice*), all presented as a form of play. Indeed, despite the resurgence in the quiz show in the late 1990s and early 2000s, largely as a result of the global success of *Who Wants to Be a Millionaire*, television studies seemed more interested in the intellectual 'buzz' surrounding reality TV. Unlike reality TV, more traditional quiz and game shows have rarely been seen as 'cool', partly because they have often been situated as family, rather than youth-orientated, fare. In the words of *Entertainment Weekly*, 'even [American] successes like *Jeopardy!*, *Wheel of Fortune* and *The Price is Right* have a stigma with youth hungry-advertisers: the viewers are notoriously gray' (Jacobs 1996).

The students on my undergraduate module 'Real TV: Television and the Construction of Popular Reality' often tell me that they rarely watch quiz shows, and many of them had not seen a full edition of *Who Wants to Be a Millionaire* before I screened it. Yet the quiz show regularly proves to be the most popular choice as an essay topic, perhaps because it becomes especially 'defamiliarised' through analysis. Part of the project of television (and cultural) studies is precisely to defamiliarise the everyday, and to make apparent the cultural politics and power relations which sit at the centre of the 'taken for granted'. Writing in *Screen Education* back in 1982 (when the idea of 'television studies' was still new), Adam Mills and Phil Rice took the opportunity to observe how:

> Nothing presents itself as a thing so familiar, so immediate and yet so intangible and enigmatic as popular television. The *same ease* with which it can be understood . . . seems to act as a barrier to its analysis – its very *obviousness* placing it in a blind-spot of intelligibility [my italics]. (Mills and Rice 1982: 15)

In this regard, it is interesting that Mills and Rice were actually writing about quiz shows, and they foregrounded the genre as exemplary of how television's 'everydayness' seems to resist analysis. When compared to other genres such documentary or news, it is easy to assume that the quiz or game show constructs only a television reality, a space with no apparent connection to the world 'out there'. Michael Skovmand outlines how the quiz/game show has been seen as an 'an unlikely vehicle for political debate' (2000: 367), while Anne Cooper-Chen suggests that the shows' apparently 'apolitical nature' appeals to television advertisers (1994: 16). Yet given that games are the product of a social and cultural construction, 'all play means something' (Huizinga 1970: 19), and Jeremy Butler observes how quiz and game shows *do* interact with social reality, but they do so on their own terms

(2002: 83). The aim of this book is to explore how and why the television quiz show represents an important and rewarding focus of study. The book is interested in the key approaches which have been used to study the genre, aspects of its historical development, and how this development has been shaped by different national contexts (Britain and America). It is also interested in what academics, critics, producers, regulators and audiences have to say about the genre, and how these perspectives can contribute to knowledge of its historical, political and cultural significance.

America: 'land of the game show'?

As the most prolific devisor of quiz/game show formats, America has historically been perceived as the 'Land of the Game Show'.[4] As a British press critic noted following the early American success of *Who Wants to be a Millionaire*, for a 'British game show to sell to the States is really [like selling] coals to Newcastle' (Barber 2000: 3). The cultural traffic in quiz/game formats has traditionally moved from America *to* Britain. As Glen Creeber describes,

> Historically, Britain has always looked to America for quiz shows, their more commercially minded broadcasting system appearing to provide the perfect breeding ground for new and original formats. In contrast, Britain's public service ethos tended to view the genre with great suspicion . . . [A] condescending attitude toward the genre stunted the creation and development of original British game shows for decades to come, consistently importing but rarely exporting its own formats. Even when successful American quiz and game shows were transferred from Britain, prizes and prize money had to be considerably lowered in order to satisfy the strict regulations of the British broadcasting authorities. (2004: 232)

There is certainly some truth to Creeber's summary here, but it also paints a picture in which British television's relations with the quiz show are awkward and uncomfortable, lacking the more 'natural' fit which is seen to characterise the American context. Perhaps most crucially, it also implies that the British history might not be too much 'fun'.

Where work on quiz show history does exist it largely refers to the American context (Anderson 1978; Hoerschelmann 2006; DeLong 1991). In fact, to bring together the period of the 1950s with the term 'quiz show' is to immediately conjure up associations of the notorious American quiz show scandals. Jason Mittell suggests, for example, that 'the scandals were certainly the most significant contribution of the quiz show genre to media history' (2004a: 32). It may be legitimate to make such a claim with respect to the *American* history of the genre, but it seems more problematic when positioned in relation to the genre as a whole, especially when so much of its history remains unwritten. Indeed, with regard to the history of the quiz show in the British context, it would be misleading to suggest that it simply offers a pale imitation of the 'real' history in the US.

To be sure, while the American history may have dominated existing academic work, its 'dominance' is cast in negative terms at the level of popular debate. America's status as the 'Land of the Game Show' is often seen as pivoting on the country's association with capitalist greed, commerciality, consumerism and media imperialism.

The power relations involved in American and cultural imperialism *do* play a role in shaping the construction of media history, but it is evidently far from appropriate to paint Britain, and British television, in the role of struggling 'underdog' here. There never has been a proportionate reciprocity of influence in the flow of quiz and game show formats where the relationship between Britain and American is concerned. As already demonstrated by Creeber's quote above, America has historically sold formats *to* Britain. Yet in wider terms, and as a developed Western nation itself, Britain is just as likely to be painted a 'surrogate American' (rather than a victim) in debates about media imperialism (Steemers 2004: 12). It would be misleading to paint British television as a 'vulnerable' repository of American culture, and it is more appropriate to suggest that there is an interesting narrative to be told about aspects of comparison, intersection and difference. This is not necessarily best characterised by vaguely held stereotypes (in which the history of British 'public service' television is contrasted with the apparently rampant commercialism of the American context). Institutional differences in broadcasting systems, as well as the significance of cultural values, *can* be revealing, but such comparisons should be based on research and analysis, rather than 'common-sense' generalisations.

Chapter summaries

When analysing a quiz show, it is possible to break the text down into aspects such as prizes, set, knowledge, host, and the roles offered to 'ordinary' people as contestants (Whannel 1992). These aspects clearly work together to produce particular connotations and effects. But as this is a longer study which deals with a number of these aspects in detail (and by chapter), it has been necessary to separate out particular themes for the purpose of analysis.

As part of a series of books about television genres, this book seeks to draw upon, and contribute to, debates about television genre as a concept. Chapter 1 thus explores how the designated object of the 'quiz show' cannot be taken for granted. Moving across the definitions used by critics, academics, regulators and viewers, it explores how the category of the quiz show is articulated and used (and this involves exploring the perceived differences between a 'quiz show' and a 'game show'). Drawing primarily on a discursive approach to television genre (Mittell 2004a), the chapter does not seek to provide a definitive and factual account of the generic elements which constitute a quiz show. Rather, it is interested in exploring how generic categories are used in this field, and how they can contribute to the study of the genre.

Although each chapter deals with questions of history and development to some degree, Chapter 2 is specifically concerned with the earlier development of the quiz show. Drawing on archival sources, it examines the disparate generic roots of the quiz show in the British and American contexts, while also considering how the development of the genre was shaped by the institutional structures of broadcasting in each case. This has a greater significance than simply indicating the 'early' history of the genre, as the book makes clear how debates or policies which were associated with the early radio quiz or television quiz show continue to have a resonance today. In this respect, while there has evidently also been a great deal of change, the earlier period is nevertheless valuable in foregrounding – often in sharper form – the debates and attitudes which continue to shape aspects of the contemporary quiz show. One of the key issues in this regard is the regulation of the genre (including, for example, the regulation of prizes). As Chapter 2 suggests, the institutional infrastructures and policies which regulate quiz shows are far from simply factual information which represents a useful 'background' to the programmes themselves. They offer insight into the cultural attitudes surrounding the quiz show, while also exerting a shaping influence on its textual form.

Chapter 3 is more concerned with the analysis of the quiz show as it appears on screen. With regard to aspects such as set design, space and colour, it examines how we can analyse the aesthetics of the genre, and the game spaces which are produced. The chapter also examines how to conceptualise these spaces – especially with regard to questions of power. Johan Huizinga's famous study of play argues that play 'is not "ordinary" or "real" life', but a 'stepping out of "real" life into a temporary sphere of activity with a disposition all of its own' (1970: 29). This description certainly captures the sometimes utopian quality of game spaces (they encourage a sense of 'what if?' and may permit rewards, actions and sentiments which are usually denied in the every-day world). Yet as the chapter explores, it is also problematic to describe game spaces as somehow separate from the social order (Dovey and Kennedy 2006: 33). Drawing on particular case studies, the chapter demonstrates how although games may have a liminal quality, they remain deeply implicated within the politics of the everyday.

One of the key themes in existing academic work has been the construction of knowledge in the quiz show. It is widely accepted that knowledge *is* power (Foucault 1990), and Chapter 4 examines how this can be applied to the quiz show. There are many different ways of approaching the significance of knowledge in the genre. It can be seen, for example, as endorsing existing social hierarchies at the level of gender or class (and the chapter gives particular attention to the politics of class in *Who Wants to Be a Millionaire*). An examination of knowledge can also provide a way of *approaching* a particular quiz show historically – linking it to prevailing political and social contexts at any one time. This is demonstrated by a discussion of the relationship between the American big money quiz shows in the 1950s and Cold War politics, as well as an analysis of the interplay between *The Price is Right* and Thatcher's Britain (the 1980s). Finally, the chapter discusses how the changing role of knowledge – in certain examples of the genre – reflects back on the relationship between knowledge and power.

We accept that people do not naturally congregate 'in television studios to demonstrate their knowledge of grocery pricing or sports trivia' (Mittell 2007), yet the spectacle of 'real' people competing in manufactured environments has historically been central to the genre's appeal. This framework has also been taken up by reality TV, yet it is in the quiz and game show that 'ordinary' people have historically appeared on television as a matter of course. Chapter 5 examines the role of 'ordinary' people as performers in the quiz show, working from the premise that the category of 'ordinariness' cannot be taken at face value. Questions of agency and power are always at stake when 'ordinary' people perform on television, and in this respect it is important to ask: how and why are 'ordinary' people constructed *as* 'ordinary' in the quiz show?

Given that quiz shows positively encourage the viewer to 'jump into the tube' (Cooper-Chen 1994: 87), it is ultimately impossible to maintain a clear separation between contestants and viewers. Chapter 6 follows on from Chapter 5 by placing a particular focus on the audience. It does not aim to offer an exhaustive insight into how quiz shows are viewed. Rather, it seeks to offer insight into particular areas of focus, such as the growth of multi-platform television and interactivity, and

1 Genre and the Quiz Show

This chapter examines the relationship between the quiz and game show and television genre, while also using the quiz and game show to reflect on the concept of television genre itself. Although Chapter 2 offers a more explicit engagement with questions of history, Chapter 1 introduces aspects of change and development in the field, such as the increased prominence of the television format, the flow of global formats, and the rise of the 'reality game show'.

Genre is a French word meaning 'type' or 'kind', and the concept has been widely used in the study of media forms such as literature, theatre, music, film and television. Nick Lacey (2000) explains how genres are constituted by 'a repertoire of elements' – setting, iconography, character types, narrative and style – as well as by the shared expectations which render a text comprehensible to its viewers. In the context of this book, it is fortuitous that Lacey applies this framework to the game show. He lists the genre's repertoire of elements as follows:

- Setting – television studio
- Characters – studio audience, 'ordinary' people for contestants and an avuncular host
- Narrative – the questions or tasks must be overcome to win the prizes
- Iconography – a high-tech, glitzy set
- Style – basic 'live' television including focus on host; audience and contestant reaction shots; segmented structure (Lacey 2000: 206).

This definition aims to attend to the attributes which make up the television text, from visual style and programme structure, to participants. But while it appears to provide a useful basis for generic classification, the framework immediately raises a number of questions. As Steve Neale observes of Lacey's paradigm:

[B]oth narrative and style here are either weakly defined or weakly specific. Is the overcoming of tasks a sufficient definition of a narrative?

11

Is basic 'live' television' sufficiently marked as a style to constitute a particular generic ingredient? (Neale 2001: 3)

This observation relates to a wider objection: that approaches to genre in television have often simply been transferred from film and literary studies, without sufficient consideration of their applicability to television. According to Neale, 'when it comes to more medium-specific genres [on television] with a less clear-cut fictional base, ambiguities can arise' (2001: 3). As Neale hints, there is a greater tendency to see visual style in non-fiction entertainment programming, and especially formatted programming, as homogenous (perhaps because it is not often seen as 'authored' like drama). Yet visual style might differ markedly between quiz shows: the use of a crane camera in *Who Wants to Be a Millionaire* (hereafter *Millionaire*) (ITV1, 1998–), diving down to the hot seat and stopping within inches of the Perspex floor, is very different to the visual style of Channel 5's relatively static, low-budget show *Brainteaser* (C5, 2002–). Furthermore, not all shows involve 'ordinary' people as contestants: panel games favour celebrities, and many shows have combined 'ordinary' contestants and famous people. Nor are all programmes set in a television studio. The 1960s American editions of *Supermarket Sweep* (it began in the US in 1965) were set in real supermarkets, while the internationally successful *Cash Cab* (ITV1, 2005–) uses a real taxi to pick up unsuspecting contestants who are quizzed as the car drives along. Given that the German translation of the show is literally 'Quiz Taxi', it would be strange indeed not to include *Cash Cab* in a classification of the quiz show.

Lacey does not just consider visual iconography and style. He also explores ideological models of genre. Structural and/or ideological approaches have illuminated how genres play out particular themes, oppositions and concerns that reflect back on the 'collective unconscious' of a society at any one time (2000: 211). For example, crime drama contains the narrative oppositions of 'police versus crime', 'law versus rule', 'authority versus technology', 'intuition versus technology' and 'comradeship versus rank' (2000: 163). But it seems difficult to advance a similar series of oppositions for the quiz or game show. While we might suggest that the shows work through concerns surrounding intelligence/luck, achievement/failure, competition/co-operation, and individualism/community, this is a very loose description, and its resonance would depend on the show in question. As Myra Macdonald observes, quiz shows 'may all . . . provide examples of competitive discourse, but they also vary in their articulation of capitalist relations or their support of individualistic as opposed to collective endeavour' (2003: 28).

Yet these objections or qualifications may seem somewhat unfair. It could be argued, for example, that the main novelty of a programme like *Cash Cab* is precisely its negotiation of difference from the longer history of the quiz show, in which contestants have indeed stepped into a carefully crafted studio space. But such qualifications still speak to long-standing debates about the problems with genre definition. There is always a tricky conceptual relationship at work between the 'generic repertoire' and the texts themselves: it is necessary to have a predetermined understanding of what a quiz or game show is in order to decide which programmes might fit into this category, yet the generic repertoire should also surely be understood as emerging *from* the programmes under review. The debate about *Cash Cab* also points to the difficulty of producing an exclusive generic category (or a definition that is widely accepted by all).

Jane Feuer argues that because television programmes do not operate as discrete texts to the same extent as films (they are part of a continuous flow), there is a greater tendency toward hybridity and intertextuality (1992: 157). Television genres thus exhibit a greater tendency to 'recombine *across* generic lines' [original emphasis], what Feuer calls 'horizontal recombination' (1992: 158). Furthermore, the discussion of *Cash Cab* above indicates how exclusive generic definitions can have difficulty in dealing with change over time. Rather than conceiving of genres as single, self-contained entities, genre critics have foregrounded the value of conceiving genre as a process in which boundaries are always subject to play and negotiation (Neale 1990).

Olaf Hoerschelmann (2006) emphasises the value of adopting the perspective offered by Jacques Derrida in his essay 'The Law of the Genre' (Derrida 1992). Derrida explains how a text cannot belong exclusively to one particular genre, and its relationship with generic categories is always multiple. As such, it is productive to think about texts as 'participating' in generic categories. Rather than asking, 'Is X programme this genre or that genre?', it is useful to ask, 'In what genres does X programme participate?' (Hoerschelmann 2006: 26). Rather than being a 'rogue' example which is breaking rank with the conventional contexts of the quiz/game show, *Cash Cab* might be seen as 'participating' in the quiz show (it asks 'ordinary' people questions and offers prizes), reality TV (it adopts the aesthetic look of CCTV), the hidden camera show (passengers are caught unawares when they find themselves 'on television'), and the travel show (we are told something of the city and its heritage and culture as we whiz around in the taxi). In participating in each of these categories, *Cash Cab* effectively keeps generic boundaries in play, renegotiating each of these categories in the process.

Is a quiz show different to a game show?

The idea of genre as a process does not render the use of generic labels or categories redundant. Both popular and academic definitions have argued that 'game show' represents the broader generic term, which then encompasses a range of subcategories, including the quiz show, within its scope (Turner 2001a: 7). The definition offered by the popular internet encyclopaedia Wikipedia subscribes to this view:

> A game show involves members of the public or celebrities, sometimes as part of a team, playing a game, perhaps involving answering quiz questions, for points or prizes. In some shows contestants compete against other players or another team whilst other shows involve contestants striving alone . . .[1]

It goes on to explain how in a quiz show, people 'compete against each other by answering quiz questions or solving puzzles', citing examples such as *Wheel of Fortune* (ITV, 1969–2001 [intermittent]), and *Jeopardy!* (1964–, US). In contrast, a panel game 'usually involves a celebrity panel answering questions', while a 'third kind of game show' – no title is given – 'involves contestants competing stunts or playing a game that involves elements of chance or strategy in addition to, or instead of, a test of general knowledge'. The example offered here is *Deal or No Deal* (C4, 2005–) which is described as combining 'luck and strategy'. The next category is the reality game show in which the 'competition lasts several days or even weeks' and a competitor's progress through the game is based on some form of popularity contest, 'usually a kind of disapproval voting by their fellow competitors or members of the public' (for example, *Big Brother*, *Survivor*, *The Apprentice*). The final category is the dating game show. This subgenre is described as 'the original reality show, in which the prize is a well-funded dating opportunity that one can only pursue with the individual [who] . . . has "won" the show' (for example, *Blind Date*).

Some of these definitions are replicated in the list of types provided by the British games consultant David J. Bodycombe, who has contributed to the design of programmes such as *The Crystal Maze* (C4, 1990–5), appeared on the BBC Radio 4 problem-solving programme *Puzzle Panel*, written thousands of puzzles for the popular press, and authored the book *How to Devise a Game Show* (2003). In offering a guide to budding game-show inventors, Bodycombe uses an extensive list of subcategories including:[2]

- action/adventure
- board game conversion

- children's
- comedy and panel game
- dating show
- educational
- family game show
- lifestyle
- puzzle
- reality
- quiz, general knowledge
- sports
- stunt/dare show
- variety.

While the Wikipedia definition was based on the textual characteristics of programmes, Bodycombe's more extensive list reaches out to a wider range of reference points. These include scheduling practices and audience address (for example, children's, family game show), the function or 'worth' of a programme (for example, educational), and extra-textual referents (for example, board game conversion).

This approach differs from the definition offered by Hoerschelmann's academic study *The Rules of the Game: Quiz Shows and American Culture*, which suggests that:

> The quiz principle primarily drives shows that deal with competitions between individuals or groups, based primarily on the display of factual knowledge. The game principle drives shows dealing with human knowledge . . . or those based primarily on gambling or physical performances. (2006: 8)

Hoerschelmann is drawing here on Fiske's (1987) taxonomy of knowledge in the genre. Fiske refers to factual knowledge, which deals with questions and answers with an empirical basis in 'fact'. This can be general knowledge, or 'everyday' knowledge, ranging across the general knowledge of *The Weakest Link* (BBC2/1, 2000–), to the guessing of consumer prices on *The Price is Right* (ITV, 1984–2001 [intermittent]). But Fiske also points to the different category of human knowledge which resides 'in the social rather than in the factual' (1987: 268). This knowledge has no absolute right or wrong answer: it depends on the ability to 'understand or "see into" people', whether in general (he gives the example of *Family Fortunes* (ITV, 1980–2002 [intermittent]), or in dating games. Thus, in drawing on Fiske's knowledge categories, Hoerschelmann implies that the distinction between a quiz show and a game show is found less in whether knowledge is actually used, than in the content of this knowledge and its role within the wider context of the game. Hoerschelmann's quote also points to the role of chance as a potential marker of difference: note the suggestion that shows involving gambling are more likely to be defined as 'games' than 'quizzes'.

This distinction is to some degree supported by the industry-related definition offered by Danny Greenstone, one of the executive producers at Talkback Thames (which in 2006 produced revamped versions of *The Price is Right* and *Family Fortunes*, and which produces the reality-talent show *X-Factor*):

> In my head, a quiz is . . . pure question and answer. *Mastermind* is a quiz . . . A game for the most part is something that doesn't rely on questions and answers, although it might have them in there. *Deal or No Deal* is a game . . .The interesting thing is of course that there is a huge grey area in the middle, where bits of both start overlapping with each other. [*Who Wants to Be a*] *Millionaire* is really a quiz, but because its got extra bits of drama bolted onto it, like 50/50, phone a friend, ask the audience, it strays into game-playing, because what you are asked to do as a contestant is to draw on elements of strategy – a bit of skill and a bit of cunning, and knowing when to play the right thing. (Greenstone 2006)

This implies that programmes drawing upon factual/academic/general knowledge are indeed more likely to be labelled as quizzes, while those relying on human knowledge, aspects of physical performance, or strong elements of chance, are more likely to be labelled games. In this regard, it is useful to note the categories offered by Roger Caillois' anthropological study of play. Although Caillois does not specifically deal with television, he distinguishes between games of 'Agon' and games of 'Alea' (see Chapter 4). Games of Agon are based on competition in which the outcome is decided by merit, while games of Alea are based more on fate or chance (*alea* is the Latin term for 'game of dice') (Caillois 1961: 17). So *Mastermind* (BBC, 1972– [intermittent]) might be aligned with Agon, and *Deal or No Deal* with Alea. But as Greenstone's description of *Millionaire* implies, these structures can be combined within a single game, and should not be used as definitive categorisations.

Formatting genre

Although categories are especially imprecise in the sphere of quiz and game shows, the fact that it is not possible to pin down a neat alignment between the terms used by the industry, academics or the popular press is not specific to the programming considered here. While earlier approaches mapped out the concept of genre as existing within a triangle of expectations between industry, text and audience, there has since been more emphasis on conflict and struggle over generic definitions. Critics, academics, fans or media producers do not all have the same investment in the concept of genre. While academics might be aiming to delimit a field of study or plan topics for an undergraduate module, media producers may be just as interested in stressing multiple generic markers in order to maximise the potential appeal of their product (Altman 1999).

Turner emphasises the difference between academic and industrial approaches from another perspective when he explains that 'there is not much evidence that the term "genre" or any equivalent abstraction is actually used on [the] . . . industrial process [of production]' (2001a: 5). Instead, he foregrounds the related, and in some ways 'competing, term "format"' (2001b: 7):

> Unlike genre, format is widely used within the television industry . . . Formats can be original and thus copyrighted, franchised and under licence, and traded as a commercial property. Genres, by definition, are not original. Format is a production category with relatively rigid boundaries that are difficult to transgress without coming up with a new format. Genre is the product of a text- and audience-based negotiation activated by viewers' expectations. Genre is the larger, more inclusive category and can be used to describe programmes that use a number of related formats, such as the game show. (ibid.)

Given that the concept of the format is crucial to the study of the quiz and game show, it is important to introduce its significance here.

Albert Moran's (1998) work on the television format complements the distinction between genre and format drawn by Turner. Although the term format can be used rather loosely, Moran emphasises the more specific meaning that it has acquired within the domain of the international TV trade. From this perspective, a format is a concept referring to the range of items which can be included in a licensing agreement in exchange for financial return (Moran 1998: 17). When it comes to the quiz or game show, these items may include a written description of the game and its rules, a list of catchphrases, information on prizes, set design and visual style, and information about software for computer graphics (1998: 17). But the concept of the format does not simply refer to textual properties which we can see or hear on screen; formats also have a legal dimension: they aim to regulate issues of copyright. This means that is problematic to position the format as being defined by any core or 'essential' characteristics. Rather, the term

> has meaning not . . . because of what it is, but rather what it permits or facilitates . . . [T]he concept of a television format is meaningful to the television industry because it helps to organise and regulate the exchange of program ideas between program producers. (Moran 1998: 18)

But this idea of organisation and regulation does not prevent the 'borrowing' of ideas across texts. Indeed, while the entire framework of format trade is now more formalised than ever before, the continued existence of copyright lawsuits attests to the somewhat leaky boundaries of this field.

An acknowledgement of this 'copycatting' also circulates within the everyday discourse surrounding format television, including the quiz and game show. The popularity of quizzes in the late 1990s and early 2000s was seen, in media discourse, to produce a rash of *Millionaire* or *The Weakest Link* 'clones' – a term which foregrounds the texts as mass-produced, factory-like products (as opposed to 'unique' texts of artistic and authorial vision). The established British website www.UKgameshows.com is a veritable celebration of the quiz and game show, but it still invokes the concept of originality as a criterion of evaluation. Endemol's rather short-lived *Shafted* (ITV1, 2001), for example, is lambasted by the site for being a 'checklist of features from more original and successful shows' ('Metallic set? Check. Industrial mood music? Check.' 'We hadn't seen that since . . . *The Weakest Link* about three hours beforehand').[3] This may also be seen as supporting Turner's point about the questionable currency of 'genre' within the industry: producers are often simply aiming to replicate the success of previous texts. Endemol even copycatted its own *Deal or No Deal* with *For the Rest of Your Life* (ITV1, 2007), simply replacing the singular contestant with couples, the boxes with cylinders, and the one-off cash reward with monthly instalments of cash. At the same time, this also demonstrates how, far from occupying an antagonistic relationship with the concept of genre, formats are also the building blocks of genre, essentially providing Neale's (1990) form of 'regulated difference'. They take existing textual elements and remould them, or combine them with new innovations on a number of different levels. So while the creators of *Millionaire* have consistently stressed its originality, it can also be perceived as '*Double Your Money* [ITV, 1955–68] meets *Mastermind*' (Beale 2006), just as *The Weakest Link* might be described as '*Fifteen-to-One* meets *Big Brother*'.[4] Turner (2001) is right to suggest that formats can be original while genres – by definition – cannot, but both are profoundly intertextual, operating at the level of relations *between* texts.

The concept of the format has become a visible area of interest in television studies, not least because of the importance of the format in the contemporary television landscape. As Chapter 2 explains, BBC radio used American quiz and game show formats from the 1930s onwards, and the use of American formats in Britain was even more visible with the advent of commercial television (ITV) in 1955. Quiz and game shows have always been popular with both service and commercial broadcasters because they are cheap to make, and one of the reasons they are cheap to make is because they are based on formats. The issue of cost has become even more crucial for broadcasters in the current television climate, with more channels competing for an audience share, and more hours to fill. In this respect, the use of formats has a clear commercial logic, representing a cost-effective way of delivering programming to audiences. The increased importance of the format also reflects the risk-averse nature of the television landscape – the desire to minimise the possibility of failure in the face of competition. If a format has been 'proven' elsewhere, it is seen as minimising (although not eradicating) the possibility of failure. The increased trade in formats also reflects the extent to which it is now crucial to derive as much financial mileage out of ownership as possible (Moran and Malbon 2006: 11). With regard to the quiz and game show, this can mean licensing a wider range of media products such as board games, internet games, interactive DVDs and books.

The increased importance of format trade is also suggested by the trajectory of business dealings at the BBC. Moving from the informal deals made with American broadcasting in its early decades, the Corporation now has BBC Worldwide, 'Europe's most successful exporter of television programmes, accounting for around half of the UK's total television exports with around 40,000 hours of programming sold in the last year'.[5] In 1994 the BBC set up its Format Licensing Division to deal with the use of its formats in other territories, and in 1999 BBC Worldwide developed a strategy with BBC Entertainment to invest more than £300,000 a year in the production of game show pilots. This produced shows which enjoyed domestic and international success, such as *The Weakest Link*, *Friends Like These* (BBC1, 1999–2003) and *Dog Eat Dog* (BBC1, 2001–2) (Moran and Malbon 2006: 88). While some format creators exist on their own without production facilities, the BBC is invariably involved in production consultancy, thus gaining both a licensing and production fee (ibid.).

If the emphasis is now on the creation of a 'global brand', it is not surprising that the increased use of television formats has prompted concerns about the global homogenisation of television. As Silvio Waisbord comments in his article 'McTV: Understanding the Global Popularity of Television Formats', 'What better evidence of cultural homogenization than format television? A dozen media companies are able to do business worldwide by selling the same idea, and audiences seem to be watching national variations of the same show' (2004: 360). Yet scholars in television and cultural studies have also painted a more complex picture of cultural exchange, and Waisbord goes on to explain how, at 'a deeper level . . . formats attest to the fact that television still remains tied to local and national cultures' (ibid.). Formats are attractive to broadcasters not only because they may have been 'tried and tested' elsewhere, but because they can be inflected by, and adapted to, different national cultures. This takes place within the parameters of the formatted framework, and format originators can keep a tight reign on the level of flexibility allowed. But it is precisely this relationship between similarity and difference which is the focus of format adaptation studies. In this sense formats can be seen to reveal less the simple (global) homogenisation of television than the dynamics of 'glocalization' (ibid.).

Yet this still needs to take account of generic differences. In his book on format adaptation, Moran finds the quiz/game show the most 'unyielding form' where cultural translation is concerned, and he notes that 'national colourings have to be sought in the interstices of adaptations' (1998: 134). In other words, national differences may not be that apparent (and viewing apparently identical replications of *Millionaire* or *The Weakest Link* in wider national contexts can certainly be an uncanny experience). Furthermore, Waisbord hints that as the bid to maximise profits from format trade accelerates, so formats are specifically designed to 'travel well' across national boundaries, meaning that 'the DNA of formats is rooted in cultural values which transcend the national' (2004: 368). As he asks, 'What is British about *Who Wants to Be a Millionaire?*'

As Waisbord hints, one of the challenges of studying format adaptations is to avoid a reductive picture in which programmes (especially to a non-native observer) are seen to reflect some kind of national 'essence'. The fact that in the Russian version of *Millionaire*, audiences in the 'Ask the Audience Lifeline' were more likely to offer the contestant the wrong answer on purpose (Hutchinson 2006) may well suggest a conflict between the programme's capitalist (individualistic) ethos and the heritage of a Communist ideology. At the same time, it might equally be read as a mark of greater playfulness, leading to a more productive discussion about how different cultures place different values on the relative 'seriousness' of game-playing (see Caillois 1961). Nevertheless, even if we take these qualifications into account, it is clear that aspects of the 'local ordinary' can inflect a quiz and game show format in different ways (Bonner 2003). Aspects such as the institutional and economic contexts of television (scheduling, programme length, channel identity, audience demographic), the selection of the host, the use of 'ordinary' people, the questions asked, and wider cultural responses to particular trends or formats can all be taken into account in this regard.

Historically, the US was the exporter, not the importer, of quiz and game show formats. But from the 1970s, European formats gradually had more success than in previous decades: the Dutch format *The Generation Game* arrived in the UK to spectacular success in 1971, while the Spanish format *3-2-1* hit British screens in 1978. British television also managed to export *The Krypton Factor* (ITV1, 1982–5, 1990–5) to America in the 1980s – a show which demanded a combination of mental and physical agility. But it was really only in the wake of the British exportation of both *Millionaire* and *The Weakest Link*, as well as the wider success of certain reality formats (for example, *Big Brother*, *Popstars*, *Pop Idol*), that contexts such as Western Europe, Australia and New Zealand gained a greater foothold in the format market (Waisbord 2004: 361). *Deal or No Deal*, like *Big Brother*, came from the Netherlands, and was then exported to over forty countries, including the USA. After selling *Millionaire* and *The Weakest Link*, British television produced a medley of re-vamped 'classics' (played by celebrity contestants) in *The Game Show Marathon* (ITV1, 2005, 2007), and then quickly sold the format to America and Germany. The high stakes cash quiz *Pokerface* was launched by the British channel ITV1 in 2006, and in 2007 it sold to territories such as Sweden, Norway, Columbia, Poland, Australia and Mexico. In 2005, British television also premiered *Cash Cab* (ITV1, 2005–), and the format was then sold to many territories including America, Poland, Germany, Norway, France, Spain, Serbia and Australia. But aspects of a national hierarchy here remain in place: while Britain created the original version of *Millionaire*, it was only after its success in America that other countries rushed to adapt the format for themselves. Equally, these shifts do not efface the inequalities which continue to exist in the global trade of television formats and programmes, especially outside the Western sphere (Waisbord 2004: 381).

Issues of format adaptation are returned to at points throughout this book, but Turner's (2001b) bid to insist on the industrial relevance of the term 'format' is useful in emphasising the danger of academic categories operating too separately from a programme's production and circulation. Much has been made of the differences between 'theoretical' versus 'historical' generic categories – with the former equated with academic definitions, and the latter associated with industrial and institutional terms. Turner's caution as to whether the concept of 'genre' has much currency within the TV industry also has some purchase. When interviewing industry professionals as part of the research for this book, I was confronted with hesitation or even resistance when I asked about labels or categories. As the executive producer of *Millionaire* explained: 'We call it "entertainment". It's a branch of entertainment. But if you want to be a bit specific, [it is] a quiz' (Hutchinson 2006).

Discursive approaches to genre

If industry professionals viewed my question with an air of bemusement or disinterest, this is not in itself an obstacle to be overcome. From the perspective of another approach to genre – a discursive approach – the conflict and struggle surrounding the use of labels represents a site of analysis in itself. Jason Mittell's *Genre and Television: From Cop Shows to Cartoons* advocates a discursive approach to genre. Although genres were traditionally understood to represent categories of texts, Mittell argues that texts do not determine or produce their own categorisation, nor mark out the boundaries of that categorisation. Generic categories need to be understood as intertextual, operating at the level of relations between texts, as well as in the material which circulates around them. Mittell asks, if 'genres are not textual properties, where exactly might we go to analyze them?' (2004a: 12):

> To understand how genre categories become culturally salient, we can examine genres as *discursive practices*. By regarding genre as a property and function of discourse, we can examine the ways in which various forms of communication work to constitute generic definitions, meanings, and values within particular historical contexts [original emphasis]. (ibid.)

Mittell is emphasising here that while 'genres do run through texts', they also operate within the reviewing practices of critics, the opinions of audiences, and the production and marketing strategies of the television industry. Thus, at the level of method and evidence, 'we might look at what audiences and industries say about genres, what terms and definitions circulate around any given generic instance, and how specific cultural assumptions are linked to particular genres . . .' (2004a: 13).

Mittell's work also alerts us to the political function of generic categories. As he explains, we 'should focus on the breadth of [categories used] . . . around any given instance, mapping out as many articulations of genre as possible and situating them within larger cultural contexts and relations of power' (2004b: 174).[6] Far from arriving at a 'proper' definition, the goal of genre analysis from this perspective is to explore the range of generic discourses in circulation, approaching them as speaking to the value systems, structures of power, and cultural climate from which the text(s) emerged.

This perspective is valuable in highlighting how the use of generic labels is often evaluative, rather than neutral. For example, in her book *Ordinary Television*, Frances Bonner's bid to distinguish between the terms quiz and game show indicates a clear hierarchy at work:

> Game shows as a category are now understood to include quizzes, though once the latter term applied to the kind with the more intellectual questions (like . . . *Mastermind*). The relegation of 'quiz' can be regarded as a sign of the increased importance of play and fun on television. 'Quiz', with its echoes of school tests, reduces the extent to which answering questions to win prizes is now just a game, on a par with spending sixty seconds in a set of stocks with a couple of dogs licking pet food off one's feet (a challenge set in an episode of the British game show *Don't Try This at Home*). (Bonner 2003: 12)

So here, the shift from 'quiz' to 'game' represents an apparent 'dumbing down' of quizzes in the contemporary television landscape. This illustrates the point that the choice of a generic label can be revealing in itself, indicating the assumptions associated with a category at any particular time (Mittell 2004a: 35). As discussed in Chapter 2, 'give-away' became a generic term for the quiz or game show in 1950s Britain, particularly after the advent of commercial television in 1955, and its investment in programmes with big money prizes. The critical currency of the term 'give-away' not only signalled a distaste for the genre, but it also aimed to shore up the notion that any money distributed was undeserved. The term was undoubtedly understood to be American in origin, and for British critics at the time, it fittingly indicated the perceived encroachment of commercial values into television programming and culture.

As this implies, channels play a role in shaping the circulation of television genres. This can be seen quite explicitly on niche cable or digital channels such as the British Challenge TV, or the American GSN: The Network for Games (formerly The Game Show Network). Although sometimes airing original formats, these channels rely primarily on quiz and game repeats, including shows from the 1950s and 1960s on GSN, and programmes from the 1980s onwards on Challenge TV. Challenge TV has featured titles such as *Play Your Cards Right* (ITV, 1990–2003 [intermittent]) *Blankety Blank* (BBC1, 1979–2002 [intermittent]), *The Crystal Maze*, *Family Fortunes*, and *Bullseye* (ITV, 1981–95 [intermittent]), as well as what it lists as 'classic' *Millionaire*. These channels are evidence of how quiz and game shows – along with other genres – have been used to brand channels within the more niche landscape of multi-channel television. This does not just offer an opportunity to exploit the libraries of quiz or game shows from the past (GSN, for example, made use of the famous Mark Goodman and Bill Todson game show library), it also enables the production of new formats with a deliberately niche address. For example, the quiz show *Legal Brain* (2006), broadcast on the Sky Channel Legal TV, seems to be a far cry from the generalist and family address of programmes such as *Family Fortunes* or *Millionaire*.

A discursive approach to genre would emphasise, however, that such channels similarly define the boundaries of the quiz and game show in flexible ways for their own purposes. Challenge TV, like most cable or digital channels, relies heavily on a rotating schedule of repeats. This means that programmes with an on-going narrative chain – as is the case with many reality game shows – are more difficult to schedule than formats which operate in relatively discrete units. As Celia Taylor, the deputy controller at Challenge TV, explains: 'For us [a programme] . . . needs a clear beginning and an end on a daily basis' (Taylor 2007). Challenge has sometimes screened programmes which might well be labelled as reality game shows, such as *Fear Factor* and *The Amazing Race*. But these are certainly outnumbered by studio-based games which, given their more discrete format, can be better exploited by the economics of the channel.

In contrast, the internet site www.UKGameshows.com, which provides information about more than 1,000 game show formats from 1938 to the present day, welcomes these newer strands of programming. It does not have to worry about the economic constraints of scheduling, and it explains that its 'definition of "game show" is wide-ranging, taking in children's television, traditional quizzes and panel games, lifestyle TV, reality TV and talent shows'.[7] Its own criteria, on at explicit level at least, is more related to questions of national context: it excludes 'imported programmes' unless a British version has been produced. Yet it too has more implicit generic criteria for inclusion and exclusion which rest upon evaluative criteria. The growth of premium-rate phone-in quiz channels, such as the Channel-4-owned Quiz Call and the ITV-owned ITV Play, are treated with suspicion and disdain, even while it lists them in its coverage ('Yet *another* premium-rate puzzle phone-in channel. What have we done to deserve this? [original emphasis]').[8] Quiz show fans, such as those who visit www.quizzing.co.uk, adopt a similar attitude, rejoicing at the axing of ITV Play in 2007 'because that programme gave quizzes a bad name'.[9]

'Call TV Quiz Services', in which viewers call a premium-rate telephone number in the hope of getting on air and winning a cash prize by answering a question or solving a puzzle, have prompted considerable regulatory concern. As discussed in Chapter 2, the relevant regulators, including Ofcom, ICTSTIS (Independent Committee for the Supervision of Standards of Telephone Information Services) and the Gambling Commission, were to decide whether 'quiz shows should be reclassified as lotteries, which would mean that 20 per cent of their revenues would have to go to charity'.[10] This indicates how, from the perspective of a discursive approach to television genre, policy practices and debates also play a role in defining genres (Mittell 2004a: 46). Not only do regulators help to steer the genre in particular directions at certain points, but they also play a role in marking out the 'legitimate' boundaries of the field. Indeed, from the perspective of www.UKGameshows.com and the regulators above, Call TV Quiz Services emerge as the 'illegitimate child' of the quiz and game show – existing on the margins of an already devalued genre.

It's only a game show!: activating and denying generic referents

If categorisations are invoked in opportunistic and flexible ways by regulators, internet sites and academics, this process is also entered into by the programmes themselves. Reality TV in particular has attracted much academic and popular attention where questions of generic hybridity are concerned. The advent of what have been referred to as 'reality game shows' or 'gamedocs' can be seen as participating in the soap opera, the documentary, the talk show and the game show. Programmes like *Survivor, Big Brother, The Amazing Race, Fear Factor* and *The Apprentice* have been classified as 'gamedocs' by some academics, and they draw upon some of the textual structures traditionally associated with the game show. Reality game formats are structured by rules, and pivot on the competitive philosophy of a winner-takes-all gamesmanship. They also use the framework of competition to capitalise on the spectacle of 'ordinary' people under extreme (television) pressure – a staple element of the quiz and game show from its earliest days. Many of the more contemporary reality formats draw upon the legacy of humiliation and extreme behaviour witnessed in the earlier 'stunt' game shows (such as *People are Funny* (ITV, 1955–6)), while the spectacle of emotional/confessional performances can be traced back to the 1950s American 'sob' or 'misery' shows (for example, *Strike It Rich* (1951–8) or *Queen for a Day* (1956–64) in which participants – often women – told personal hardship stories in exchange for money or prizes (see Cassidy 2005). Money is still on offer in reality game shows, but contestants also compete to win something which is now seen as more desirable. They compete to become a celebrity – the owner of a brand identity that can in itself be used as exchangeable capital.

Reality TV producers have dubbed the combination of drama and 'reality' as a form of 'dramality', the use of casting and structuring to 'elicit and intensify drama without actually scripting it' (Haralovich and Trosset 2004: 80). This suggests a further connection with the quiz and game show. As the quiz show scandals of 1950s American television made clear, the promise of liveness and authenticity is central to the genre's appeal. When it was revealed in the late 1950s that certain shows were rigged (and that contestants were cast as winners and losers), a social and televisual contract with the audience was broken (ibid.). But this was in itself a debate about the relative balance of drama/'reality' ('dramality'), prefiguring the cultural debate surrounding reality TV. In fact, these discourses have become central to the interpretive frameworks used to approach reality texts, while they are also self-consciously debated within the programmes themselves. Thus, while we might suggest that, as with the quiz show, the impact of reality TV ultimately depends on a belief in the 'authenticity of the contrived reality' (Haralovich and Trosset 2004: 80), the popular discussion surrounding it has interrogated precisely this contradiction.

It is useful to set out these intersections, as while it is often suggested that reality formats draw upon the precursor of the quiz and game show, the textual relationship at work here has not really been explored. Jack Z. Bratich offers a brief but useful comparison when he emphasises what he sees as the *difference* of the reality game shows:

> Past game shows worked with a high level of abstraction . . . from reality. This earlier generation of game shows . . . [were] characterized by digitized number displays, hyper artificial spaces . . . and disembodied skills (trivia retrieval, price estimation, relationship knowledge, word association). These programmes established a clear distinction between contestants (with individual seats, boxes, or desks) . . . [They] created a sphere severed from everyday life by taking contestants and viewers into a hyper virtual space. (2007: 13)

Bratich suggests that today's 'gamedocs' pursue the opposite trajectory: they seek to immerse the game dynamics within 'lived' contexts – however fabricated these contexts may be (for example, the *Big Brother* house). Bratich is keen to emphasise, in answer to the accusation that reality shows are 'unreal', and that they abstract their participants and games from the world 'out there', that they simply offer 'distillations of scenarios occurring across other social sites' (2007: 14) (for example, work communities). This defence seems entirely reasonable, but what Bratich refers to as the 'traditional' quiz and game show is surely given short shrift in his argument, and the suggestion that they are an 'earlier/older' phase of the genre, apparently now defunct, is not supported by the television schedules. Simply because such programmes predominantly occupy 'hyper artificial spaces' does not mean that they have ever severed a connection with everyday life. Furthermore, this viewpoint too readily endorses the assumption, as outlined in the Introduction, that quiz and game shows are not about 'anything much' at all.

But just as this chapter has noted similarities, it is worth noting the potential differences between what Bratich refers to as the 'earlier generation of game shows' and reality formats. Reality shows differ in the extent to which they invoke the discursive framework of a game. In *Survivor*, *The Apprentice*, *Unanimous*, or *The Games*, the idea of the game is always self-consciously present, with a competitive game ethos, and an emphasis on winning or losing, structuring each episode. In comparison, *Big Brother* exploits long periods of observation and participation in which the framework of the game is not the dominant force. Furthermore, rather than a central game, reality contestants play 'layers of games' (entering into individual tasks or competitions within the context of a wider competitive trajectory) (Haralovich and Trosset 2004: 78), and the game structure can become secondary to, or is used to stage, interpersonal interactions. Reality shows have also been more successful in attracting a youth audience, and the extent to which people emerge as 'characters' in such programmes differs from encountering contestants within a studio-based quiz. While quiz shows have long since beckoned the possibility of returning contestants ('Are you going to come back next week?'), the 'dramality' of reality TV typically plays out in a more extended time-frame (of weeks or months). When compared to the tightly structured competition of the quiz and game show, the wider game structures of reality TV offer their competitors what Haralovich and Trosset term 'an enormous scope of action' (2004: 78), although these contexts are, of course, ultimately also bound by rules (evictions, voting regimes, no contact with the outside world, rationing of food).

As with all the definitions discussed in this chapter, and returning us to a discursive approach to genre, the programmes activate and suppress their association with game shows as needed (Mittell 2004a: 198). The UK version of *The Apprentice*, dealing with the traditionally 'masculine' sphere of business and originally screened on BBC2, aims to position itself as a more 'serious' form of reality TV. To this end, it often aims to de-activate its generic association with the game show. As the central figure of Alan Sugar explains to the new candidates at the start of series three: 'This is not a game show. There are no blonde women to lead you off when you don't win the prize . . . This is the hardest interview of your life' (28 March 2007). In contrast, in the UK version of *Big Brother*, the contestants have periodically chanted 'It's only a game show, it's only a game show' in a bid to diffuse tension within the house, or to downplay the power of both producers and viewers in shaping their fate ('It's *only* a game show so we don't care'). At the same time, participants seen to be openly 'playing the game' are often judged negatively by fellow housemates and viewers (as such a strategy is seen as compromising the authenticity of the self on display).

Rather than attesting to the demarcation of clear boundaries, this discussion endorses the view that texts, generic categories, and the relations between texts occupy a place on a sliding continuum. But in mapping out the focus for a book such as this, it is necessary to draw up boundaries for inclusion and exclusion (just as the TV channels, fans, internet sites, academics and reviewers do above). Indeed, I am not quite convinced that the notion of a sliding continuum can stretch to meet Hoerschelmann's point that 'the bulk of reality television appears to be quiz shows in disguise' (2006: 150), precisely because of the differences outlined above. Given the emphasis placed on knowledge in scholarly work on the quiz show, its relative marginalisation in reality formats is worth some note. To be sure, *Big Brother* and other programmes may incorporate elements of quizzing, whether spontaneously played by the participants or set as a task by the production team. The fact that reality shows often test contestants (toward the end of a show's run) on their accumulated knowledge of fellow participants indicates that knowledge, in the form of 'human knowledge', has a role to play within the game. Participants also consistently speak of 'personal growth through self-knowledge' (Bratich 2007: 9). But it is not unfair to suggest that this is stretching the comparison to its limits.

It is also notable that attempts to mix a more specific emphasis on quizzing with a 'reality' framework, such as with *24 Hour Quiz* (ITV1/2 2004) and *The People's Quiz* (BBC1, 2007), have not so far proved to be that successful (although we can doubtless expect to see more such experiments in the future). Endemol produced the *24 Hour Quiz* for ITV1. Hosted by ex-*EastEnders* actor Shaun Williamson, the programme aired for five weeks, with contestants living in a small 'Quiz Pod' around the clock. They were asked questions by a disembodied voice for up to sixteen hours a day, and sleeping, eating or showering cost them (prize) money. One of ITV's digital channels, ITV2, continued the possibility of offering round-the-clock coverage of the live-in quizzers, and given the Endemol link, it is not surprising that the low-grade visual aesthetic was reminiscent of *Big Brother*.

Scheduled on a weekly basis, *The People's Quiz* – screened as one of the BBC's National Lottery quiz programmes – was structurally and visually similar to reality talent shows such as *Pop Idol* and *X-Factor*. With a jackpot of £200,700 and a serial narrative structure, the aim was to find Britain's 'brightest brain'. But the early elimination stages were more like auditions than rounds. In the absence of a buzzer or set behind which to stand, the hopeful contestants faced a panel of three judges (including quiz show host and producer William G. Stewart) and had to give ten correct answers in a row to go through to the next stage. In a similar manner to the pop programmes, we are taken to visit regional auditions, with the host, Jamie Theakston, mediating the personal dramas of the winners and losers as he catches them entering and exiting the room. As with pop programmes and their judicious editing of bad and good auditions, we are invited to marvel at talent and to laugh at the 'losers', while enjoying the performances of those who largely participate in order to give a comic turn.

A further example of cross-over between quiz and reality is ITV1's *Don't Call Me Stupid* (2007). Two celebrities seek to teach each other about one of their hobbies or interests, usually not related to their media career. So darts player Bobby George teaches television presenter Vanessa Feltz about fishing, while Feltz teaches George about the literature of Geoffrey Chaucer (9 October 2007). The programme begins in the studio, and we are shown video clips of the tutoring process as the celebrities induct each other into their new sphere. This concept draws much from a reality format such as *Wife Swap* (C4, 2003–) (swapping an aspect of your lifestyle with someone else), as well as *Faking It* (C4, 2000–) (in which contestants are required to occupy a new role which is often at odds with their own class background, knowledge and interests). The quiz element then emerges from the fact that the two contestants are tested on their new interest in the studio by the host, Alexander Armstrong, and the celebrity with the highest score is the winner. Existing quiz show formats are also invoked here: the idea of being tested on a 'specialist subject' references the long-standing series *Mastermind*.

Yet these shows have not garnered the popularity of quiz shows or reality TV. *Don't Call Me Stupid* aired in ITV1's 'graveyard' slot of 10:00pm (Tuesday evening), and *The People's Quiz*, which was pitched as a 'big' Saturday night offering, was far from a runaway ratings success. An even worse fate struck *The 24 Hour Quiz*, as it was abruptly axed mid-series after failing to find a loyal audience. Gauging why a programme succeeds or fails is always an elusive business, but the relative failure of these examples may point to the fact that there are still different expectations, and perhaps different audiences, associated with quiz/game and reality shows.

Genre in practice

This discussion has moved a long way from a debate about a genre's 'repertoire of elements' (Lacey 2000), and the emphasis on how a vast range of textual sites participate in genre definitions is doubtless frustrating for anyone wanting a clear definition of the 'quiz' and 'game' show, and the potential distinctions between them. But by engaging with recent debate in television genre studies, the purpose of this chapter has been to show how generic definitions cannot exist outside particular historical, institutional and cultural contexts, and to explore the relationship between the quiz/game show and the concept of genre (rather than exploring 'the genre of' the quiz/game show). Not only do genres need to be conceived as processes in which the boundaries are always malleable and in play (Neale 1990), but they can also be understood as practices of interpretation and evaluation. It should also be clear that a discursive approach to genre may have a different aim than a textual approach. While a textual approach may seek to group together texts in order to understand their commonalities and cultural functions, a discursive approach is more interested in struggle, generic circulation and power. As students and theorists of quiz and game shows, we can look at the labels used to define programmes, and how terms might be used differently by industry professionals, critics, fan sites and academics (and for what purposes).

Academic definitions are part of how genres are constituted as cultural categories, and it is still clearly necessary to delimit one's focus when writing a book. In general, this book places a particular emphasis on programmes dealing with the production of knowledge through question and answer. For programmes with a significant component of question and answer, the preferred term adopted is 'quiz', while if a significant questioning component is absent, the preferred term adopted is 'game'. (If the phrase 'quiz and/or game show' is used, then this indicates that programmes which might be related to both categories are being discussed.) The book also draws on the perception that quizzes are in themselves games (hence the discussion of 'game spaces' or 'game worlds' in Chapter 3). But in retaining a self-reflexive and discursive emphasis on the use of generic categories, the book still attends to struggles surrounding generic terms, whether at particular junctures, or with respect to particular programmes. It is also in examining these discourses that it is necessary to range outside programmes with a significant focus on question and answer. For example, the early discussions at the BBC over competitions and prize-giving in broadcasting emerged from disparate programme roots quite unrelated to 'quiz' programmes (not least of all because the idea of the 'broadcast quiz' was not yet a recognised term). Equally, programmes which might be described as reality game shows are not the major focus of the book, although given the suggestion that they occupy relations with the quiz show on a generic continuum, they are regularly referred to in order to bring out points of comparison or difference.

Notes

1. http://en.wikipedia.org/wiki/Game-shows [accessed 30 October 2006].
2. http://www.tvformats.com [accessed 10 February 2007].
3. http://www.ukgameshows.com/page/index.php/Shafted [accessed 22 May 2007].
4. http://www.ukgameshows.com/page/index.php/The_Weakest_Link [accessed 22 May 2007].
5. http://www.bbcworldwide.com/tvsales.htm [accessed 29 March 2007].
6. Mittell is drawing upon Michel Foucault's (1990) conception of discourse: the construction of specific frameworks of thinking which take place within wider systems of social power.
7. http://en.wikipedia.org.wiki/UKGameshows.com [accessed 30 October 2006].
8. http://www.ukgameshows.com/page/index.php/Quiz_Call [accessed 29 March 2007].
9. http://www.iqagb.co.uk/trivia/viewtopic.php?t=5999 [accessed 29 March 2007].
10. *Broadcast*, 29 September 2006, p. 22.

2 Quiz Show Histories

In the year 2000, Judith Keppel became the first contestant to win the top prize on the UK version of *Who Wants to Be a Millionaire* (hereafter *Millionaire*). Keppel's win boosted media interest in the already popular show, and press critics continued to discuss the influence of the programme in 'injecting new life into the genre and pitching it back into prime-time' (Thynne 2000: 22). In the UK, a number of new quiz shows emerged in the wake of *Millionaire*, ranging across *The Weakest Link* (BBC1/2, 1999–), *The Syndicate* (BBC1, 2000), *The Chair* (BBC1, 2002), *No Win, No Fee* (BBC1, 2001), *The Biggest Game in Town* (ITV1, 2001), *The Enemy Within* (BBC1, 2002), *The Vault* (ITV1, 2002–4) and *The Big Call* (ITV1, 2005). While *Millionaire* enjoyed astonishing global success (as early as 2003, it had been taken up in over fifty territories), its impact was especially apparent in the US, largely because the quiz show had not been seen as a prime-time genre for some years. Although the quote above describes *Millionaire* as pitching the genre '*back* into prime-time [my emphasis]', it would be unfair to suggest that it had ever disappeared from this slot in the UK. Certainly, there was a sense in the late 1990s that traditional forms of light entertainment, especially quiz shows and sitcoms, were being overtaken by the rise of popular factual programming. But the quiz show has always had a presence in daytime and prime-time slots on British terrestrial television. In America, shows such as *Jeopardy!*, *Wheel of Fortune*, and *The Price is Right* have long since been syndicated as popular daytime fare. But the emphasis on a prime-time 'resurrection' was particularly visible in the late 1990s.[1]

The American resurgence in the genre included NBC launching *The Weakest Link* and reviving *Twenty-One* (2000), CBS launching *Winning Lines* (2000), and the Fox network scheduling *Greed* (1999). A key attraction here where producers and channels were concerned was simply cost. While *Millionaire* had upped the stakes in terms of production values (including a very expensive set), quiz shows were typically costing $150,000 per show, versus $1 million per hour for prime-time drama (Mahoney 2000). But just as American critics described *Millionaire* as a 'surprise hit', so its American executive producer, Michael Davies, explained how 'everybody said . . . "Oh, a prime time quiz show? Are you crazy?". . . But people forget that in the 1950s . . . this [was] . . . the foundation of American television'.[2] Davies' description here confirms Boddy's observation that the history of the quiz show in America is marked by peaks and troughs of popularity. As Boddy explains:

> [T]he quiz show has endured long periods of critical disdain or indif-ference, interrupted by infrequent moments of generalized and often hyperbolic critical reaction to the spectacular success of a specific show or format, before the genre recedes again into fringe-time invisibility and *critical* obscurity [original emphasis]. (2001: 79)

But while television channels in the US and UK eagerly cashed in on the quiz show boom, critics in the press sometimes produced a more negative discourse – what *The Independent* described as 'the usual har-rumphing about the morality of giving away such sums of money on television' (Hughes 1998: 12). In fact, 'traditionalists . . . waxed lyrical about the days when contestants were happy to go home with a food mixer or a toaster . . .' (ibid.). Academic commentary was not immune from such expressions of distaste. Mike Wayne's analysis '*Who Wants To Be a Millionaire?*: Contextual Analysis and the Endgame of Public Service Television' foregrounded the programme as evidence of how 'the gravitational pull of commercialisation . . . is warping what is left of public service television' (2000: 197). On a wider scale, Wayne's analysis implicitly reflects a history which has emphasised the differ-ences between British and American quiz shows, and this history con-flates perceptions of different broadcasting systems (public service versus commercial) with perceptions of cultural values. For example, although the two contexts have rarely been compared in any detail, comments such as 'American game shows . . . tend to be more harshly competitive . . . and winning is everything' (Cowdery and Selby 1995: 204), abound in academic literature. References to format and title adaptation – the American *Family Feud* became the British *Family Fortunes*, and the American format *Card Sharks* became the British *Play Your Cards Right* – have also been used to attest to these differences. In this regard, while American shows apparently celebrate ruthless competition and the acquisition of commodities or money, the British programmes are more invested in maintaining the social aspects of competition, and focusing on participation rather than reward. From the perspective of Wayne's argument above, *Millionaire* appeared to be a regrettable attempt to buck this trend.

This brief discussion of the institutional and cultural impact of *Millionaire* carries a weight of history behind it, and this history contextualises many of the comments and judgements which attended its emergence. In this respect, the advent of *Millionaire* points to the importance of understanding quiz show history. Chapter 2 begins by exploring the somewhat disparate generic roots of the quiz show in the British and American contexts, while examining how the development of the quiz show was shaped by the institutional structures of broadcasting in each case. This includes exploring how public service and commercial broadcasting systems approached the regulation and development of the genre, including, for example, the regulation of prizes. This is far from simply factual information which can be used to contextualise a programme before the 'real' analysis begins. The institutional infrastructures and policies which regulate quiz shows can themselves offer insight into cultural attitudes toward the genre, while they also exert a shaping influence on its textual form. Yet the chapter does not aim to offer a neat and exhaustive chronological history which leads up the contemporary moment. Even if this were possible, many of the debates surrounding the genre are cyclical, re-emerging in new contexts. In this regard, while Chapter 2 does seek to indicate key stages of generic development, it also aims to demonstrate why studying the history of the genre has a vital role to play in quiz show scholarship.

Historical precursors

As Thomas DeLong has explained, the term 'quiz' is a word with an uncertain origin. In the eighteenth century, it was linked to the idea of a practical joke, but by the twentieth century it was associated with the idea of questioning ('to quiz . . . a person to learn the extent of his or her knowledge') (1991: 1). Academia has reinforced this connotation and, in the American context, to 'quiz' the students means to 'test' (for example, a 'pop quiz'). Quiz and game shows on radio and television also appropriated an existing cultural appetite for games, and they find their roots in the diverse contexts of the fairground sideshow, the Victorian/Edwardian parlour game, and the popular press (Whannel 1992: 181). With the growth of newspapers in the early twentieth century, publications also adopted the quiz or question-and-answer feature as a means to attract audience interest and boost circulation (DeLong 1991: 1). Furthermore, theatrical performers in music hall or vaudeville had previously incorporated games into their stage numbers (ibid.: 2), while gambling had long since had a presence in cultural life, much to the concern of nineteenth-century reformers.

As these precursors and contexts make clear, it is important to approach quizzes and games as a wider cultural practice which have a life outside of broadcasting (and we can note the popularity of quiz books, board games and pub quizzes). Yet while broadcasting did not 'invent' quizzes and games, it was radio and television which transformed them into 'programmes'. Furthermore, the influence of broadcasting is especially crucial given that the quiz show is one of few broadcast forms which did not emerge as an adaptation of existing entertainment in literature, cinema or theatre (Mittell 2002: 320).

The broadcast development of the quiz show begins with radio, and in the UK and the US, television emerged from the same institutional infrastructure as sound broadcasting. British television, as presided over by the BBC, developed under an ethos of public service, while US television was in the hands of the commercial networks. The British government had deemed that the wavebands necessary for broadcasting be regarded as a 'valuable form of public property' (Scannell 1990: 11), and felt that such an 'important a national service ought not to be allowed to become an unrestricted commercial monopoly' (ibid.: 13). The government awarded a public service monopoly to the BBC, and the licence agreement required the BBC to 'inform, educate and entertain'. This differed from the complex, competitive and commercial network of radio's infrastructure in the US which was established by the mid-1930s. Yet simply because broadcasting was in the hands of commercial networks did not mean that it was not charged with public service responsibilities to inform, educate and entertain. In fact, while this chapter indicates how the institutional differences between British and American broadcasting are relevant when examining the development of the quiz and game show, it also suggests that the use of sharp contrasts is not always helpful.

Until 1955, the BBC was the sole broadcaster of television in the UK. This monopoly came to an end when commercial television (ITV) was launched in 1955. The BBC was awarded the right to broadcast a second channel in the early 1960s, and BBC2 went on air in 1964. This followed the findings of the Pilkington Committee (the Pilkington Report was published in 1962), which famously contrasted the BBC and ITV, accusing ITV of screening a preponderance of 'trivial' fare, and suggesting that the channel had failed to realise the powerful social and cultural effects of the television. As is often noted (Sendall 1982; Whannel 1992), quiz and game shows featured heavily in the Pilkington Committee's scathing assessment of ITV, held up as the essence of its innate 'triviality' and appetite for 'cheap' and populist fare. This has cemented the quiz show's identity in Britain as a 'low' cultural form, while it has also fostered a tendency to discuss ITV as the early home of the genre in British television history. This, however, effaces the BBC's role in establishing the possibilities of the quiz and game show in Britain, at least two decades before ITV arrived.

'Buying the audience': regulating reward

With regard to the BBC, one of the earliest references to competitions in broadcasting, and thus prizes or rewards, appears to be in 1926. A memo from the BBC's Board of Governors notes that: 'It [is] . . . felt that the conduct of competitions should be carefully considered by the Programme Board before they were entered into by any department, and that under any circumstances no more than one a month should be held'.[3] The need for careful consideration was clarified in 1930 when a producer enquired about including a puzzle competition in *Children's Hour*:

> While I entirely agree with the [BBC's] Board [or Governors] that competitions of any obvious type, which are more in the nature of lotteries than anything else, are to be deprecated, I feel that the right kind of competition which stimulates thought and creates intelligent interest has something to recommend it.[4]

The aim of fostering 'intelligent interest' sat at the core of the BBC's idea of public service, and this was in itself imagined as the chief 'reward' for listening. As a further memo expands, programmes containing prizes 'inevitably introduce an element of bribery rather than adequate reward as a means of stimulating interest'.[5] The use of prizes and competitions in broadcasting is here seen as a deplorable means of 'buying' the audience, something which sits in tension with the BBC's public service ideals. Programmes dealing with prizes also posed further problems for the Corporation: they could be construed as a form of advertising, and this was prohibited by the BBC's official charter.

In contrast, the emergence of the quiz show in America, which developed with the rise of commercial radio broadcasting, operated as a vehicle for commercial messages from the start (Hoerschelmann 2006: 40). On 1930s radio, quiz shows promoted particular products by linking the sponsor or advertiser names to the game ('*your brand* jackpot', '*your brand* prize winner' [original emphasis]) (ibid.: 55). Later examples have also explicitly used prizes as a form of product placement (for example, *The Price is Right*, *Supermarket Sweep*). The boundary between programme material and advertising has always been subject to stricter regulation in the UK, and this has meant (although the BBC's early concerns anticipate the future of a genre which would always, to some extent, *blur* the boundaries between advertising and entertainment) that such commercial relationships have been less overt in Britain.

The BBC's concern about the relationship between listening, viewing and winning ('bribing' or buying the audience) had also been debated in America – an example of why sharp contrasts between the two contexts are not always helpful. The concept of the radio 'give-away' had created controversy in the late 1930s when programmes such as NBC's *Pot O' Gold* debuted with a new gimmick: calling people from the telephone book and awarding them $1,000 just for answering (Mittell 2002: 320). The regulations imposed by the Federal Communications Commission (FCC) prevented the existence of on-air lotteries, and the FCC encouraged the Department of Justice to prosecute the show on these grounds (ibid.: 321). Although this was not carried through, the FCC's attitude was enough to dissuade other networks from pursuing such programming, at least until the late 1940s when there was again a radio upsurge in the 'give-away'. This time the FCC aimed to ban the genre, again on the grounds that it constituted an on-air lottery that was not 'in the public interest' (ibid.: 320). What is notable here is that such programmes were seen as the ultimate attempt to 'buy the audience', with the FCC deeming them to be 'illegitimate broadcasting rather than "proper" entertainment' – an attempt to lure an audience with the promise of 'easy money' (ibid.: 332). In this regard, although the radio 'give-away' could not have emerged in Britain at this time (with the publicly funded institution of the BBC representing the primary radio broadcaster), the FCC in fact uses the same terminology, and expresses the same distaste, as the Corporation. Indeed, while the term 'give-away' was later used by the BBC to signal all that was distasteful about American broadcasting and values, there is actually nothing intrinsically 'American' about the idea of giving away money. In fact, programmes labelled as 'give-aways' in America were criticised for promoting the ' "Un-American" value of receiving something for nothing' (Mittell 2003: 35), not least because they appeared to *undermine* the myth of the American Dream (in which success is deemed to follow hard work).

'The BBC can be accused of using licence-holders' money wrongly'

The chapter has so far outlined the extent to which, according to early debates at the BBC, the quiz and game show is seen as having an uneasy relationship with the concept of public service. In fact, in 1957 the BBC's Deputy Director of Television Broadcasting set out in more detail the 'difficulties and dangers associated with money giving programmes':

(a) The BBC can be accused of using licence-holders' money wrongly

(b) The possible effect on the contestants of being given a large money prize (for example, prize winners in the 'Pools' and in the Irish Sweep have become dissolute) can be unfortunate.

(c) Audiences can be wrongly moved by the desire for unearned money . . .[6]

The second and third of these points appear to rest on a middle-class disdain for an (implicitly) working-class audience, while the first point refers to the BBC's status as a public institution funded by the licence fee. The memo goes on to gesture toward the Corporation's 'ban' on prizes, which it suggests has been in place before the Second World War. But even within the existing trail of memos relating to the BBC's early radio and television quizzes, the idea of a ban is undermined. In 1954, when the BBC were facing the impending arrival of a competing television channel in the form of ITV, the controller of television programmes, Cecil McGivern, spoke of how the Corporation needed to decide on a policy about these programmes before ITV began. He went on to say that the arguments against prizes were valid, but so were the arguments *for* prizes:

> Even the BBC offers bonuses – which are prizes – for good work. But prize programmes can also be fairly intelligent! It can be argued that the sensible way is to admit a human weakness [the desire to win a prize and get something for nothing] and, while catering to it, at the same time try and control it and try to keep it decent.[7]

What might be described as this negotiated approach (trying to 'control it' while keeping it 'decent') characterises the BBC's involvement with the quiz and game show on both radio and television in the 1940s and the 1950s, and to some degree ever since this time. In order to demonstrate this, it is necessary to outline the range of programmes on offer in this early period.

Game on: the range of programmes

Although quizzes had a certain presence on local British radio stations before the establishment of the BBC, they had an earlier start in America. American historians have pointed to the growth of quiz programmes on 1920s local radio stations (such as *Pop the Question* in 1923); 1930s radio forms such as *Vox Pop*, which incorporated elements of interview, quiz and human interest; and programmes such as *Uncle Jim's Question Bee*, which selected contestants from the audience to answer a range of general knowledge questions for monetary reward (Hoerschelmann 2006).

From the earliest days, the BBC used a number of formats from the US. The Corporation claimed that radio's 1937 *Inter-regional Spelling Competition* in Children's Hour, inspired by an American format and indicating an early example of format adaptation, represented the birth of the 'quiz programme' on British radio.[8] This was followed by the efforts of the BBC's fledgling television service which had commenced transmission in 1936. *Spelling Bee* was broadcast on BBC television, transmitted live from Alexandra Palace, in 1938. Hosted by Freddie Grisewood, the programme featured a panel of children who were asked to spell a series of words.[9] But television did not get a chance to explore such programming before the service was closed down for the Second World War, and it remained closed until 1946. The majority of long-running quiz formats thus initially emerged on radio in the 1940s, and after the restructuring of the BBC's radio service (see Crisell 2001), they primarily appeared on the Home and Light Programmes.

First, there was a strand of programming which focused on general knowledge and competition. This could encompass competition between teams, whether in *Transatlantic Quiz*, which aired simultaneously over BBC and the American NBC network during the war, or the regional *Round Britain Quiz* (Light, 1947–present). Other programmes focused on competitions between individuals, perhaps most famously in *What Do You Know?* (Light, 1946–present), where the aim was to find the 'Brain of Britain'. *Puzzle Corner* (Light, 1946–8) was a combination of general knowledge and crossword puzzles, and the *ABC Spelling Bee* for adults was another example of British broadcasting adapting the American spelling bee craze (Home 1947). *Top of the Form* was an inter-school quiz with teams of four pupils (Home 1947–75), and there were many quiz formats aimed specifically at children.

Adapted from the American radio programme *Information Please!*, the BBC's *The Brains Trust* began on radio in 1941 (and the British version was also re-broadcast in the US). Although originally conceived as a quiz format, *The Brains Trust* ultimately became a discussion programme, with questions sent in – as in America – by the listening audience. Deliberately positioning itself at the opposite end of the class spectrum was the popular *Have a Go!* (Light, 1946–67). Including a quiz based on general knowledge which largely focused on popular culture,

Have a Go! was presented by the popular Yorkshireman Wilfred Pickles. With the tag-line 'Presenting the People to the People', it was organised around the idea of allowing 'ordinary folk' to perform, and the quiz element was really secondary to the banter between contestant and host. *Have a Go!* did involve economic reward, and the programme's famous catchphrase was 'Give' 'em the money, Barney' (which referred to the producer, Barney Colehan). The conventional prize, however, was a modest 38s 6d.

From sound to vision . . . 'The programme is the thing, not the prizes'

When the quiz show came to television, certain BBC personnel felt that, with its verbal basis in question and answer, it had a certain 'non-visual' quality.[10] While it is true that the 1950s saw many of the radio programmes transfer to television, new formats also emerged. The popular 'Brain of Britain' competition (*What Do You Know?*) made the shift in 1955, and in *Ask Me Another* (BBC, 1955–63), intellectual geniuses competed in teams of three. Prior to this, *The Brains Trust* (BBC, 1955–61) and *Top of the Form* (BBC, 1953–75) had already made the transition to television.[11] By 1950, the radio title of *Puzzle Corner* was re-used as the name of a quiz section in the magazine programme *Kaleidoscope* (BBC, 1946–53). Presented by MacDonald Hobley, this again incorporated a prize element. The offer of £2–4 for answering general knowledge questions may sound like an incredibly small sum today. However, in 1954, the chief wage earner in a working-class family would bring home around £9–10 week (Hoggart 1958: 9), so the prize in *Puzzle Corner* was not insignificant. Yet such examples of prize-giving seem to be overlooked in the BBC's emphasis on a self-imposed 'ban'.

The Charlie Chester Show (BBC, 1951–60) also began in 1951, and it included a 'Pot Luck' section in which members of the public participated in games for forfeits and prizes. *Know Your Partner* (BBC, 1951) quizzed couples about their knowledge of each other, and the early 1950s also saw the flourishing of the television panel game. The most popular of these was undoubtedly the American-invented *What's My Line?* (BBC, initially 1951–62). Hosted by Eamon Andrews and featuring panel members such as Gilbert Harding, Isobel Barnett, Barbara Kelly and David Nixon, the task was to guess the unusual occupation undertaken by a member of the public.

What is important here is that the BBC's negotiated approach to prize-giving in the quiz or game show, whether on radio or television, fosters essentially two strategies. First, there are programmes in which the competitors win prestige and a symbolic prize, rather than a consumer-orientated prize or a cash reward. This applies to programmes such as *What Do You Know?* and *Ask Me Another* (which offered a diploma and book tokens), and it has continued with programmes such as *Mastermind* and *University Challenge*. Second, there is the offer of limited cash or commodities only when the programmes are not really about the prizes (or even knowledge), but pivot on participation, camaraderie and the experience of meeting the host. Radio's *Have a Go!* offered monetary reward, but everyone appeared to be given the same sum of money. When speaking in the press, the host Wilfred Pickles would also emphasise how the money was 'just for fun', and that 'often it is returned at the end of the programme to help some good cause'.[12] There was equally a persistent fudging of where the money actually came from – Pickles would joke about 'Father Christmas'[13] – and it was unceremoniously produced from a brown paper bag.

Have a Go! was a radio show, and the idea of aiming for an image of restraint necessarily took on new meanings where television was concerned. Produced by the Light Entertainment Department, *The Charlie Chester Show* was greeted with some surprise by the press, attracting such headlines as 'New TV Show Will Give Presents: BBC Breaks Rules for Quizzers', 'First TV Gift Show', or simply (referring back to *Have a Go!*) 'Give Em the Money, Charlie'.[14] In this regard, early debates about prize-giving on television circled around more of a 'game' show segment than a quiz show. Comedian Charlie Chester had previously fronted successful radio shows such as *A Proper Charlie* and *That Man Chester*. When Chester's programme was adapted for television in 1951, the 'Pot Luck' saw members of the studio audience at the King's Theatre, Hammersmith, compete in a range of games and party forfeits (which critics often cited as humiliating). The prizes on offer ranged across cosmetic pearls, ties, handkerchiefs, nylon tights, a lamp and a razor blade, as well as football, boxing or theatre tickets. These choices also anticipate the ethos of later BBC shows such as *Blankety Blank*, which deliberately made jokes about the 'naffness' of its prizes ('A *Blankety Blank* cheque book and pen!').

With regard to *The Charlie Chester Show*, the head of light entertainment, Ronald Waldman, was keen to frame the programme's image of restraint in more earnest tones. He told the press how the 'prizes would be severely limited in cost . . . No big American stuff here . . . We don't want to buy viewers . . . The programme is the thing, not the prizes. We can't have people queuing for tickets to furnish their homes'.[15] Waldman's comment is an important reminder of the still austere conditions of everyday life in Britain in 1951: many wartime rations were still in force (see Addison 1985). His bid to distance *The Charlie Chester Show* from American programmes also speaks to a long history in which the BBC has invoked the 'other' of the American quiz or game show in order to shore up its own sense of public service difference. Here, America provides a contrast in terms of its television system (which is apparently driven by rampant commercialism), as well as of cultural values (the apparently insatiable pursuit of consumer desires).

The Charlie Chester Show was clearly wary about showcasing its goods, and there were particular concerns that television, with its visual aesthetic, would only increase the dangers of advertising and promotion. Several press reviews reported how 'complaints came from viewers' because the prizes were handed to the on-screen participants in boxes.[16] The BBC claimed that this aptly reflected the theme of 'pot luck', while it also indicated that participation (not prizes) was the point of the show. In this regard, *The Charlie Chester Show* is a clear example of the BBC negotiating its relations with the genre (catering to a prize-giving desire while 'trying to control it and keep it decent'). Yet the outcome of this for *television* was the sight of hidden prizes in boxes being shuttled across the screen.

Quiz shows as 'cultural uplift'?

Although *The Charlie Chester Show* was frowned on by critics (and even by personnel within the BBC), it would be misleading to suggest that quiz and game shows only carried negative cultural associations. One of the challenges of studying programming in this area (and in mapping an early history) is the sheer diversity of programmes which might come under the umbrella of 'quiz' or 'game'. The Introduction to the book noted Mittell's observation that quiz shows have 'alternately been hailed as cultural enrichment and educational, or as corrupting influences encouraging gambling . . . and dumbed down intellects . . .' (Mittell 2007). For example, while this chapter has discussed the rise of the radio 'give-away' on US radio, the dominant incarnation of the genre on 1930s and 1940s American radio 'focused . . . upon the intellectual challenge of contestants competing for modest prizes' (Mittell 2002: 322). As Mittell expands in relation to American radio shows such as *Professor Quiz* and *Dr I.Q.*, the genre was 'socially validated through the framework of educational appeals and cultural uplift . . . focusing on fact and objective knowledge' (2002: 325). This is where a comparison with British broadcasting is particularly interesting. With regard to 1940s BBC radio, it is true that critics or listeners could occasionally praise quiz shows as a legitimate form of broadcasting, citing children's quizzes as evidence of 'the good work of the teacher', while also emphasising their educational value.[17] But the BBC did not really seek to promote its quizzes in terms of 'cultural uplift'. In fact, the Corporation was more likely to play down these possibilities.

For example, radio's *Round Britain Quiz* (which focused on a general knowledge competition between teams) was conceived as 'primarily an entertainment and not a competitive examination',[18] while radio's *Top of the Form* was keen to ensure that it was not 'too academic' and that the questions were kept 'as general as possible'.[19] Even with the more discursive format of *The Brain's Trust* – for which listeners sent in often philosophical questions such as 'What is happiness?' and 'Are thoughts things or about things?'[20] – the BBC was not excessively keen to foreground its educational significance. In fact, it emphasised how it was not the aim of the series to allow 'clever people to show listeners how really clever they are'.[21] It was for questions to be answered concisely, so 'that as many [listeners] as possible may hear their questions asked' (ibid.). In terms of a connection with public service values, it is audience participation which is foregrounded here.

This can be interpreted in different ways. Despite the emphasis on the BBC's class elitism and paternalism in institutional histories of broadcasting, it is clear that the BBC was often well aware of such perceptions, and worked hard to address its more negative associations. But the BBC's hesitation in stressing the educational value of the quiz show was perhaps also shaped by the fact that this was a subject of considerable cultural debate at the time. As Chapter 4 outlines, many critics and 'experts' doubted the educational value of the genre (and this debate continues until this day).

Thus, while it would be untrue to suggest that the early radio and television quiz in Britain was purely seen as a 'low' cultural form, it did not appear to carry the potentially positive social values of 'educational appeals and cultural uplift' which could be associated with some of the shows in the American context (Mittell 2002: 325). This is a further example of how the 'common-sense' oppositions which are often drawn between British public service television and the American commercial networks (as well as the British and American quiz show), reward a more critical eye.

ITV and the quiz and game show

As the 1950s progressed, the Conservative government re-opened the monopoly debate, and pressure grew for an alternative service. In 1954, the Television Act made the coming of commercial television a reality, and the service began broadcasting in the London region in September 1955. ITV was to be funded by spot advertising during commercial breaks, and with regional programme contractors making up the service, the channel was supervised by the Independent Television Authority (ITA). Furthermore, it was a measure of the prevailing strength of a public service ethos that ITV was actually set up as an extension of this concept: the new channel still had to conform to a public service remit, with a duty to educate and inform as well as to entertain (Scannell 1990). Nevertheless, existing broadcast histories have emphasised the differences between the BBC and ITV, and the quiz and game show has played a prominent role in this respect.

The quiz and game show, or to use the dominant term from the time, the 'give-away' show, is often used in existing histories of the 1950s to represent ITV giving the audience what it wanted, apparently untroubled by concerns about critical distaste and cultural value (Sendall 1982). The genre is also invoked as the epitome of ITV's claim to be 'people's television', addressing the working-class audience in ways which it found more appealing. The emphasis on Americanisation is also important. While the previous discussion of the BBC points to a much longer history of British disdain for American culture, the post-war period is widely recognised as a time when fears about the Americanisation of British life and culture were particularly apparent. Britain's status as a declining world power and its substantial war debt created a dependency on American finance for post-war reconstruction. This fostered (or accelerated) the feeling that British values, histories and forms of culture were under threat. In introducing advertising to British television, the emergence of ITV fed into these debates, and the channel was associated with the 'Americanisation' of British broadcasting from the start. Its use of American quiz and game formats, and the fact that America is often identified as the home of such programming, meant that ITV's association with Americanisation was doubly consolidated. (This is despite the fact that, as the preceding discussion has noted, the BBC had long since used American formats.)

It is certainly true that quiz shows were central to the building of the audience for commercial television. By early 1957 there were between eight and ten such shows a week (depending on the region), a move which later prompted the ITA to demand a reduction to one per day. The first three shows to achieve popularity were *Double Your Money* (ITV, 1955–64) hosted by Hughie Greene, *Take Your Pick* (ITV, 1955–68) hosted by Michael Miles, and Tommy Trinder's *Beat the Clock* section in the popular *Sunday Night at the London Palladium*

(ITV, 1955–67). ITV adapted a number of formats from the US, including the big money programmes such as *The 64,000 Question* (ITV, 1956–8), and *Twenty-One* (ITV, 1957–9), which were hugely popular on American television in the 1950s. Almost immediately after ITV began, it adapted the American radio success *People Are Funny* (ITV, 1955–6). Referred to as one of the 'stunt' shows in the US (Mittell 2002), and downplaying question and answer in favour of set-ups and 'daffy' tasks, such programmes challenged the dominance of the question-centred quiz on American radio in the 1940s. The UK version of *People are Funny* was also controversial, and it was quickly pulled from the schedules after its mix of 'ordinary' people, prizes and pranks was deemed by critics and MPs to be in 'bad taste'. *Take Your Pick* similarly included forfeits (as did the BBC's *The Charlie Chester Show*), and the cultural debate shifted to a dominant emphasis on the 'dumbing down' of knowledge, and a distaste for the apparent humiliation and ridicule of the contestants (Holmes 2008).

The changing debate surrounding the programmes also focused on money. When compared to previous programmes on the BBC, there was certainly a big leap in the prizes on offer. ITV's *Double Your Money*, for example, boasted a jackpot prize of £1,025. However, the jackpot was rarely won, and the British prizes were still far smaller than those offered in America. The British adaptation of *The $64,000 Question* paid its top prize in sixpences (amounting to £1,600) and the lavish prizes on the American version of *People are Funny*, such as houses or aeroplanes, were replaced in the UK with washing machines, radios and refrigerators. But it is important to bear in mind that, with the more prosperous 'age of affluence' only reaching Britain by mid-decade, these commodities were then seen as symbols of the high-consumption way of life. In reading the press commentary at the time, we get glimpses of how the genre was discussed as part of a wider distaste for a shiny new consumerism. A critic in *The Times* observed how, 'Collectively, these . . . programmes leave a dominant impression of money and goods changing hands at a feverish tempo, a symbol of our buy now, buy quick (and pay later) society'.[22] To some degree, this distaste for consumerism has shaped attitudes toward the quiz show ever since that time.

So although some of these concerns over prize-giving and the promotion of acquisitive desires had structured the BBC's circulation of the genre long before ITV emerged, the new channel did mark a shift in the cultural visibility of the quiz and game show, and the cultural associations it carried. In the mid to late 1950s, the quiz/game show became a repository for British fears surrounding the commercialisation of television and its development into a truly mass medium. But it was in America that this relationship would be most visibly explored: enter the quiz show scandals.

The scandal of it!: quiz shows and 1950s American television

In the US, the ruling of the Supreme Court in 1954 that quiz shows were not a form of gambling paved the way for the high stakes prizes on the Big Money television shows. The first big television show, *The $64,000 Question*, was adapted from the radio format, *Take It or Leave It*, but on radio, the top prize had been $64. Suddenly, with the advent of television, it was possible to win the huge sum of $64,000. Produced by Louis G. Cowan, television's *The $64,000 Question* was first broadcast on CBS on 5 June 1955. The contestant was required to answer a series of questions of escalating monetary value. It took eleven correct answers to win and there were no multiple choices, and the programme adopted the serial structure of the hangover – a contestant's appearance could stretch across more than one edition. With audience figures exceeding 50 million, *The $64,000 Question* was an immediate success, prompting other networks to pursue quiz shows. Many new shows premiered, including the spin-off *The $64,000 Challenge*, and other titles such as *The Big Surprise*, *Dotto*, *Tic Tac Dough*, and *Twenty One*. *The $64,000 Question* also offered an early case study of a format's global circulation. Adaptations of the programme 'spread around the world, without regard for nationality or ideology' (Anderson 1978: 30). The Italian version, *Lascia O Raddoppia* ('Double or Nothing'), is even said to have stimulated the rise of television ownership (ibid.: 35).

The programmes represented an important juncture in the adaptation of the genre for television, as they exploited the visual possibilities of the medium in ways which radio had not required. They relished the possibility of exploring the possibilities of quiz show aesthetics: cross-cutting between battling contestants, or placing the contestants' faces next to dollar signs (Boddy 1990: 104). The iconography of the progammes was also intended to convey the seriousness of the proceedings and the genre's claim to fairness and authenticity. Contestants were sequestered in sound proof booths while bank executives and armed guards made on-air deliveries of sealed questions. On *The $64,000 Question*, the first four questions were provided by an IBM sorter – this was intended to create the impression that the questions were selected randomly without human intervention.

The fact that the programmes are now primarily associated with corporate greed stems from the role that sponsor control played in the scandals. The Big Money shows were often sponsored by a single company, such as Revlon's sponsorship of *The $64,000 Question*, or Geritol's sponsorship ('America's number one tonic for tired blood!') of *Twenty-One*. On one level, there were explicit economic motivations for producers wanting to exercise control over what were promoted as unwritten contests. In a testimony to the Congressional subcommittee, the former *Twenty-One* contestant Herbert Stempel explained how the producer of the show, Dan Enright, had told him that,

> [h]e received approximately $10,000 a week [from the sponsor] . . . as prize money, and he had to arrange the games in such a way as to not go over the budget, because any monies which were expended over $10,000 . . . came out of his pocket, and if he could keep the budget down, he made a little gravy, to use the phrase.[23]

Control manifested itself in other ways. Contestants would be taught how to produce a tense and anxious performance, or could even be provided with the answers in advance. Such strategies ensured that producers could exert a greater control over the life-span and popularity of their on-screen 'characters' and narratives. Fiction provides the certainty of suspense, drama and clearly delineated characters. In comparison, quiz shows, much like reality shows today, are structured to 'elicit and intensify drama without actually scripting it' (Haralovich and Trossett 2004: 80) (see also Chapter 1). But while this unwritten quality is integral to the genre's appeal, it also represents a risk for producers: how do they know that the 'characters' and their 'narratives' will be exciting/compelling/dramatic? In this regard, the desire to exercise producer or sponsor control pointed to the contradictory demands placed on the quiz show as a television form.

While in some shows the contestants were unaware of producer intervention, this was not ultimately the case with *Twenty-One*. Conceived and created by Dan Enright, a producer at NBC, *Twenty-One* utilised soundproof booths and the game was played with two contestants in isolation. The contestants had to answer questions which were valued in difficulty (worth between one and eleven points) and the winner was the first contestant to reach twenty-one points. When the show failed to attract the desired ratings, its sponsor, Geritol, instructed the producers to 'take any measures to make it a success' (Venanzi 1997). The first big winner on the show was Herbert Stempel and the producers presented him as a 'man next door' or an 'average Joe' – a move which sought to capture audience interest and identification. This involved crafting as well as casting his identity, and Stempel was fashioned to present an image of a 'penniless ex-GI working his way through college' (Anderson 1978: 49). But Stempel was also seen as 'a high-IQ eccentric' (Doherty 2007), and his apparent unsuitability for the sponsor's image was sealed when Charles Van Doren appeared on the scene. Van Doren, a lecturer in English at Columbia University and son of a prestigious literary family, was perceived by Geritol to offer a more desirable contestant image, a 'clean-cut intellectual . . . instead of a freak with a sponge memory' (Anderson 1978: 69). The fact that Van Doren was described as more 'tele-genic' than Stempel also had class and ethnic implications. After all, the battle was between 'the tall hand-some, young Ivy Leaguer with the engaging smile versus the stout Jewish student from CCNY' (ibid.: 56). In 1956 viewers saw Stempel lose to Van Doren (with Van Doren ultimately scooping $129,000), but Stempel's loss was scripted by the producers.

The 1956–7 season saw the first public surfacing of the idea that the quizzes were not the straightforward contests of knowledge they appeared to be. Articles in national magazines such as *Time* and *Look* bluntly asked 'Are TV quizzes fixed?' (Anderson 1978: 88), and the dis-gruntled Herbert Stempel aimed to expose the cheating scam to the media. His story was not accepted until August 1958, and by this time it was increasingly corroborated by other contestants. Ratings fell, many prime-time quiz shows were taken off air, and in October 1958, a New York grand jury heard the testimonies of those involved. The contestants and producers all committed perjury by protesting their innocence. When the judge ordered the grand jury report sealed, 'Washington smelled a cover up and a political opportunity' (Doherty 2007). Thus, 1959 saw federal intervention, with the House Committee on Legislative Oversight holding hearings on the scandals. At this stage, contestants and producers confessed to the rigging – including the popular *Twenty-One* winner, Charles Van Doren. The main people prosecuted after the hearings were contestants, but they were not convicted for television fraud, but for lying to a grand jury (Anderson 1978: 182). This was because the rigging was not illegal, and also because it was not seen to constitute 'fraud' in the traditional sense (it lacked a clear victim) (ibid.: 134).

The legacy of the scandals

It is widely perceived that the scandals prompted a re-examination of national and cultural values in America. Amid discussions over 'moral illiteracy' and the privileging of consumer values over intellect, Van Doren occupied centre-stage – positioned as a starting point for debates about the ethics of television, and the state of US society in general.

In 1960 a bill was passed in the US which declared it illegal to run a game or contest on television with intent to deceive (Anderson 1978: 163). While this clearly occurred after the fact, the scandals highlighted how the rapid growth of television had outstripped the speed with which its regulatory framework had developed (DeLong 1991: 223). It is with respect to the institutional and economic framework of television that the clearest legacy of the scandals is seen to reside. The fact that the television networks could *deny* knowledge of the rigging seemed to highlight, on a broader scale, the potential dangers of a system driven by advertising profit, and which pivoted on a separation between programme production and network. It is now conventional to suggest that the quiz show scandals were instrumental in prompting a change in the economic and institutional infrastructure of American television. Instead of buying space to produce an entire programme, advertisers were to buy time to screen adverts in the separate slots of 'commercial breaks' (the system adopted from the start by commercial television in the UK). If advertisers no longer had direct involvement with a show, it was perceived that such a structure would eliminate the desire to 'meddle' with content in order to boost ratings.

Yet Boddy has sounded a note of caution here, arguing that the impact of the scandals may have been overstated. The demise of single sponsorship and the rise of multiple sponsorship, as well as the rising power of the networks in shaping programme licensing and scheduling, 'are all developments which predate . . . the public calamities of the quiz shows, already anachronisms in their mode of production in the second half of the 1950s' (Boddy 1990: 109). He does observe, however, that the quiz show scandals provided something of a 'reformist gloss on long-running network efforts to rest control programme procurement and scheduling from sponsors and advertising agencies' (ibid.).

The scandals also had a direct impact on the genre itself, at the level of scheduling, production and textual form. In this regard, policy regulation again influenced the parameters of the genre, as winnings were to be capped at $75,000. (This rose again in the 1980s, until the winnings cap was gradually removed.) The American television industry sought to reshape the circulation of the genre, rebranding 'quiz' shows as 'game' shows. While panel shows remained popular, the new definition of 'game shows' foregrounded programmes with:

> smaller monetary prizes, merchandise, and the centrality of audience participation. The emphasis on the new term *game* also indicates a

move away from the serious connotations of the term *quiz*, which granted the genre a significant degree of cultural centrality. (Hoerschelmann 2006: 92)

This decline in prestige was also marked by a shift in scheduling. Over the next three decades, the majority of new shows in the genre premiered in daytime, rather than prime-time, and were primarily geared toward a female audience (Hoerschelmann 2006: 92). While the initial run of *The Price is Right* (1956–63) actually commenced during the period of Big Money shows, it was joined in the 1960s by programmes focusing more on the 'female' domain of shopping and consumption, such as *Shopping Spree* and *Supermarket Sweep* (ibid.: 99). This did not, however, necessarily reflect a long-term shift in generic terminology and textual form. With the advent of the American version of *Millionaire* in 1999, it was not uncommon to see the term 'quiz' in circulation, and knowledge-based quizzes in prime-time were once again in vogue. But the attempt to rename the genre indicates how producers were engaged in a struggle to shape its cultural associations (ibid.: 17).

The American scandals were only the most high-profile example of concerns surrounding authenticity and ethics where the quiz show was concerned, and the British version of *Twenty-One* also faced accusations of foul play (see Holmes 2008). Despite this, the British commentary on the US events was smug and moralistic, aiming to shore up the difference of a television system with an overriding investment in public service. When it comes to prize-giving in British quiz shows, the juncture usually mentioned is the moment when the ITA, and then the Pilkington Report (1962), suggested that the value of prizes be reduced, and their distribution more 'closely linked to *skill and knowledge* [original emphasis]' (Whannel 1992: 184). The ITA had already announced in 1960 that there would be 'no more big money', and it stipulated that prizes should be limited to £1,000.[24] In a way not dissimilar to the American context, the ITA conducted a review of the arrangements governing prize-giving and competitions on quiz shows. Producers would have to produce a leaflet which explained the nature of the game and the rules under which it operated, as well as the process via which contestants were selected. This tighter regulatory framework was in part prompted by the American scandals, and the extent to which they had apparently dramatised the worst excesses of a system driven by corporate and commercial greed.

The American context may have been invoked to reassure British critics, audiences and regulators of the relative acceptability of the British TV system. (One critic commented how 'television really is an entertainment *business* in the US – we may have gone "commercial", but we are a long way from all that'.)[25] Yet the fact that this chapter has observed as many *similarities* as differences between the contexts may reflect back on the relatively close cultural relationship between British and American culture. Comparisons with how different national television systems have developed the quiz show may offer sharper contrasts. Cooper-Chen's cross-cultural comparison, written in the early 1990s, found that contexts with state-run broadcast systems which were geographically distant from the West (she lists territories in Africa and India) adopted games and quizzes which eschewed expensive consumer goods, which pivoted solely on the display of knowledge, and which emphasised teams of young people competing for their schools (1994: 254). This balance may be changing with the increased global flow of quiz and game show formats (see Chapter 1), but it does highlight how each national context has its own quiz history to reveal.

Now and then

The trajectory of how the quiz show developed in Britain after the 1960s does not have the distinct contours of the American context. But in subsequent decades, and building on the perceptions already evident in the 1950s, it is ITV which has continued to be associated with the highest-profile, and often critically reviled, examples of American formats. Adapting commodity-orientated programmes such as *Sale of the Century* (ITV, 1971–83, Sky 1989–92), and *The Price is Right*, the channel was accused by regulators of 'gloating over the high value' of the prizes – something considered to be the 'height of vulgarity'.[26] The BBC's shows of the 1960s and 1970s (from *Ask the Family* (BBC1, 1967–84, BBC2, 1999) and *The Generation Game* (BBC1, 1971–82, 1990–2002) to *Mastermind*) continued to display the 'negotiated' approach to prize-giving established in the 1940s and 1950s. Depending on the show in question, the emphasis was on winning prestige or participating 'just for fun' ('Didn't they do well?').

But there have clearly been considerable changes in the television environment since this time, especially when compared to the earlier period discussed in this chapter. We have moved through what John Ellis (2000) coins the 'era of scarcity' in television broadcasting (with many national contexts having access to one to two channels) to the 'era of availability' (the rise of satellite and cable TV in the 1980s), and then onto the 'era of plenty' (the proliferation of channel choice in the digital age). The shift toward the multiplication of channels was also facilitated by the deregulation of television. In a wider analysis of the

UK *Millionaire*, Wayne reflects specifically on how this institutional and economic framework has impacted upon the quiz and game show. The 1990 Broadcasting Act favoured deregulation and increased competition between channels, and it replaced the Independent Broadcasting Authority (IBA) with the Independent Television Commission (ITC). Until that time, the channels regulated by the IBA (ITV and Channel Four) could only give away prizes that were equal to the value of a small new car (Wayne 2000: 206). By 1993, this limit was £6,000. But after this stage, the lighter regulatory touch of the ITC saw a gradual relinquishing of these limits, and prize values slowly increased. It was in 1998 that British television saw the unprecedented offering of £1 million on ITV1's *Millionaire*.

As this chapter has outlined, the BBC has always self-regulated, imposing its own 'bans' and limits as it saw fit. Yet according to Wayne, the increasingly competitive and deregulated television environment has prompted considerable change in the construction and circulation of the genre across the board:

> Under public service broadcasting, examples of the quiz/game show genre tend to foreground such values as camaraderie, for example, *It's Knockout* and *The Generation Game*, or specialist knowledge, e.g. *Mastermind* or *University Challenge*, or physical/problem-solving skills such as *The Crystal Maze* . . . but the more exchange values permeate television, the more we can expect consumerism, consumer goods, individualism and hard cash to be at the centre of the game show. (2000: 197)

On one level, we can find evidence to support this argument. A programme such as the BBC's *The Weakest Link* could be perceived as confirming what Wayne sees as the decline of public service values (and the format also attests to the BBC's contemporary status as a key player in the international format trade – (see Chapter 1)). With the concept of camaraderie replaced by a ruthless battle for supremacy, Jerome Bourdon observes how the 'international success of *The Weakest Link* . . . is witness to the sense of defeat of public service television, which no longer knows how to extol its old ideals' (2004: 289). This may also speak to wider shifts in the social values of genre (as primarily examined in Chapter 4).[27]

What is of interest here is the extent to which Wayne's discussion of change in the genre indicates the value of returning to the early development of the quiz and game show. In fact, it suggests how the historical trail left by the BBC memos is still relevant to the understanding of the genre today. Despite Wayne's assertion that values such as camaraderie and 'specialist knowledge' are somehow tied to public service broadcasting, there is really no *inherent* relationship between the values of a quiz show, the prizes on offer, and their association with a public service or commercial broadcaster. As Matt Hills points out in his discussion of the relationship between ITV1 and *Millionaire*, there is no 'natural affinity' between big prize quiz/game shows and commercial television: this is the product of a cultural and institutional construction (2005: 179). The same can be said of the values which Wayne associates with the public service quiz and game show. In this regard, what is valuable in returning to the earlier broadcasting context is that it offers the opportunity to see this cultural construction *in process*. From Wilfred Pickles's references in *Have a Go!* to how the prize money came from 'Father Christmas', to the BBC's emphasis on how 'there will be no "Big American stuff" over here', to the frustrated viewers watching gifts in boxes on the BBC's 'Pot Luck', we see a deliberate *performance* of restraint, an attempt to shape the public perception of how the BBC spends its funds. To be sure, the BBC could not have matched the thousands of dollars offered by American quiz and game shows on radio and television, but it could have afforded more than it spent.

The value of returning to this earlier history can also be highlighted in other ways. The contemporary television environment has seen the proliferation, on an international scale, of Call TV Quiz channels, which pivot on viewers phoning in to answer questions or solve puzzles in the hope of winning a cash prize on air. In the UK, and following the success of the (now defunct) Channel-4-owned channel Quiz Time, ITV launched the digital service ITV Play. The channel largely screened gaming shows from other channels, while some of the titles, such as *Quizmania*, *The Mint* and *Glitterball*, were also transmitted in fringe slots (for example, 12am–4am) on ITV's terrestrial channel, ITV1. In programmes such as *Glitterball*, there are no on-screen competitors, but only excitable hosts who continually solicit the viewer to 'call in and play'. These programmes fill extended air-time, while also capitalising on the lucrative push toward transactional TV (you pay to 'play').

In the UK, these channels and programmes have attracted acute regulatory concern, as well as much media debate. The trade paper *Broadcast* announced how 'premium rate call TV shows have been accused of ripping off punters, but they are big business for [the channels], but with regulators mooting tougher regulation, could the good times be over?' (29 September 2006: 22). The programmes were variously accused of being too easy (in order to encourage people to call in) or too hard (making it impossible to win once you had paid to call in). In 2007, this took place amidst a much wider surge of concern surrounding the regulation of premium-rate phone lines on British television, with a range of popular magazine, quiz and entertainment shows all investigated for various shades of malpractice. These investigations variously focused on channels over-charging callers, using fake winners on air, and advertising competitions after a winner had already been selected.[28] In doing so, they effectively provided an occasion for the much wider expression of concern about the extent to which transactional TV has become a dominant means of funding programmes in an increasingly commercialised television landscape. As one viewer notes with a critical tone, phone or 'text to vote' has become 'a way of life now' (see Chapter 6).[29]

The Call TV Quiz channels were undoubtedly at the forefront of this wider surge of concern. But while the channels may be new and the formats different, we have to some extent heard these debates before. On one level, the whiff of rigging and malpractice harks back to the American quiz show scandals of the 1950s. On the other hand, the cultural and regulatory concern surrounding these shows is reminiscent of the earlier controversy over the radio 'give-away' in America. Indeed, it once more suggests that, in an increasingly commercialised broadcast environment, the audience is being 'bought' by the lure of 'easy money' and is being denied 'proper' entertainment in the process (only this time, they are paying for it). This is certainly *not* to suggest that there was no case to answer here: the breach of public trust involved in the phone-in scandals as a whole – spanning children's television, magazine and cookery shows and entertainment formats – reflected some truly serious lapses in television's regulatory frameworks. But it does suggest that, especially with regard to the Call TV Quiz channels, there were echoes of earlier concerns about the very idea of playing for money on television, and the apparent address to a nation of viewer/consumers rather than 'citizens'.

The debates surrounding these newer programmes also hark back to the BBC's initial concerns in the 1920s about 'buying' the audience (and the BBC has notably stayed well away from the Call TV Quiz phenomenon). Yet despite the repeated use of this phrase, the idea of 'buying the audience' has always had vague and ambiguous connotations. Does it refer to the possibility of the audience actually winning a prize while listening/viewing at home, or does it express a more general distaste for *any* broadcast programme which deals with money or prizes? While the television environment may have changed substantially since the BBC first contemplated prizes in programmes, the cultural attitudes speak to the past as much as the present.

Conclusion

This chapter has not aimed to offer a definitive overview of how the broadcast quiz show has developed through time. Even if this were possible (which seems doubtful given that the reality of generic development speaks to a messier terrain of affairs), subsequent chapters continue to explore issues of historical change and development. Topics discussed in the rest of the book include the increased investment in the 'unsociable' aspects of competition, the decline of commodities as prizes (Chapter 4), changing conceptions of appearing on television (Chapter 5), and the 'new' media contexts in which audiences now navigate their relations with the genre (Chapter 6).

This chapter has also aimed to approach history less as objective 'fact' than as a site of contestation, debate and interpretation. For example, rather than accepting the prevalent historical perception that the quiz show in Britain 'really' begins with the advent of ITV, re-inserting the BBC back into the picture points to a more on-going line of debate about the relationship between quiz shows, commercialisation and public service. Equally, the chapter has aimed to explore how there are a number of parallels to be drawn between the British and American contexts, as well as points of exchange or influence. In this respect, it has aimed to question 'common-sense' perceptions of the relationship between the British and American interpretation of the genre (and thus between public service and commercial television).

This chapter began with an emphasis on the '*Millionaire* effect' in the late 1990s and early 2000s. Trends in television programming change rapidly, meaning that academic publishing is always catching up with the flux and flow of the television schedules. At the time of writing this book, *Millionaire* is still on British television screens on a Saturday night, although it attracts a far smaller audience than in its initial years (approximately 5 to 6 million as compared to 11 million in the late 1990s/early 2000s). In 2006, the international popularity of *Deal or No Deal* marked a further interest in television games, although this did not necessarily signal a resurgence in knowledge-based games. Success continues to be unpredictable, with the next hit format just around the corner. In America, 2007 saw the huge success of Fox's *Are You Smarter than a Fifth Grader?* when it premiered as the number one network show in the first half of that year. The show sees adult contestants asked questions from the fifth-grade curriculum, and the format was also sold to the UK, where it was taken up by Sky and re-titled *Are You Smarter than a Ten Year Old?* (2007).

Although a 'peak and trough' picture does not adequately capture the history of the quiz show, it is true that a perennial problem for the genre is its relative lack of flexibility. Once the audience tires of a set format, it is hard to 'fix it'.[30] But the emphasis on quizzes as a 'fad' or 'addiction', indicating both a childish interest and a potentially 'dangerous' over-investment, also speaks to an unwillingness to take the genre's social and cultural significance seriously. As the next chapter explores, analysing quiz shows is a serious business.

Notes

1. 'TV's final answer?', *On-line NewsHour*, 19 January 2000, found at http://www.pbs.org/newshour/bb/entertainment/jan-june00/quiz_show_1–19.html [accessed 18 March 2007].
2. Cited in 'TV's final answer?' (ibid.).
3. 'Minutes of Control Committee Meeting', 13 January 1926. R19/989. BBC Written Archive Centre (hereafter 'WAC').
4. 'Competitions', D. P to D. G, 3 July 1930. R19/989 (WAC).
5. J. P. Clarke to Head of Talks, R19/989 (WAC).
6. 'News Chronicle competition', Deputy Director of Television to Director General, 7 August 1958. R34/595/2 (WAC).
7. Cecil McGivern to George Barnes, 29 November. 1954. T16/160 (WAC).
8. 'And that's how quiz kids were born!', *Evening Express*, 7 November 1958.
9. http://www.ukgamehsows.com/page.index/php/History_of_the_Game_Show [accessed 30 October 2006].
10. Ronald Waldman to Kenneth Adam, 29 June 1955. T12/455 (WAC).
11. Although it has been suggested that *Top of the Form* did not make the transition to television until 1962 (when it was called *Television Top of the Form*), this was not the case, although its television appearances were intermittent in the 1950s.
12. *Yorkshire Evening News*, 30 January 1950.
13. *The Evening Telegraph and Post: Dundee*, 29 December 1949.
14. See BBC Press Cuttings, Television, 1951–2 (WAC).
15. 'New TV show will give presents: BBC breaks rules for quizzers', *News Chronicle*, 6 December 1951.
16. *Daily Herald*, 27 December 1951.
17. 'Too much quiz?', *Birmingham Mail*, 15 October 1946.
18. 'Round Britain Quiz', Acting Controller, Light Programme, 23 March 1948. R51/519/2 (WAC).

19. 'Headmaster with a class of 12 million', *Daily Mirror*, 10 October 1950.
20. See Frank Gillard, 'The story of "Any Questions?"', *Radio Times*, 18 September 1953, p. 3.
21. 'The Brain's Trust talks too much', undated memo. R41/22/2 (WAC).
22. *The Times*, 22 October 1958.
23. Source: Congress, House, Committee on Interstate and Foreign Commerce, *Investigation of Television Quiz Shows*, 86th Cong., 1st Sess., 6–10, 12 October 1959 (Washington, DC: US Government Printing Office, 1960), reprinted at http://historymatters.gmu. edu/d/6557/ [accessed 3 April 2007].
24. *Daily Express*, 13 July 1960.
25. *Birmingham Mail*, 16 March 1959.
26. http://www.ukgameshows.com/page/index.php/Sale_of_the_ Century [accessed 18 March 2007].
27. It should be noted, however, that the BBC still guards its use of prize money quite carefully: *The Weakest Link* started out offering up to £10,000 per show, while the highest sum awarded by the Corporation to date is £200,700 (in *The People's Quiz*, 2007).
28. 'ITV suspends premium phone-lines', BBC News on-line, http://news.bbc.co.uk/1/hi/entertainment/6420885.stm [accessed 18 March 2007].
29. 'Roll up, roll up for multichannel television's latest money-spinner', *The Guardian*, 28 November 2005, p. 22.
30. Robert Thompson, cited in 'TV's final answer?'.

3 Quiz Show Theory: Approaching the Programme Text

Play is both liberty and invention, fantasy and discipline. (Roger Caillois 1961: 58)

The previous chapter examined some of the contexts from which the broadcast quiz show emerged, but this chapter is more concerned with the quiz show as it appears on screen. This involves asking questions about how we approach the analysis of the quiz show text, and what the purpose of this analysis might be. What critical and theoretical approaches can be used to analyse the quiz show, and what does their application reveal about its generic conventions, aesthetic construction, cultural politics?

In studying the quiz show, we have at our disposal a range of approaches which are used more widely in television studies. For example, the present chapter outlines how perspectives on quiz shows and 'power' have been influenced by changing approaches to ideology in television and cultural studies. Equally, Chapter 1 has explored the relationship between the quiz and game show and genre theory, as well as the branch of study interested in format adaptation. Chapter 2 has examined how the genre can be illuminated by historical, archival research and a focus on the institutional contexts of broadcasting, while Chapter 6 explores how work on fandom can be applied to the quiz show. But there are also critical approaches which can be applied to the quiz show, and which are arguably more specific to the genre. In this regard, we can point to anthropological and cultural studies of play offered by Johan Huizinga (*Homo Ludens* ('Man the Player') (1938)) and Roger Caillois (*Les Jeux et les Hommes* ('Man, Play and Games') (1958)). Huizinga and Caillois made important contributions to 'ludology': the study of games,[1] and if used selectively, their work can offer illuminating insights into *television* quizzes and games. Given that quiz shows have been described as difficult to analyse as television 'texts' (when compared, for example, to fiction) (Skovmand

2000: 367), drawing on wider disciplinary approaches can prove to be particularly fruitful.

Paradigms of power

Earlier approaches to quiz shows in television studies were often influenced by Marxism, not least of all because it represented a key paradigm of thought in television/cultural studies when academic work on quiz shows began to emerge. But Marxism has also been important in quiz show criticism in so far as, like the quiz show, it deals explicitly with questions of money, consumerism, opportunity and class. Detailed introductions to Marxism can be found elsewhere (see Turner 1996), but the crux of Marx and Engels's critique in *The German Ideology* was that the ideas of the 'ruling class are in every epoch the ruling ideas, i.e. the class which is the ruling *material* force in society, is the same as the ruling *intellectual* force [original emphasis]' (1968: 64). What they meant by this is that those who control the means of economic and cultural production in society also control the circulation of ideas. These 'ideas' are often referred to as ideologies, and while the concept of ideology can be defined and approached in different ways (see Storey 2001: 2–5), it can broadly be conceptualised as a set of dominant value systems and beliefs. Although often presented as 'natural' or 'common sense', ideologies offer particular ways of seeing the world (which support dominant structures of power). In this regard, television can be seen to produce a multitude of ideological discourses ranging across capitalism, consumerism, work, individualism, class, gender, sexuality and ethnicity (and so on).

Earlier approaches to the quiz show tended to see the genre as a site of ruling ideological power. Writing in *Screen Education* in 1976, and comparing the intellectual *Mastermind* with the more populist *Sale of the Century*, John Tulloch was interested in exploring how 'ideology is reproduced in two current quiz programmes' (1976: 3). As the use of the term 'reproduced' suggests, Tulloch asserts that both programmes express ruling class values. *Sale of the Century*, for example, is seen as suturing a passive audience further into the capitalist system:

> Placing contestants in a situation where goods that represent hard saving, HP debts or wistful dreams to a large part of the audience are available at 'give-away' prices is a superb stroke of gimmickry. In a sense it is a delivery of the promises that advertisers make. (1976: 9)

Earlier versions of Marxism perceived ideology to operate as a kind of 'veil' over the eyes of the working-class – a filter that disguised people's 'real' relations with the world around them. In this regard, it is no coincidence that Tulloch focuses on the construction of consumerism (or 'leisure') here, and Marxism has often offered a very gloomy perspective on consumerism (Edwards 2000: 18) (see Chapter 4). A classic Marxist reading would expect consumerism and leisure to be foregrounded over work or labour, in large part because 'the effacing of work from our screens . . . effaces the fact that industrialized work benefits one class rather than another . . .' (Fiske 1987: 275).

In fact, Matt Hills has more recently described a trajectory in which quiz and game shows have been devalued by 'left-wing "radical" academics on the basis of their supposed vulgarity and because they are assumed to be overly concerned with cash prizes and consumer goods' (2005: 178). In terms of quiz show scholarship, there is still some evidence to support Hills's description of academic perspectives on the genre (for example, see the analyses offered by Missen (2001) and Wayne (2000)). At the same time, his assessment of the field relies on a rather limited (and negative) conception of Marxism which irons out significant developments and differences *within* this sphere.

Later revisions of Marxism, especially those described as 'neo-Marxist', differed in how they understood the concept of power. Important in this regard is the work of the Italian sociologist Antonio Gramsci (1998) who developed the concept of hegemony. This concept is not based on the assumption that domination is achieved by the powerful controlling the world view of the 'masses'. Rather, it suggests that the dominant group has to engage in negotiations with opposing groups, classes and values, and that these negotiations must result in some genuine accommodation (Turner 1996: 194). In the words of Tony Bennett, this paved the way for cultural production to be perceived as a 'battleground' on which 'dominant, subordinate and oppositional cultural and ideological values . . . are "mixed" in different permutations' (Bennett 1980: 17). To be sure, this was not necessarily conceived as an equal battleground: neo-Gramscian Marxism was often interested in *how* dominant views secured their dominance. But Gramsci's model did offer a more complex, flexible and dynamic understanding of how cultural production works. Furthermore, the focus was no longer specifically on class, as this neo-Marxist framework was increasingly applied to other aspects of identity and representation (such as gender, sexuality and ethnicity).

The influence of this shift can be seen in British work on the quiz show in the late 1970s and 1980s. For example, Adam Mills and Phil Rice find in their analysis 'Quizzing the Popular' that cultural 'forms comprise a contradictory and uneven balance of elements' (1982: 25).

In fact, during the second half of the 1980s, television studies and British cultural studies became increasingly interested in how dominant ideologies were resisted or subverted. John Fiske's work is now often seen as representative of this shift, and he opens his book *Television Culture* by explaining how 'Programs are produced, distributed and defined by the industry: texts are a product of their readers' (1987: 13). Reflecting the title of his chapter 'Quizzical Pleasures', Fiske argues that the 'motivations of the producers of quiz shows that determine the . . . characteristics of the genre do not . . . determine the ways that they are read and used by viewers' (ibid.: 272).

Although Fiske's work was subsequently accused of offering an uncritical celebration of popular pleasures, of implying a simplistic opposition between dominant and subordinate cultures, and of neglecting the contexts in which texts are produced and consumed (see McGuigan 1992), Graeme Turner justifiably observes how it is by no means 'serving of the bogeyman status it seems to have acquired' (1996: 204). In fact, with regard to the quiz show, Fiske's chapter 'Quizzical Pleasures' is probably *the* most influential piece of scholarship on the genre. It mapped out categories of knowledge in the genre, while also examining what can be described as the quiz show's key ideological themes. When it comes to analysing the programmes, Fiske's view of power also has much in common with Gramsci's emphasis on an unstable and contradictory framework of ideological discourses. For example, Fiske spends considerable time setting out how the genre appears to endorse dominant ideological meanings, while he also goes on to examine points of ideological ambivalence or rupture.

Fiske's work continues to be influential in quiz show scholarship, while Gramsci's neo-Marxist conception of ideology continues to influence the wider field of television and cultural studies. Indeed, when introducing his *Rules of the Game: Quiz Shows and American Culture* in 2006 (one of few single-authored academic books on the quiz show), Olaf Hoerschelmann begins by describing how:

> [quiz shows] need to be understood in terms of the textual structures that enable audiences to engage with them in a variety of ways that are not determined by texts, but that are also not independent of them . . . [Q]uiz shows [also] need to be understood within a larger system of cultural production that exerts an influence above the level of a narrow text-audience relationship . . . The . . . relationship among institutions, texts and audiences . . . needs to be understood as a historically specific relationship and as such includes elements of dominance and subversion in numerous ways. (2006: 7)

In broad terms, this book shares Hoerschelmann's conception of the genre, and the method and approach it implies.

But while the book as a whole seeks to question a 'narrow text-audience relationship' (Hoerschelmann 2006: 7), this particular chapter *is* concerned with what we see on screen. When analysing the quiz show, it is possible to break a programme down into aspects such as prizes, set, knowledge and host, as well as the roles offered to 'ordinary' people as contestants. These aspects clearly work together to produce particular connotations and effects. But as this is a longer study which deals with a number of these aspects by chapter, the present chapter concentrates on the construction of the game space. In doing so, it explores how we might approach the semiotic analysis of the quiz show (examining aspects such as time, set, camerawork and host), before considering how this analysis can be used to examine the relationship between games and power.

Playing for time

Games are played out within certain limits of time and place (Huizinga 1970: 28), and the temporality of the quiz show deserves particular note. Although quiz shows can be pre-recorded *or* live, they are all 'performed live' – using the codes of direct address, and references to 'now', 'here' and today (Bonner 2003: 35). This is characteristic of television's address as a medium. Yet with regard to the quiz show, Fiske describes how a sense of ' "liveness" and "nowness" ' is 'crucial to . . . [the genre's] appeal . . . The narrative appears unwritten, the resolution is as much a mystery to the characters as to the viewer . . .' (1987: 272). Fiske indicates here how liveness functions as a code of authenticity, assuring us that events in the programme are not planned or controlled (although, as the discussion of the quiz show scandals in Chapter 2 makes clear, there is no inherent relationship between live transmission and 'authenticity').

In fictional genres, time is often seen as a vehicle for narrative events. Yet the quiz show foregrounds time in its own right, making it a central feature of the game itself. In fact, titles such as *Every Second Counts* (BBC1, 1986–93), *The Waiting Game* and *Countdown* (C4, 1982–) attest to this fact. The setting of deadlines is used as a means to generate tension in many television genres (for example, hospital drama, reality TV, make-over shows), but this is especially evident in the quiz show. In the word game *Countdown*, the title of the programme finds its visual and aural referent in a huge ticking clock which hangs over the contestants throughout the game, and it is conventional in many shows to have on-screen graphics or sound effects which track the movement of time in 'rounds'. As Lury observes, in this sense, the quiz show can be:

> [a] kind of chase narrative, a 'race against time' where time is . . . broken up into successive, or clearly delineated periods . . . Since time is valuable . . . it may actually feature as something that can be 'won' by individuals as they progress through the game . . . [Time may be] accumulate[d] . . . [in order to] to chase the 'big prize' . . . (2005: 119)

Time can thus also be invoked as a marker of failure in the genre (as indicated by the phrase 'I'm sorry, but you've run out of time . . .'). Given its role in constructing a sense of liveness and tension, it is unusual for a quiz format to entirely relinquish time-based constraints. Although *Millionaire* dispensed with a time restriction to some degree (there is no time limit placed on asking and answering the questions and this is used to actually *build* tension), time constraints still punctuate the format at certain points (for example, 'Fastest Finger First', 'Phone a Friend').

Analysing the game space: examples and issues

Games are played out within particular limits of time *and* space, and this chapter goes on to discuss Huizinga's famous conception of the game space as a form of 'consecrated spot' (1970: 28). With regard to the quiz show, the 'consecrated spot' is usually a television studio. The genre has traditionally found its base in highly abstract spaces, or what Baudrillard (1994) would call 'simulations'. That is not to suggest, however, that such spaces do not 'refer' to the real world in their own way. Quiz shows articulate relationships with a variety of different domains, ranging across work/leisure, schooling and education, interrogation and punishment, 'carnival' and celebration, shopping and consumerism, and family and social relationships (Fiske 1987: 274). An important question to ask of any quiz show – and especially one which involves attention to set construction, colour, editing, sound, lighting and camerawork – is to what does its game space 'refer'?

Mastermind

In the 1970s, *Mastermind* was one of the most popular quiz shows on BBC television, attracting an average of 13 million viewers each episode (Brayfield 1976). The first producer of the show, Bill Wright, described how its thematic and visual inspiration was the 'Spanish Inquisition' ('I suddenly had a vision of the Inquisition – a chap sitting

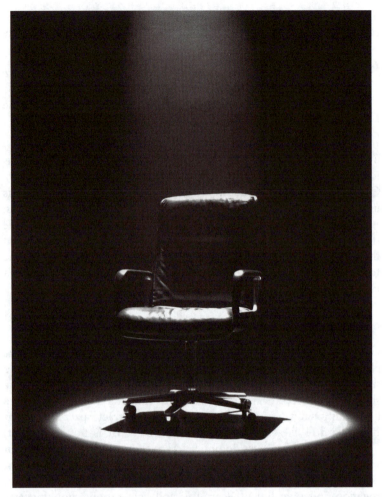

Figure 3.1 The *Mastermind* chair: 'I suddenly had a vision of the Inquisition'. Credit: Rex Features

in a chair and cardinals all in red questioning the guy' (ibid.)), and the initial plan was to have the contestant dragged onto the set by costumed guards. The visual imagery of *Mastermind* clearly reflects the referent of interrogation, with a single white light trained on a solitary black chair. The simplicity of the set was also shaped by practical concerns. Not only did the programme have a slim budget, but the set needed to be mobile, as *Mastermind* was shot at a different university or college each week. The portable kit included the inquisitor's desk, the black walkway, the chair, and long velvet drapes. The context of the show's setting, as well as the bid to foster the impression of 'intellectual terror', clearly also refers us to education. The first host to preside over the programme was the sombre Magnus Magnusson, and he was initially described by the press as a 'fair but stern schoolmaster', able to extract nuggets of information with 'steely pressure' (ibid.). Indeed, at least from the perspective of the contestant, the premise of the programme also departs from (or even reverses) the logic of interrogation: the competitors aim to display, rather than withhold, as much knowledge as possible.

Are You Smarter than a Fifth Grader?

Whether the quiz show has a positive function in promoting education and knowledge has long been subject to debate (see Chapter 4), but the genre can certainly draw upon the imagery of education. Whannel describes how the general knowledge quiz *Fifteen-to-One* (C4, 1988–2003), in which William G. Stewart questioned fifteen contestants in a round, evoked the 'rote interrogation of the Victorian classroom' (Whannel 1992: 18) (despite the neon green/blue lights which adorned the 'pupil's' 'desks'). Although far more punitive in both structure and tone, *The Weakest Link* is indebted to *Fifteen-to-One*. Both shows offer an image of education as a 'trial by ordeal, in which the contestant is publicly examined, with a clear divide between success and failure' (ibid.). Other programmes may draw upon the referent of education only to recast its meanings, while others actively de-articulate themselves from an educational context (Fiske 1987: 274).

In the American hit of 2007, Fox's *Are You Smarter than a Fifth Grader?*, contestants are asked questions relating to the first–fifth grade curriculum. A group of ten-year-olds are referred to as the contestants' 'classmates', and sitting at school desks, they can be asked for assistance in various ways. The entire set is constructed like a school: there are shelves to place school bags, an American flag, and the questions are displayed on a screen 'blackboard'. The opening graphics wrap the title of the show around a red apple, an object which is traditionally seen as a present for the teacher. Yet while pivoting on the residual humiliation of the adult contestants (who often find that they are not 'smarter than a fifth grader'), the opening trailer foregrounds moments of comedy and interaction between contestants, classmates and host (Jeff Foxworthy). The voice-over booms, 'It's the easiest, funniest, and most embarrassing game show ever!', while the red and green spotlights swirl around the illuminated studio.[2] There is a long history of quiz and game shows marrying the discipline of the schoolroom with the 'trappings of showbiz' (Fiske 1987: 277): after all, they are intended to function as part of television entertainment. Nevertheless, programmes which most clearly embrace the 'trappings of showbiz' (and *The Price is Right* is considered later in the chapter) often find themselves placed at the bottom ('tacky') end of the generic continuum.

The Enemy Within

In comparison, *The Enemy Within* (BBC1, 2002) draws upon the referent of surveillance, rather than education or leisure. One of the contestants has been given the answers in advance. If, after several general knowledge rounds, the other contestants can pinpoint the 'enemy', they share out the money. If they fail to pinpoint the cheat, then the cheater scoops the cash. As the host Nigel Lythgoe encourages the participants to 'flush out the faker', the home and studio audience are also given the opportunity to vote on who the person might be. To assist in this task, the contestants are tracked by personal surveillance cameras which record them from different angles as they answer questions and interact. Thus, as the host insists that 'cleverness is not what it seems', the viewer is encouraged to scrutinise the identity of the participant from all angles. The visual design of the set, which favours sharp lines and transparent Perspex sheets, seems to reinforce this obsession with an omniscient, penetrating gaze. In fact, the introduction to each participant explicitly draws on the referent of police work and interrogation. The contestants' faces are placed next to on-screen graphics which mimic the layout of a criminal profile (as might be imaged by a police computer), while details of their occupation, hobbies and 'attitude toward cheating' are displayed on screen. As Chapter 4 examines in more detail, this rather disconcerting game, and of course the entire concept of 'the enemy within', takes on a new resonance within the current climate of global terrorism.

The Chair

The examples discussed so far indicate how games 'test' their competitors in different ways, and it is this process which plays a significant role in shaping the construction of the game space. In this regard, we can also consider the impressive aesthetic of *The Chair* (BBC1, 2002) – a format which requires the contestant to answer general knowledge questions while withstanding blasts of heat or cold ('heart-stoppers') and the baiting of the host, John McEnroe. (*The Chair* can be grouped together with Fox's *The Chamber* (2002), which similarly combined general knowledge with aspects of physical endurance.) In *The Chair*, 'keeping the heartbeat under control is the difference between winning and losing'. The contestant must maintain a steady heart-rate throughout their game, and this is monitored by graphics at the side of the screen. If their heart-rate exceeds a certain level, the contestants can 'red-line' their winnings away, only halting the loss if they manage to lower their beats per minute.

This set-up invokes a number of cultural referents. The chair itself, and the body angle it fosters, is not dissimilar to a dentist's chair – expressing the apparent vulnerability of the contestant, and the some- what masochistic experience offered by the game. The chair itself jolts and swerves in a robotic manner, amplifying the concept of 'man' being at the mercy of a machine. The sound of the amplified heartbeat also directs us to another site which dramatises the vulnerability of the human body: the television medical drama. The title of *The Chair* is mapped across the screen in a luminous green light, the hue and quality of which is more characteristic of horror, while in a flash of white light, the letters are scored through with a jagged line, as if recorded by an ECG monitor or life-support machine. The chair itself also has con- notations of a psychiatrist's couch, pointing to the fact that the format is as much about psychological control as displaying one's general knowledge. Yet, in terms of the referent of torture, and the staging of a public spectacle, the set itself has connotations of a gladiatorial, Roman amphitheatre, a space which, in Roman times, pitted gladiator men against wild animals for the entertainment of the 'masses'. As a new contestant is introduced, and the host bellows, 'Bring me another chal- lenger . . . It's game time!', the chair rises up from within a cylinder bor- dered by flames, with the set bathed in red light.

Who Wants to Be a Millionaire?

The set of *The Chair* was surely in part also inspired by *Millionaire*'s 'Perspex and chrome amphitheatre' (Sutcliffe 2000). While pivoting on a less punitive ethos than *The Chair*, *Millionaire* still drew upon the visual contours of a Roman spectacle or what Creeber calls a 'post- modern coliseum' (2004: 235). But according to the set designer, Andy Walmsley (and the set cost £150,000 against a conventional budget of £18,000), it was actually inspired by cinematic referents: the Riddler's lair in *Batman Forever*, the courtroom scene in *Judge Dredd* and the incubation room in *Jurassic Park* (McGregor 1999: 29). As Walmsley explains, it was 'really unusual . . . for a quiz show set to be based on science fiction, but the best designed films are almost always sci-fi so it made sense' (ibid.).

Although the concept of the 'cinematic' is clearly aligned here with high production values, Walmsley does not indicate why sci-fi was seen as an appropriate referent for *Millionaire*, nor the connotations the producers were seeking to convey. But, across programmes such as

The Weakest Link, Shafted, 1 Vs 100 and *Pokerface*, it is an aesthetic which has been taken up more broadly by the genre, and critics have referred to 'sci-fi zaps of . . . light' (Thynne 2000: 22) or 'technopods' (Missen 2001) when discussing the aesthetics of modern quiz shows. In the words of *Independent* critic Thomas Sutcliffe, *Millionaire* instigated a trend for 'icy blue lights that glare at the contestants and ricochet off the chrome and metal fittings', and he described how 'angles are sharp and surfaces highly reflective' (Sutcliffe 2000). In observing the various shows which mushroomed in the wake of *Millionaire*, Sutcliffe also noted how the 'colour of mental effort' appears to be blue (ibid.). While this demonstrates the essentially arbitrary relationship between denotation and connotation (mental effort has no obvious 'colour' in cultural discourse), Sutcliffe's observation does emphasise how blue was not a colour conventionally used in the quiz show. More often associated with ' "serious" news programmes', this brought a new seriousness to the genre (Creeber 2004: 235).

The shift at work here is highlighted if we compare more contemporary shows with those at the height of their popularity in the 1970s or 1980s. The beige, gold and brown hues of programmes such as *The Golden Shot, Blankety Blank, The Price is Right* and *Sale of the Century* indicate how television set design is shaped more broadly by 'fashions' of the time: the hosts, for example, are often attired in beige suits which complement the colours of the game environment. But the colours also connote a sense of warmth which differs markedly from the metallic, reflective and cold aesthetic of the newer incarnations. At the very least, this shift attests to the fact that the quiz show is no longer seen as a 'safe' place. Indeed, if the modern quiz show celebrates the fact that the 'unsociable aspects of competition' can no longer be disguised (Bonner 2003: 168) (see Chapter 4), then this is clearly played out at the level of aesthetic construction.

The use of lighting can also mark out a contrast between earlier and later formats. Quiz and game shows traditionally made use of high-key lighting, with notable exceptions such as *Mastermind* which used low-key lighting to create its 'searchlight' aesthetic. In contrast, and involving a fixed key light and a range of fill lights, high-key lighting offers bright, saturated colours and even illumination across the set. The effect of this is described by Lury as 'deliberately non-atmospheric and apparently neutral' (2005: 39). But, as Lury expands, despite its often 'invisible' appearance, high-key lighting:

[i]s not naturalistic . . . Instead, the purpose may be more akin to certain kinds of window or shop display, where every object and

detail is made visible and attractive to the viewer; this kind of lighting has strong associations with consumption, and is therefore particularly obvious on home shopping channels . . . (2005: 39)

It is thus not surprising that such an aesthetic is most identified with the commodity-oriented shows of the 1970s and 1980s – *The Price is Right*, *Wheel of Fortune*, *Family Fortunes* and *Sale of the Century*. Given the direct product placement in the American version, *The Price is Right* indeed functions as a 'national shop window for commodity producers' (Fiske 1987: 276). Furthermore, in programmes such as *Family Fortunes* and *Sale of the Century*, this consumer aesthetic is reinforced by the use of a 'promotional' voice-over and the strains of 'browsing' or 'shopping' music.

Millionaire's bid to distance itself from its generic precursors ('aspirational' versus 'tacky', cash versus commodities) was in no small part shaped by its use of lighting. In pursuing what was perceived as a more 'classy, aspirational' feel, the producers of the format sought to avoid high-key lighting. The initial pilot, which had the less aspirational title of *Cash Mountain*, relied heavily on high-key lighting and, along with the upbeat music, the lighting was cited by the producers as a key 'problem' to be rectified.[3] As the programme's executive producer, Colman Hutchinson, confirms, the 'whole idea was to make it less glitzy, and less light entertainment' (Hutchinson 2006). Along with the use of a camera crane, which enables the camera to swoop in and out in tandem with the rising and lowering of the bold orchestral score, *Millionaire* adopted the use of 'varilites'. More commonly seen at rock concerts, the width, direction and intensity of the beams can be used to create patterns, or to effect a rapid change of atmosphere on set (McGregor 1999: 35; see also Creeber 2004: 235). Although most clearly 'borrowed' by *The Weakest Link* (Creeber 2004: 235), this aesthetic has since pervaded many quizzes and light entertainment formats.

Lighting can also be used to express the meanings of the game space in other ways. For example, the use of varilites on *Millionaire* symbolically express the focus on the individual. High-key lighting is used for 'Fastest Finger First' and for the 'Ask the Audience' lifeline, but as the game progresses, the varilites cascade down to highlight the interaction between the host and contestant. The other competitors, as well as the studio audience, are thus 'disempowered by the lighting design' (Lury 2005: 84) – denied studio, and thus television, visibility. This works in tandem with the structural presence of 'Fastest Finger First': part of the function of this round is to accentuate the spotlighting of the individual, and the 'specialness' of *actually* appearing in the chair.

Finally, in addition to lighting and set constriction, the shape of the game space also functions as a potential signifier of social meanings. It may be no coincidence that programmes with multiple contestants (for example, *The Weakest Link, Millionaire, Fifteen to One*) often use a circular shape as the basis for the set. The very shape of a circle eschews the possibility of a privileged point, conveying the idea of equal opportunity for all. As Fiske observes of the quiz show, 'individuals are constructed different but equal in opportunity' (1987: 266) (a problematic ideology which Chapter 4 takes to task). In contrast, programmes pivoting on groups tend to prefer straight lines which emphasise the unity of the team (for example, *Eggheads, University Challenge*), but the separation between groups.

Hosting quizzes: 'I've started so I'll finish . . .'

The construction of the game space also directs us to the role of the host. Part of the power of broadcasting, like many institutions, is found in its ability to designate roles and hierarchies (Scannell 1991) (and the fact that the role of the host has historically been occupied by white males is examined in the next chapter). Although there are evidently many different ways in which the role can be inhabited, the host always functions to direct and control the game. Whether the host is conceptualised as a 'familiar jolly uncle' (Fiske and Hartley, discussing Bruce Forsyth, 1978: 148), or a cross between a 'sympathetic helpmate and cruel inquisitor' (Boddy, discussing Chris Tarrant, 2001: 80), depends on the person and format in question. The host may use the codes of touch and space to establish a familiarity with the contestant – the hand on the shoulder, the feeling that they are 'rooting' for the contestant (for example, Les Dennis in *Family Fortunes*) – or the relationship may be marked by a social and physical distance, or even a playfully antagonistic air (Anne Robinson in *The Weakest Link*).

Quiz show hosts usually have multi-functional roles. They function as a presenter (addressing the home audience), a referee (overseeing the game), and an evaluator-expert (presiding over the facticity of knowledge and the scoring of the game). Like a referee, the host must always avoid intervening in the outcome of the game. At the same time, while the concept of liveness and 'unwrittenness' is central to the genre's appeal, the host functions to manage this uncertainty. The outcome of the game may be unknown, but it is intended to proceed in a certain manner and within a certain time-frame. Thus, one of the functions of the host is to keep the unpredictable nature of the game within the prescribed limits of the format design.

Bill Lewis has also drawn attention to the physical positioning of host and contestant which 'indicates elements of control within hierarchical structures' (1984: 42). The host enjoys 'the power and freedom of movement', while contestants are always allotted a more circumscribed mobility. It is often only the most 'successful player [who] gain[s] . . . the right to move . . . to another playing space and with it, the right to play for greater rewards' (ibid.). In *Millionaire*, Tarrant asks, 'Do you want to play for a million?', as he leads the contestant from the outer ring to the hot seat – thus linking physical and economic mobility. Other programmes reverse this structure, which is not to say that they also reverse the power hierarchy on which it is based. In *The Weakest Link*, the host Anne Robinson remains static, and to remain behind one's podium (like the host) is to remain within the cut-throat circle of the game. In contrast, movement, as played out by the 'walk of shame', represents punishment, expulsion and failure. But as Lewis observes, whatever the show, the host ultimately remains subordinate to the 'hegemony of the game' (1984: 43). The host too must return to his or her set position, or obey the programme's temporal regimes. In *Mastermind*, for example, Magnus Magnusson's famous catchphrase was 'I've started so I'll finish', uttered when the end-of-round buzzer interrupted his questioning in mid-flow. This phrase marked out his authority (it is hard to imagine a contestant saying the same thing), while it also spoke to his powerlessness to defy the temporal regime of the game (Magnusson has to explain what he is doing, while accepting that the current question will be his last).

As Fiske and Hartley observe, hosts also bring with them 'a cultural accumulation of past usages' (1978: 152), and they refer here to wider intertextual meanings (whether on-screen or off-screen associations). This accumulation can sometimes be explicit, as suggested by the choice of the tennis player John McEnroe as the host of *The Chair*. In *The Chair*, the contestants aim to keep cool under pressure, but it was McEnroe's inability to 'keep cool' on the tennis court that contributed to his international fame (and an acknowledgement of this fact often shapes the banter between McEnroe and contestant). The 'accumulation of past usages' can also be more implicit. On *University Challenge*, Jeremy Paxman's identity as a journalist, author and newsreader – he is famous for interrogating politicians on the BBC's *Newsnight* – is an underlying referent which anchors his authority as a host. While evasive politicians are chased for an answer on *Newsnight*, so flustered students can receive a withering stare on *University Challenge* as Paxman demands, 'Oh *do* come on . . .' Paxman took over from the less aggressive, and more openly cerebral, Bamber Gascoigne. This also indicates how a change of host can inflect the meanings of a format in new ways, even if the role itself remains the same. Indeed, the existing meanings that a host brings with them *cannot* be formatted, and this enables *national* variations to register across the same format.

Bonner states that 'British presenters are generally much less bland than Americans . . . "niceness" may be required of daytime ones, but at least half of the evening presenters are allowed a different persona: abrasive, zany, camp, sly, even morose' (2003: 182). Regis Philbin was the first presenter of the US *Millionaire*, and he emerged from the televisual context of a morning chat show – maintaining what Bonner calls 'the soft, avuncular manner proper to that' (ibid.). The UK host, Chris Tarrant, has an edgier style – something especially apparent in the early years of the show when the contestants could not be sure that he was on their side. In the UK, Tarrant was already well-known from his work as a TV presenter on shows such as the Saturday morning children's programme *Tiswas* (ITV, 1974–82) and *Tarrant on TV* (ITV1, 1992–),[4] and he was also familiar from his role as a radio broadcaster on Capital FM. Tarrant exudes a playfully arrogant self-confidence which enables him to be mildly insulting to contestant and/or studio audience. This bold, loud and brash approach also has class undertones, conveying a certain 'common touch' which fosters an illusion of connection with working-class life. This is despite the fact that it was essentially *Millionaire* which catapulted Tarrant into a higher stratosphere of stardom and wealth. But in this sense, Tarrant is also emblematic of the success myth, working from 'ordinary' beginnings to become a millionaire. Indeed, this more 'humble' discourse was often invoked when he responded to criticisms about the programme promoting a 'windfall mentality' or a culture of 'wealth without work' (Holmes 2005b). Even though there is no necessary correlation between Tarrant's career trajectory and the promise of the show, this indicates how meanings can move from one context to the other.

'High marks for the new set': questions of value

This chapter has taken time to reflect on the aesthetic construction of quiz shows, precisely because this is not often deemed worthy of attention. This may speak to wider perceptions of formatted television: once a programme is designed, each edition follows a set formula at the level of structure, 'narrative' and shot construction. Indeed, unlike fiction or documentary, formatted television appears to offer little scope for discussions of authorship, creativity and 'art'. In this regard, it is interesting to briefly consider how industry personnel view their work in this field (although as the following responses make clear, these perspectives do not necessarily challenge the often low cultural status afforded the quiz show).

When asked about the relative creativity of format design, the industry professionals interviewed for this book discussed the production of quizzes and games as akin to developing a well-oiled machine, something that needs to function in a reliable manner with no glitches or 'malfunctions'. According to Danny Greenstone, 'you need to know that the format you have come up with is so solid that it would take an army of gibbons to actually wreck it' (Greenstone 2006). Others play down, or even dismiss, an emphasis on aesthetic creativity. As Mike Beale, executive producer of the British general knowledge format *Eggheads* (BBC2, 2003–) comments,

> Sometimes we get designers . . . who come and say 'this door opens and this goes up', but we don't want any of that. When you are pushed for time that is one of the first things that goes in an edit, and the viewer doesn't care, they just want the questions, or the game or the resolution. They don't care about someone coming up behind a puff of smoke . . . or the camera whirling around this way. In *Eggheads*, we don't feel there is the need for clever gimmicks. (Beale 2006)

With regard to *Eggheads*, Beale dismisses set construction, special effects or mobile camerawork as 'clever gimmicks', essentially because the 'game is the thing' (ibid.). *Eggheads* is indeed a show which primarily pivots on a contest of knowledge (pitting a team of 'professional' quiz champions against a team of amateur quizzers). But this points to the diversity of the genre given that other programmes, from *Millionaire* to *The Chair* to *The Price is Right*, embrace the idea of producing an evocative game space (and this chapter has discussed the careful attention to aesthetic detail which shaped the development of *Millionaire*). Of course, it is also possible to suggest that Beale's comment reflects a disjuncture between industry and academic discourse. In the quote above, Beale appears to resist the idea that analysing the game space is even possible, never mind worthwhile. From a wider perspective, 'studying' the quiz show would doubtless be viewed by some industry professionals as 'over-analysing' the genre (and industry professionals may not always welcome academic analysis, precisely because it involves adopting a critical or questioning attitude toward the programme or genre in question).

But if industry professionals seem reluctant to engage with questions of creativity, judgement or value where quiz show aesthetics are concerned, Hills (2005) has complained that academic criticism has similarly avoided these issues – largely discussing quiz or game show aesthetics as 'vehicles' for ideological meanings (for example, the distaste for the camera 'gloating' over the prizes). It is true that the increasing interest in aesthetics in television studies has focused its attention on particular spheres (for example, the analysis of 'American quality television'), and when debates about 'quality' in television studies have been entertained, the quiz show has been positioned as beyond the pale (ibid.). But as Hills acknowledges, one of the few spaces to offer a more *evaluative* recognition of quiz show aesthetics is the established British website, www.UKGameshows.com, designed for interested viewers and fans, as well as the quiz and game show industry. In the extensive entries for each show written by the owners of the site (Chris M. Dickson and David J. Bodycombe), we come across such comments as:

> [*Dirty Rotten Cheater*] is a stylish show, with some very interesting camera angles, and a nifty little logo of a cartoon villain . . . In the endgame, the cheater is revealed in a funky manner – the pyramids into which [the] cash is thrown contain trapdoors, and the losing contestant sees $100,000 literally vanish in front of their eyes.[5]

UKGameshows.com refers here to the US version of *Dirty Rotten Cheater*, and in judging the show, it uses the criteria of innovative camerawork, impressive set design, and effective graphics and iconography. To be sure, the site often injects a heavy dose of irony and/or playfulness into its discussion of the shows, thus ensuring that its approach is not seen as too 'serious' or 'arty'. But it nevertheless offers an example of aesthetic evaluation which is rare in wider discussions of the quiz show.

If quiz shows are to be treated equitably with other genres, Hills is right to point out that the analysis of power and ideology need not be seen as the endpoint for quiz show analysis, nor the only reason why we might want to engage closely with the analysis of the game space. But the evidence above does not suggest that the interest in quiz show aesthetics and the interest in power can ever be *separated*. In other words, set, lighting, camerawork and so forth are never 'neutral' carriers of meaning where questions of power are concerned. The discourse on UKGameshows.com actually attests to this. In discussing the revamping of *University Challenge* in 2000, it observes,

> High marks for the new set . . . and a background that's a combination of artwork, lighting and mirrors, best described as a sort of giant academic lava lamp . . . We can't say we're fans of the new

music – the old one was refreshingly bouncy, but this remix seems to emphasise *the upper class nature* of the quiz rather too much. [my emphasis][6]

As this description recognises, the aesthetic elements of quiz shows play a role in constructing and expressing relations of power. So while it is certainly true that we should be aware of how we evaluate, as well as interpret, the visual and aural construction of quiz shows (what makes a 'good' quiz show, and how can this be related back to questions of aesthetic form?), this does not necessarily mean sidelining questions of ideology.

Theories of play

This chapter began by outlining the relationship between popular culture and models of power, before moving on to discuss the analysis of the quiz show, or more specifically, the concept of the game space – breaking it down into aspects such as set construction, lighting and colour. But thinking about the connotations of the game space is really only stage one, and it is important to bring together the spheres discussed so far in this chapter in order to offer a more advanced analysis. As already discussed, ideology need not be conceived in purely repressive and homogenous terms. Power can often work in contradictory ways, and produce contradictory texts, and quiz show scholarship has reflected this fact. The final section of this chapter seeks to expand on this perspective by drawing on anthropological or 'humanist' theories of play. Rather than simply examining the immediate connotations of this game space, these wider perspectives enable us to ask broader questions about the relationship between games, power and the everyday.

In his book *Homo Ludens* (first printed in 1938), the Dutch historian and theorist Huizinga explored the significance of the play element in culture and society. Huizinga defines play as a temporary and voluntary activity in which participants willingly submit to the 'rules' of the game. The rules determine what 'holds' in the temporary world of play, and as soon as they are given up or transgressed, the play-world collapses and 'real' life gets going again (1970: 30). Huizinga thus conceives of play as a temporary sphere of activity which is separate from 'ordinary' or 'real' life. As such, he emphasises how all games are played out within certain limits of time and space, and he influentially described what this chapter earlier referred to as the 'consecrated spot':

The arena, the card table, the magic circle, the temple, the stage, the screen, the tennis court, . . . are all in form and function playgrounds

. . . All our temporary worlds within the ordinary world, dedicated to the performance of *an act apart* [my emphasis]. (ibid.: 28)

This idea of an 'act apart' directs us toward the potentially liminal quality of the game world – a space which (as developed below) might license behaviours, actions and attitudes which would not be accepted, or at least interpreted in the same way, in 'real' life.

But Huizinga's argument also seems contradictory. He emphasises how, as a social construction, 'all play means something' (1970: 19), while also insisting on its separation from the 'real' world. In this regard, there is a danger of seeing play as apolitical, somehow separate from the social order (and we have already seen the tendency to assume that quiz shows are about 'nothing much'). This conception of play was challenged by the French intellectual Roger Caillois in his book *Man, Play and Games* (first published in 1958). Caillois paid tribute to Huizinga's conception of play, while also reworking and challenging some of its basic premises. In particular, Caillois argued that there was a need to pay attention to different forms of play and, most crucially, their relationship with social and material contexts. Chapter 4 discusses how Caillois differentiates between games based on competition, in which the outcome is decided by merit ('Agon'), and games based on chance ('Alea') (for example, lotteries, roulette), and he argues that games of chance have quite different social meanings and functions than merit-based games. As Caillois points out, Huizinga also saw games as being 'denuded of all material interest' (Caillois 1961: 5), a perspective which would problematically exclude everything from gambling and casinos to television quizzes.

What is most useful about Caillois' conception of games is that he sees them as both separate from, yet deeply implicated within, the politics of the everyday. Of course, it is useful to bear in mind that these anthropological studies had little to say about mediated games. Although Caillois briefly mentions the American Big Money quiz shows of the 1950s (1961: 118), Huizinga had nothing to say about broadcasting at all, despite the fact that radio games and quizzes were hugely popular when he wrote *Homo Ludens* in the late 1930s. Quiz shows only exist *for* radio and television, and as this chapter has outlined, we need to pay careful attention to their televisual construction. But if used selectively and supplemented with an attention to television form, these seminal works can offer useful insights into the study of the quiz show.

With regard to the liminal qualities of game worlds, this chapter goes on to discuss the anarchic offer to go 'wild in the aisles' in *Supermarket*

Sweep (something that would likely get you arrested in your local supermarket), or the attraction of 'the only taxi that gives *you* money' (*Cash Cab*). Certain formats can also license cheating, even though this action would probably be punished in real life (Chapter 4). Although in a different way to *Supermarket Sweep* or *Cash Cab* (which use or construct recognisable social spaces), *Millionaire* also presents itself as a space apart from the everyday, 'workday' world. Not only is it constructed as a spectacle of entertainment/leisure in which money is given away for 'free', it is very much framed by what Dovey and Kennedy have more widely described as a 'lusory attitude' – a sense of 'what if?' (2006: 29). Tarrant introduces the programme with such comments as 'Who'll be the first to have a chance to wave good-bye to the bills, the job and the 9–5?' (26 April 2003), while he also refers to the show as the 'Saturday night cashpoint'. Unlike real cashpoints, however, which offer you access to your own money and then deduct it from your account, *Millionaire* spews out money for 'free'.

Yet rather than representing a simple escape from the real world, these are also clear examples of how, in the words of Richard Dyer, 'entertainment provides alternatives *to* capitalism, which will then be provided *by* capitalism [original emphasis]' (1992: 25). This comes from Dyer's famous analysis of 'Entertainment and Utopia' (originally written in 1977, reprinted in 1992) which deals with light entertainment in general. But when related to the quiz show, his analysis usefully complements the emphasis on the social dimensions of the game space. Dyer argued that light entertainment exhibits a utopian sensibility, and that this sensibility responds to what he calls 'specific inadequacies in society'. So the social tension or inadequacy in real life might be Scarcity (that is, poverty, economic hardship) while the utopian solution might be Abundance; the social tension might be Exhaustion, while the utopian solution might be Energy. Further binaries discussed by Dyer include Dreariness/Intensity and Fragmentation/Community (ibid.). Crucially, Dyer argues that these values can be communicated by a text's 'affective code', as articulated by the signs of 'colour, texture, movement, rhythm, melody, camerawork . . .' (ibid.: 18).

The Price is Right and *Supermarket Sweep*[7] offer instructive examples of this paradigm. In the 1980s editions of *The Price is Right* (UK), the arena is adorned with strips of metallic gold paper which match the glittering gold graphics of the opening titles. Evocative of a staged public spectacle such as a circus, the strips rustle and twinkle as people joyously 'come on down!'. The opening graphics also announce 'It's Saturday night alright!', positioning the programme as a space of leisure and entertainment (not work). Invoking Mikhail Bakhtin's (1993

[1941]) concept of carnival which refers to a space or time when 'the constraints of the everyday are evaded and its power relations are temporarily reversed' (Fiske 1987: 277), Fiske describes how the 'excitement and frenzy separates the game off from "normal" shopping and shifts it toward the carnivalesque' (ibid.). Although the programme involves a range of different games for the competitors, in one edition a contestant called Rachel has to guess the price of a new car. If she gets four of the five figures correct, she gets to buy the car from the host for £1 (he gives her coins in her hand) (21 March 2001). In this regard, competitors are seemingly released from the economic constraints of the real world, and shopping knowledge, which might usually be used to count or 'save the pennies', becomes an 'agent of empowerment' (ibid.). At least in terms of domestic products, such skills have traditionally been associated with women, but rather than rendering them invisible (or 'taken-for-granted'), *The Price is Right* celebrates them with noisy and public acclaim (ibid.).

This gendered emphasis can also be applied to *Supermarket Sweep* which celebrates knowledge of supermarket pricing, shelf layout, and the calorific content of foods ('Which food has the most calories? (A) 100g of pineapple (B) 100g of strawberries (C) 100g of banana?'). The programme also sets itself up as a space which sits outside the routines of the everyday. The opening of the British version begins with a flashing image of a barcode and a loud 'beep', simulating the sound of a supermarket till. The camera then swoops down from an aerial shot into the middle of the supermarket set. We initially see images of 'ordinary' shoppers milling around the aisles, thus establishing the 'normal' and conventional rules of everyday shopping. These rules are then disrupted as the sequence takes on a faster pace, and the 'ordinary' shoppers are replaced by images of contestants running around the supermarket in pairs. The sequences feature the contestants hugging, rejoicing and leaping into the air, thus shifting the emphasis from the mundanity and drudgery of the everyday to the province of intensity, energy and celebration. This shift is also visualised by the positioning of a camera inside the front of a trolley, offering the viewer the sensation of careering around the aisles.

This visual perspective is to some degree sustained throughout the programme, as the contestants are chased around the aisles with handheld cameras. The voice-over and commentary offered by Bobby Bragg is loud and booming yet light-hearted, and he tells us that 'shopping has never been so much fun!'. The opening sequence concludes with a cartoon graphic of a middle-aged woman dashing across the screen with her trolley, making the letters of 'Supermarket Sweep' sway precariously

Figure 3.2 Dale Winton goes 'wild in the aisles' with *Supermarket Sweep*.
Credit: Rex Features

as she runs past. The idea of creating mayhem in a highly regulated, public space is thus established, and the British host Dale Winton affirms this when he runs out to exclaim in his characteristically camp style: 'This is the show that lets you do what your supermarket won't – run through these aisles . . .'. Winton's camp persona eschews the connotations of 'gravitas' and seriousness associated with more elite, prime-time quiz hosts, and he emphasises an ethos of fun. His persona also invites readings of excess and irony (and *Supermarket Sweep* was notably recognised as a 'cult' student programme on British television in the 1990s).

In terms of Dyer's emphasis on the utopian qualities of entertainment, the *Price is Right* equally provides 'intensity' as well as 'energy'. It has a frenetic and hectic pace, and it involves exaggerated demonstrations of elation from contestants and host. The programme also clearly provides 'community'. Far from the individualising 'trial by ordeal' offered by a programme such as *Mastermind*, *The Price is Right* invokes the participatory quality of (traditionally) working-class leisure culture. Not only does the contestant emerge from the audience, but the audience shouts out the answers and roots for the contestants, and the host (Leslie Crowther in the earlier editions) makes frequent references to work or friendship teams which have travelled 'down together' to enjoy the show. (The reference to travelling 'down' in itself speaks to class identities, implicitly suggesting a trip from the 'North' to the 'South'.) *The Price is Right* uses a camera crane to sweep across the studio audience, the extreme mobility of which was unusual for a quiz or game show in the early 1980s. This connotes a sense of kinetic energy, while also visualising the enigma of who will be chosen next ('It's time for the next contestant . . . *who*ever you are!). The high-key lighting illuminates the metallic gold decor as the camera careers by, and we are given a sense (in contrast to the solid monochrome appearance of *Mastermind*) of impermanence, frivolity and fun. In short, the aesthetics of the game space in *The Price is Right* promise a temporary yet intense experience for all concerned.

Dyer's paradigm would suggest that this is not the whole story. The utopian solutions offered by light entertainment only reflect wishes that capitalism itself can fulfil, while the social tensions and inadequacies are actually caused *by* capitalism in the first place (for example, scarcity, exhaustion). As *Supermarket Sweep*, *The Price is Right* and *Millionaire* make clear, the quiz show responds to scarcity with abundance, but this abundance comes in the form of commodities or swathes of cash. Furthermore, Fiske acknowledges how the 'carnival' of consumerism offered by *The Price is Right* is not a space of total license: the prices and values to be guessed on the show are of course set by commodity producers, and the player is 'rewarded for knowledge of *their* system [original emphasis]' (1987: 278) Equally, *Supermarket Sweep* may license 'unruly' behaviour, but it also instils its own regimes of capitalist discipline. Although predominantly positioning its contestants as supermarket shoppers (consumers), it also curiously sets tasks which require contestants to demonstrate their skills as efficient workers. While the contestants are scooping items off the shelves, they can also be asked to stack tins at speed, pricing them up with a pricing gun.

This confirms the argument that while play may require a 'lusory attitude' (a sense of 'what if?'), the game arena is *not* a utopian space – it is still located within the world of social reality (Dovey and Kennedy 2006: 29). At least with respect to the two shows examined here, it is precisely the invocation of the everyday (and then the promise to turn it 'upside' down) which makes the game space inviting – something elided by Huizinga's (1970) insistence on the separation between 'ordinary' and game worlds. Dyer's conception of light entertainment as utopian complements the trajectory of my argument here:

> To be effective, the utopian sensibility *has to take off from the real experiences of the audience*. Yet to do this, to draw attention to the gap between what is and what could be is, ideologically speaking, playing with fire [my emphasis]. (1992: 25)

Dyer suggests that the need to refer to the 'real' conditions of experience may admit contradictory and resistive discourses (reflecting back on the debates about contradictory nature of ideological power introduced at the very start of this chapter). So alongside the guessing of 'real' prices, *The Price is Right* invites contestants to buy a 'car for a pound', effectively drawing attention to the arbitrary value which capitalism places on commodities (and which is usually concealed) (Marx 1967). As Chapter 4 examines in more detail, *Millionaire* might present itself as a 'special' cashpoint, an escape from the economic relations which govern real work. But the very appeal of this offer also depends on the programme's ability to invoke the world which is being 'escaped' *from*. For example, contestants in low-paid jobs are asked 'how many years' it would take them to earn £32,000 ('How many yoghurt pots do you fill at the factory each hour?'). In Dyer's terms, this could well be seen as 'playing with fire', as it is precisely such inequalities and divisions which the programme otherwise seeks to elide.

This insertion of games into everyday life, or the recognition that games emerge from the fabric of everyday life, is taken to its logical conclusion in the internationally successful format of *Cash Cab* (ITV1, 2005–), invented by the British company Lion TV. In *Cash Cab*, 'the only cab that pays YOU!', the taxi visits a particular region each time looking for unsuspecting people to play the game. When a passenger hails the taxi (assuming it is a normal cab) and asks to be taken to a destination, the driver (John Moody) turns around and says 'Welcome to Cash Cab – it's like no other cab you've ever been in'. The interior of the taxi flashes with coloured lights and the sound effects mimic the noise of a fruit machine as it pays out a big win. After consenting to take part, contestants are then asked a series of general knowledge questions by a disembodied female voice.

The programme clearly draws upon a reality TV or documentary aesthetic. Although we see exterior shots of the taxi as it speeds along, the interior shots have a deliberately low-grade, blurry quality, as if shot from the car's security camera. The use of an unknown face to play the taxi-driver/'host' also adds to this sense of realism (in the UK version, John Moody's persona also draws on the somewhat stereotypical image of the 'cockney' cab driver). Contestants have three lives and, if they are defeated, they are asked to exit the taxi and to 'walk the rest of the way' to their destination. In this regard, it is the passenger's journey which provides the temporal frame: the time it takes to reach the destination is the time allotted to the contestant to play the game. The onscreen graphics track the 'miles travelled', while the taxi's meter, which normally measures how much the passenger must pay, is used to record the contestant's winnings.

As Chapter 1 observed, *Cash Cab* indicates how the boundaries of genre are always in play, subject to renegotiation and change. But the format is also a useful reminder of the need to continually reassess the debates, tools and theories used to study the genre. *Cash Cab* embraces reality TV's interest in 'fully immer[sing] game dynamics into everyday life' (Bratich 2007: 13), and it clearly eschews the light entertainment, 'showbiz' aesthetic that Dyer explored in 'Entertainment and Utopia'. Dyer was initially writing in the 1970s, a time when many quiz and game shows were more clearly indebted to established entertainment traditions (such as variety). His emphasis on 'intensity', 'energy', 'community' and other utopian values may still be applicable to *The Price is Right* and *Supermarket Sweep* (and these formats are clearly not defunct: in the UK, *The Price is Right* was re-made in 2006, and *Supermarket Sweep* in 2007). But the paradigm may work less well for the greater realism of *Cash Cab*, or when faced with the shift toward the metallic/reflective/cold aesthetic of certain contemporary shows (which also promote more unsociable and ruthless competitive relations). It would be hard indeed to argue that *The Weakest Link* offers an ethos of community, or in fact any of the other utopian values described by Dyer.

The implications of this shift are examined in more detail in Chapter 4, which explores the possibility that such shows may be more invested in, or reflective of, contemporary work cultures. This could be interpreted as reflective of changing cultural imaginaries and utopias: the fantasy may now be less about winning a new car, than about beating your work colleagues to the 'top'. But simply because certain shows may no longer reflect the traditionally utopian qualities of light entertainment, does not render the dialectic discussed in this chapter redundant. Quiz and game shows can still beckon an escape from the everyday, while pivoting on this very same context in the process.

The release of formats such as *Payday* (C5, 2007) and *Win My Wage* (C4, 2007), both of which revolve around guessing what people earn, attest to this fact. *Payday* and *Win My Wage* are both British formats, and although *Payday* was released first, *Win My Wage* has achieved international success (in territories such as Turkey, Australia, America, Holland and Germany). *Payday* is played by eight contestants, while

Win My Wage has one contestant who must guess the wages of the other participants. In *Win My Wage*, the contestant is given a list of the participants' salaries on a board, and their aim is to locate the highest earner. They are then given information about the participants in each round, as pertaining to their hobbies, lifestyle, home or car. They must then gradually eliminate the contestants and aim to scoop the highest wage (for example, £65,000 as opposed to £3,000). *Payday* is slightly different. It begins with eight contestants, and includes a conventional quizzing component based on general knowledge. In the knowledge rounds, the contestants accrue money in their 'payday account'. In banking the money, they select whose weekly wage they would like to be paid ('Pay me John'). This decision is based on the contestant's assessment of who they think earns what: so who might be the IT consultant, the lawyer, the white van driver, the cleaner or the policewoman, and which of these jobs would earn the most? This in itself trades upon the appeal of being 'nosey' about what others earn (particularly when, in Britain, asking about someone else's wages 'just isn't done'). The contestant who accrues the most money in the general knowledge rounds then goes through to the final, and their task – as in *Win My Wage* – is to match up each person with the list of salaries on screen. This assessment is based on 'clues' such as physical appearance, general demeanour, lifestyle information, as well as the display of general knowledge. If the contestant manages to match the names and salaries correctly, they scoop the highest wage earner's salary as the prize.

On one level, these programmes appear to operate in a kind of fantasy space: you can temporarily be paid someone else's wage, with the clear hope that it is larger than your own. Yet on another level, and given that the salaries vary from £2,000 to £75,000 per annum, the different earning capacities, and the lifestyles they may offer, are self-consciously foregrounded for all to see. Furthermore, while the programmes occasionally intend to confound the assumptions which are made on first impressions (so the 'twenty-eight-year-old blonde' from Essex is not the hairdresser but the lawyer), the judgements often made by the contestants, such as the tendency to assume that middle-aged white men are at the top of the earning ladder, *do* reflect the inequalities and disparities which exist in real life. In fact, *Payday* and *Win My Wage* provide the clearest evidence of why it is problematic to conceptualise games as 'a stepping out of "real" life into a temporary sphere of activity with a disposition all of its own' (Huizinga 1970: 29). In stressing this separation, Huizinga argued that 'we do not *play* for wages, we *work* for them [original emphasis]' (1970: 71). The titles of *Payday* and *Win My Wage* would suggest otherwise.

Conclusion

This chapter has paid particular attention to the semiotic analysis of the game space, while also examining how neo-Marxist perspectives, as well as theories emerging from anthropological studies of play, can illuminate the relationship between quiz show aesthetics and discourses of power. Both spheres suggest that quiz shows can be conceived as an often contradictory 'battleground' on which 'dominant, subordinate and oppositional cultural and ideological values . . . are "mixed" in different permutations' (Bennett 1980: 17). The potential for such readings will of course still vary between formats. But if we simply saw the purpose of quiz show analysis as aiming to locate the genre's relationship with 'dominant' structures of power, it would be a joyless task indeed.

Although emerging from different perspectives, the work of Caillois (1961) and Dyer (1992) suggests the importance of seeing the game space as offering an escape from the routines and relations of the world, while its imaginary still remains deeply structured within the everyday. After all, and as the next two chapters go on to explore in more detail, the power relations which structure the circulation of gender, class or ethnic identities are hardly rendered erased within the generic parameters of the quiz show. Furthermore, while quiz shows have often been aligned with consumerism (and television in a wider sense often disguises work as 'play or leisure' (Bonner 2003: 156)), discourses of *work* have never been entirely evacuated from the genre. The political implications of this fact are explored as part of the study of knowledge in the next chapter.

Notes

1. In the context of media and cultural studies, 'ludology' is a sphere most associated with the study of computer games. This chapter aims to demonstrate how certain debates and approaches in this sphere can be applied to television.
2. http://www.youtube.com [accessed 23 April 2007].
3. Cited in the documentary on *Millionaire, Is That Your Final Answer?* (ITV1, 24 February 1999).
4. Usually screened after 10:00pm, *Tarrant on TV* takes a comedic and often mocking look at bizarre TV programmes or adverts from around the world – sometimes permeated by an emphasis on the sexual and the risqué.
5. http://www.ukgameshows.com/page/index.php/Weaver%27s_ Week_2003-04-26 [accessed 11 June 2007].

6. http://www.ukgameshows.com/page/index.php/University_ Challenge [accessed 11 June 2007].
7. Although both shows have gone through different phases, *The Price is Right* began on American television in 1956 and British television in 1984, while *Supermarket Sweep* began on American television in 1965, and first aired on British screens in 1993.

4 Knowledge in the Quiz Show

In the 2002 Christmas Special of the British sitcom *Only Fools and Horses* (BBC1, 1981–2003), the central character of 'Del Boy' Trotter appears as a contestant on a big money quiz show called *Goldrush* (hosted by Jonathan Ross). Clearly intended to be *Millionaire* in all but name, Del is hopeful that the show will make the Trotter family 'millionaires', a dream which represents an ongoing narrative in the sitcom itself. Del is confident that he is doing well and when the host asks him, 'What state was President Kennedy in when he was shot?', Del responds, 'Well, he was in a terrible state, wasn't he?' (BBC1, 25 December 2002). The joke emerges from the fact that Del's response is not only deemed to be wrong, but it is also understood to be in poor taste. As such, this is also in part a class 'mistake', as the confusion arises from Del's more collo-quial use of language (in which the word state is more likely to refer to personal well-being than to geography or history).

This example usefully introduces a number of key themes which structure the relationship between quiz shows and knowledge, and which will be explored in this chapter. Del is an emblematic figure when it comes to the promise of the genre. The idea that 'anyone' can make it 'big' and hit the jackpot has historically been central to the quiz show's appeal. But what is less conventional is Del's response to being questioned by the host. Del may well offer what Chapter 5 will discuss as an example of 'disorderly ordinariness', when 'the very qualities that make [ordinary people] . . . "real" make them more difficult to manage in routine ways' (Grindstaff, cited in Macdonald 2003: 80). Del's 'dis-orderly' behaviour foregrounds the extent to which the apparently neutral power of facts sits at the core of the quiz show, rigidly delimit-ing interpretation and other ways of seeing. Del fails to master this system and he goes home with nothing, returning to his job as a wheeler-dealer street-seller.

It has become commonplace to suggest that knowledge is power, and to see these concepts as inextricably linked (Foucault 1980). The relationship between knowledge and power has also been a key theme in the analysis of the quiz show. Chapter 4 investigates this relationship, asking such questions as: how does knowledge express, and endorse, existing social hierarchies (such as class)? How can we read knowledge historically in the quiz show – as situated in relation to different political or cultural contexts? How does the circulation of knowledge in the genre also shape the quiz show's discursive links with work and consumerism? What can the changing role of knowledge in contemporary formats tell us about change in the genre itself?

Question and answer

Question and answer exchanges are taken for granted in Western society, and we enter into such exchanges in a number of different contexts (from consumer questionnaires, exams, and job interviews to weddings) (Bell and Van Leuwen 1994). In Western schools and universities, questioning is also 'the dominant mode of teaching – but not learning' (ibid.: 3). As Bell and Van Leuwen observe, the power of questioning resides in its ability to exercise 'control over meaning' (ibid.: 225) – as exemplified by the fate of the hapless Del Boy above. While question and answer contexts are inflected by their own rules and regulations, the form of the question always instructs the answerer to give a particular kind of response. In this way, questions aim to delimit the potential answers which the respondent can provide. With regard to the quiz show, correct answers are not rewarded by access into the 'ritual realm in which testing occurs' (ibid.: 15). This is because the realm of ritual testing is occupied by the figure of the host.

'The man with the questions and the money': hosts, knowledge and power

In the introduction to a 1978 (UK) version of the *Sale of the Century*, the host, Nicholas Parsons, is introduced as 'the man with the questions and the money' (12 March 1978). While the popularity of *Sale of the Century* may have waned, its introduction remains apposite, in so far as men are still far more likely to occupy the role of the quiz show host. The introduction to Parsons refers us to the host's association with both knowledge and money, which in turn can be related to cultural expectations surrounding gender roles. To be sure, men have a much longer historical status as breadwinners than women, but it should be pointed out that the host merely *presides* over the distribution of the money (it is not 'his'), and women actually have a long history as money-managers in the family. So does the gender imbalance where hosting is concerned reflect on perceptions of knowledge and intelligence?

The quiz show has often been accused of sexism, most visibly, perhaps, in its use of female assistants to demonstrate prizes and to add 'glamour'. Changing conceptions of gender politics have rendered this role less visible. Although the figure of the hostess can still be seen on versions of *Wheel of Fortune* and *The Price is Right*, there has also been an attempt to use male models to balance this fact (however unsuccessful these efforts may seem). It would also be unfair to suggest that women never host quiz shows. In the UK, the highest-profile example in recent years has been Anne Robinson on *The Weakest Link*, and the vast majority of countries used a female host when they adapted the format. Davina McCall, host of the UK version of *Big Brother*, has hosted the Saturday night quiz show *The Vault* (as has Melanie Sykes), while Kay Adams has presided over the tea-time quiz *The People Versus* (ITV1, 2000–2). Comediennes Ruby Wax (*The Waiting Game*) and Rhona Cameron (*Russian Roulette*) (ITV1, 2002–3) have also hosted quiz shows, while Alex Lovell and Rachel Pierman have hosted Channel Five's *Brainteaser*. In the US, examples from more recent quiz show history include Meredith Vieira taking over as the host of *Millionaire* (a show which has predominantly used male hosts around the globe), and Nancy Pimental co-hosting on *Win Ben Stein's Money*.

Although examples are less than plentiful, there is also a gendering of domains where hosting opportunities are concerned. From Arlene Francis to Cilla Black, female hosts have been most prominent on dating game shows, precisely because such programmes deal with the apparently more female domain of relationship knowledge. In contrast, prime-time quiz shows are more likely to be entrusted to a male,[1] and when women do host quiz shows, they are usually programmes with less prestige and visibility. Female hosts have been more slightly visible on daytime quiz programmes, and it is certainly revealing that when the US version of *Millionaire* moved to a daytime, syndicated slot, Meredith Vieira took over from Regis Philbin as the host. In 2005, Vieira actually won the Daytime Emmy Award for 'Outstanding Game Show Host', but ABC never considered a female host when the show was screened in prime-time (Hutchinson 2006). Lastly, women have been more visible as hosts on the much derided Call TV Quiz shows, which are always screened in fringe slots in the schedules. Not only are these programmes positioned at the 'lowest' end of the genre (if they are deemed to count as quiz shows at all) (see Chapter 1), but their very nature – they involve soliciting the viewer to call in and do not require a host to 'manage' a game in the studio – means that the role they offer is in any case more akin to a hostess. Indeed, the women are clearly intended to add 'glamour' and sex appeal to otherwise extended periods of on-screen repetition or inactivity.

Mike Beale, deputy managing director of the British independent company 12yard Productions, explains how one of the 'problems' with using a female host relates to credibility: 'You always want to believe that the person giving you the answer knows the answer' (Beale 2006). In suggesting that this is less likely to be the case with a female host at the helm, Beale's comment attests to the sexism which has traditionally shaped the casting of hosts in the genre. Someone such as Carol Vorderman, co-presenter (although not host) of the British word and numbers game *Countdown*, would appear to contradict Beale's statement. She is widely acknowledged as being more intelligent than her male co-host, and she initially became famous for her displays of mathematical skill. Yet as Chapter 5 outlines in its discussion of female contestants, the perception that intelligence is not 'very feminine' – woman defined as 'body' rather than 'brain' – still has a surprising currency, and it might argued that Vorderman was seen as 'novel' and 'interesting' precisely because she combined a conventionally attractive image of femininity with displays of intelligence. When it comes to investigating women's more 'uneasy' status in the quiz show space, there is certainly some overlap between the debates about female hosts and female contestants. But unlike the contestant, the role of the host is invested with discourses of power.

Despite the suggestion that perceptions of knowledge and intelligence play a role where hosting opportunities are concerned, the gender imbalance is more often explained away by vague references to 'control' or 'gravitas'. For example, 'The problem is . . . that there aren't that many women with fantastic gravitas . . . When women are perceived as having gravitas, they host [quiz shows]' (Beale 2006). The reference to 'gravitas' here is interesting, especially given that the genre most associated with this term is television news. Women have enjoyed a much greater presence as newsreaders and reporters since the 1970s, but as Patricia Holland explores in her article 'When a Woman Reads the News', this did not occur without considerable ideological struggle. As Holland observes, the forms of 'femininity and sexuality required of women are not readily compatible with the solemn business of news' (1987: 133). Women are rarely presented as 'controlling and competent, grey-haired and unruffled' (ibid.: 137), and this again points to the tendency to define women in terms of their visual presence and sexuality.

There is certainly an element of crossover between the genres in so far as newsreaders, as well as journalists, sometimes host quiz shows – perhaps evidence of a wider blurring between different forms of 'factual' television output. As Chapter 3 outlined, hosts are associated with wider intertextual meanings, and this framework includes existing career personae. In the UK, newsreaders such as Angela Rippon, John Humphrys, Sophie Raworth, Dermot Murnaghan and Krishan Guru-Murthy have all hosted quiz shows, suggesting a generic commonality in the desire for an apparently objective, detached and serious presence. In terms of journalistic backgrounds, Meredith Vieira, host of the US *Millionaire*, was originally a news reporter for CBS, although she later worked on *60 Minutes* (CBS, 1968–), *The View* (ABC, 1997–), and as an anchor on *The Today Show* (NBC, 1952–). Interestingly, when it was announced that Vieira would host *Millionaire*, some critics suggested that it may undermine her status within the sphere of current affairs (Hutchinson 2006), an example of a genre hierarchy (current affairs above quiz show) being foregrounded over a gender hierarchy.

This also suggests that more mature women (Vieira is fifty-three at the time of writing) fare better in the genre than younger female hosts, although this is clearly a double-edged sword, as it implies that their sex appeal may no longer be a 'distraction' when it comes to claiming authority and control. To be sure, the highly attractive and blonde Vieira might well contradict and confound these expectations, but it is Anne Robinson (aged sixty-one at the time of writing), host of *The Weakest Link*, who also provides an interesting example here. Robinson's status as a quiz show host certainly prompted discussion when the programme first aired. There were some differences between the UK and US responses, in so far as some American critics wondered whether the British sense of irony would 'work' in the US, and there was a wider emphasis on how the ridiculing of the contestants was more of a challenge to American cultural ideals. As Ken Tucker observed in *Entertainment Weekly*, 'The British are used to the stinging lash of boarding school bullying and House of Commons wig pulling; they groove on vicarious masochism. Americans, by contrast, feel self esteem stroking is an inalienable constitutional right' (Tucker 2001). But the initial response to Robinson in both contexts appeared to find the 'wig pulling' somewhat distasteful, not least of all because it broke gendered conventions of politeness. As Sara Mills explores in her book *Gender and Politeness* (2003), the concept of politeness is deeply gendered. The qualities of being direct and 'rude' – interrupting and answering back – are still more associated with masculinity than femininity. With her harsh, clipped tones and long dark overcoat, Robinson was quite clearly masculinised, and the masculinisation of 'strong' women in television often means that existing gender binaries are not really disturbed. While female sexuality is described above as being somehow incompatible with intelligence and 'gravitas', the initial responses to Robinson actually sought to foreground her sexuality. Yet they did so in ways which smacked of a generic male fantasy. As Tucker described in *Entertainment Weekly*, 'Redheaded Robinson presides dressed in schoolmarm long black dresses, sensible shoes, and steel rimmed glasses to match her steely glare: Think Mary Poppins as a dominatrix' (Tucker 2001).

If this discussion suggests that quiz shows may be out of step with shifts in gender politics in other television genres, similar claims could perhaps be made about sexuality and ethnicity. Quiz show hosting is primarily the province of white, straight males (and as Chapter 5 outlines, this is again paralleled by the demographic of quiz show contestants), and this contrasts with the greater ethnic diversity found in other television genres (reality TV, news, drama). In Britain, the popularity of white heterosexual hosts, such as Bob Monkhouse, Bruce Forsyth, Magnus Magnusson or Chris Tarrant, have largely been paralleled by America's Alex Trebek, Wink Martindale, Pat Sajak or Bob Barker. In fact, in a culture increasingly nervous about discussing ethnic difference, it seems notable that while the dearth of female hosts in the genre can at least be discussed in newspaper and online pop culture articles, no such debate seems to surround the marginalisation of hosts from ethnic minority groups.

In scanning the BBC Audience Research reports on quiz shows across the decades, it is clear that viewers were always asked to comment on the host. Hosts are described as 'friendly, yet . . . always in complete control,[2] 'scrupulously fair, able, courteous, efficient and altogether charming', 'in full command as always' or as simply 'just perfect'.[3] But what are presented as desirable qualities attached to particular individuals are still seen as best entrusted to a white male. In this regard, knowledge functions here as part of a wider framework which invests the role of the host with authority and power.

This presents us with a seeming paradox, in so far as while the host may be positioned as guardian of the questions, there has long since been a debate about whether quiz shows offer displays of knowledge or intelligence at all. Knowledge in the quiz show has been described as an accumulation of facts, severed from any context (Tulloch 1976; Whannel 1992: 187), and this was observed by critics of the genre from the start. In the early 1940s, British critics and viewers could certainly praise quiz shows as a legitimate form of broadcasting, citing children's

quizzes as evidence of 'the good work of the teacher', while also emphasising their educational value for all listeners.[4] But there was also a
chorus of criticism surrounding the quiz show's relationship with education. Providing a variation on the long-standing argument that the
genre promotes 'wealth without work', the appeal of the quiz show was
linked to a form of 'social malady'. Rather than reflecting an 'insatiable
thirst for knowledge', the genre apparently encouraged an 'easy sense
of education' without effort.[5] Some fifty years later, psychologists still
make such comments, suggesting that quiz shows, apparently accelerated by the internet, are confusing intelligence with 'the ability to
absorb and retrieve nuggets of information' (Hill 2000: 23). Such
responses also in part reflect the extent to which television, which has
historically attracted monikers such as 'the idiot's lantern', 'the goggle
box' or the 'boob tube' (Holderman, forthcoming) has not readily been
connected to perceptions of education or intelligence. But either way,
these claims about the questions should not be taken at face value, as
they effectively complement the genre's promotion of an egalitarian
myth of opportunity ('It's so easy "anyone" can win'). This debate is the
focus of the next section.

Competition: Everybody's Equal?

In thinking about the role played by knowledge in genre, it is useful
to set out what Fiske (1987) defined as the categories of knowledge in
the quiz and game show (see also Chapter 1). Fiske distinguished
between 'factual knowledge' and 'human knowledge', and he then
divided each category into two further groups. Factual knowledge
can be categorised as 'academic' knowledge, such as in *University
Challenge*, *Mastermind* or *Are your Smarter than a Fifth Grader?*, or it
can be categorised as 'everyday' knowledge, as in *The Price is Right*,
Supermarket Sweep or *Wheel of Fortune*. The knowledge in this category (guessing the prices of consumer goods, demonstrating knowledge of words and popular sayings) is not gained through school or
reading, but through 'common social experience and interaction'
(Fiske 1987: 267). Precisely because it is available to a wide range of
people, this knowledge is seen as 'democratic, rather than elitist in
temper' (ibid.). The second main category, human knowledge, can be
split into 'knowledge of people in general' (predicting 'what 100
people said' in *Family Fortunes/Family Feud*), or 'knowledge of a specific individual' (as in programmes such as *The Newlywed Game* or *Mr
and Mrs*, in which points are scored by demonstrating knowledge of
one's partner). Human knowledge has its basis in the social rather than

in the factual, and depends on one's ability to 'understand or "see into" people' (ibid.: 268).

Fiske does note that there is an internal hierarchy within his category of 'academic knowledge', as it can also include programmes with a more 'populist inflection in "general knowledge"' (1987: 269). This qualification would seem to be particularly important today. Most general knowledge quizzes pivot on a mixture of received academic subjects, such as geography or history, and what Fiske sees as 'general knowledge', ranging across current events, popular culture and cookery. Furthermore, even *Mastermind* would no longer (if it ever did) sit squarely as an example of 'elite' knowledge, given that it now includes specialist subjects based on popular culture (for example, 'The films of Jim Carrey'). In light of the growth of film, media and television studies, such knowledge can of course now be classified *as* 'academic' knowledge, although such disciplines certainly still struggle for legitimacy when faced with the traditional judgements of 'high' and 'low' culture. Indeed, with the suggestion that *Mastermind* should be re-named 'Master-lite',[6] this shift has been to the regret of some scholars, critics and viewers, and quiz shows are often doubly invoked to demonstrate the 'dumbing down' of social intelligence, as well as of television itself.

One of the key aims of Fiske's article is to question the ideologies of competition in the genre, and their relationship with structures of power. Fiske draws on Lévi-Strauss's definition of the difference between 'games' and 'rituals': games move from similarity to difference (a winner emerges), while rituals perform an equalising function, bringing together different individuals and implying commonality. In applying this to the quiz show, Fiske points to the introduction of each competitor by name, occupation or anecdote, a 'ritual recitation' which moves them from differentiated individuals to apparently equal competitors (1987: 265). But as fiske observes, this structure enables the quiz show to function as an 'enactment of capitalist ideology' in which:

> Individuals are constructed as different but equal in opportunity. Differences of *natural* ability are discovered, and the reward is upward mobility into the realm of social power which 'naturally' brings with it material and economic benefits . . . Such an ideology . . . grounds social or class differences in individual natural differences and thus naturalizes the class system. [original emphasis] (Fiske 1987: 266)

In so far as this reproduces the structure of the education system in Western societies, Fiske's point is that it is ideological to perceive the chance of success in the quiz show as related to 'natural' ability, given that all individuals are not – and cannot be – equal in opportunity. This explains why it is more acceptable for contestants to tell us about their families or 'amusing' stories than it is for them to tell us about their educational qualifications. While stories about holidays and weddings aim to establish a sense of a 'shared' culture between contestant and viewer, educational qualifications might be seen as divisive, revealing some contestants as more advantaged than others in a context which claims that all have an equal opportunity to win (Bonner 2003: 141).

This chapter aims to demonstrate how Fiske's argument remains applicable to contemporary quiz shows. But his approach has also been criticised for abstracting programmes from their social, cultural or political contexts (see Turner 1996). Given the extent to which quiz shows might appear to be about 'nothing much', this is a potentially serious omission. The very form of quiz show knowledge (fragmented, decontextualised, often recycled across different programmes, across decades) may seem to resist contextualisation. Yet it is precisely in relation to knowledge that scholars have aimed to make connections between quiz shows and their contexts. The next section thus draws upon two case studies which demonstrate how Fiske's knowledge categories can be related to particular social, political and ideological contexts.

Reading knowledge historically: Thatcherism and *The Price is Right*

Whannel (1992) has reflected on how the politics of Thatcherism (Margaret Thatcher became British prime minister in 1979) may have influenced the quiz and game shows of the time. The major task of the Thatcher revolution was arresting Britain's economic decline, and the aim of the Thatcher government was to curb growth in public spending in order to 'liberate the entrepreneurial energies of the British people' (Kavanagh 1987: 244). But the idea of an economic boom also fostered a 'greed is good' ethos, and historians now associate Thatcherism with an 'I, me, mine' economic egoism, or a 'Get what you can' individualism (Driver and Martell 1999). In the context of this chapter, it is interesting that a BBC documentary series (*Andrew Marr's History of Britain*) made a link between this ethos and the much vilified *The Price is Right*. As the presenter of the documentary, Andrew Marr, explains: 'The raucous game show *The Price is Right* showcased near hysterical contestants trying to win luxury goods by guessing their value. The passive studio audience was transformed into a baying, greedy mob' (12 June 2007).

Yet Whannel's earlier analysis (1992) indicates how Thatcherism may have had a more contradictory influence on the quiz and game show than this argument would suggest. The start of the 1980s saw a significant move away from an emphasis on factual knowledge to what Fiske (1987) labels 'human' or 'everyday' knowledge (*Family Fortunes, Play Your Cards Right, Blankety Blank, The Price is Right*). Just as these shows relied to some degree on the 'common sense' of the 'ordinary' people, so part of the Thatcherite project was to challenge the conventional wisdom of the experts, and to address the populace in terms of 'common sense'. As Thatcher insisted, 'Every housewife knows you can't spend more money than you have' (cited in Whannel 1992: 198). As the presenter of the BBC documentary above also notes, the idea of conspicuous consumption and personal excess actually ran *counter* to Thatcher's traditional values. She wanted to 'shrink the state and free the people in order to create a harder working, harder saving, self-reliant, thrifty nation'. Although this qualification is not used by the documentary to complicate its reading of the greed-driven *The Price is Right*, the format might actually be seen to illustrate Thatcher's 'thrifty' values: while contestants may be guessing the prices set by the capitalist system (Fiske 1987: 277), you are never allowed to be *over* the value in your estimation (even though this rule does not change the nature of the game).

Reading knowledge historically: America, anti-intellectualism, and the 'Big Money' quiz shows

Whannel is careful not to imply any simple idea of 'reflection' here, and he acknowledges that there is no easy way to make a connection between text and context. Popular culture may address, work through or even defuse ideological and political themes, but it does so in indirect and complex ways (Whannel 1992: 197). One of the most detailed attempts to read knowledge historically in the quiz show is offered by Hoerschelmann's analyses of the Big Money shows on 1950s American television (especially *The $64,000 Question* and *Twenty-One*) (see also Anderson 1978). Hoerschelmann reads the programmes in relation to the field of knowledge and education in 1950s America, especially as this was related to the Cold War. But in order to consider this relationship, it is first necessary to outline the heritage of what is known as 'anti-intellectualism' in America.

In his famous book *Anti-Intellectualism in American Life* (first published in 1963), Richard Hofstadter argued that anti-intellectualism had a long historical background in America, and he defined the term as indicating a 'resentment and suspicion of the life of the mind and those who are considered to represent it . . .' (1974: 7). According to Hofstadter, intellectualism sits uneasily with the American emphasis on egalitarianism, and the ideology of American society as intrinsically democratic and open. It is not difficult to see the continued resonance of this tension today. Popular lore in America distinguishes between 'book smarts' and 'street smarts' (college educated versus 'life' educated) (Holderman, forthcoming). The later US series of *The Apprentice* (2006) pitted a team of 'book smarts' against a team of 'street smarts', and the programme clearly held little faith in the perception that scholarly intelligence was going to be a particular advantage. The hit show *Are You Smarter than a Fifth Grader?* also suggests a playful doubt that American citizens *are* smarter than ten-year-old children, while it also suggests a willingness to hold them up to (good-natured) ridicule. Furthermore, when American television signed up *The Weakest Link*, there were frequent references to how the 'high culture' questions expected by the '[British] contestants ("What was the nationality of the artist Gustav Klimt?"'), would have to be 'dumbed down for Joe Six Pack over here . . .' (Tucker 2001).

This is interesting in indicating American cultural perceptions of Britain: British viewers may be surprised to see the questions on *The Weakest Link* positioned as a bastion of esoteric, 'high' culture. Hofstadter did not suggest that anti-intellectualism was exclusive to America, and he listed it as present in much of Anglo-American experience, including British culture. Even though Britain has always understood itself to be a more class-stratified society than America, Whannel reminds us that British presenters and audiences on quiz shows rarely like 'a clever dick' (1992: 197). A more obvious contrast might be found between America and France, given that France sees intellectualism as key to its cultural heritage. Wendy Pfeffer's analysis of French and American quiz shows emphasises how French quiz shows traditionally reflected the scholastic tradition: '[P]rograms emphasize intellectual ability and discount the show-business aspect of television in their design. They tend to have amateurish sets, and lack electrical buzzers, flashing lights, or fancy props' (1989: 26). She contrasts this with the American pursuit of dollars rather than intelligence. As this suggests, anti-intellectualism can be an attitude claimed *by* America, while it can also be used to negatively *judge* its identity, and the cultural value of its media products.

But in terms of situating this attitude in relation to knowledge in the quiz show, as well as historical readings of the genre, it was primarily in the 1950s that the term anti-intellectualism became what Hofstadter calls a 'familiar part of national vocabulary' (1974: 2). In the early part of the decade, it was McCarthyism[7] which fostered the idea that there was a clear connection between intellectuals and the 'Left', intimating a connection between intellect and potential Communist sympathisers. In the early 1950s, the word 'egghead' acquired negative connotations, delineating someone who was seen to be 'pretentious, conceited, effeminate, and snobbish; and very likely immoral, dangerous, and subversive' (ibid.: 18). In the early part of the decade, anti-intellectual sentiment also shaped contemporary theories on schooling and education. 'Life adjustment education' advocated practical training ('ethical and moral living, citizenship'), over the significance of intellectual development and cumulative knowledge (ibid.: 344). In fact, the acquisition of knowledge was seen as having little to do with life values, and these new educational practices were seen as more democratic in temper.

In this respect, the rise of the Big Money television quiz shows developed in an ambiguous cultural space where attitudes toward knowledge and education were concerned. On the one hand, it is clear that they cannot squarely be aligned with intellectualism. Hofstadter's book seeks to differentiate between intellect and intelligence, in that intellect is a 'critical, creative and contemplative state of mind [which] . . . wonders, theorizes, criticises', while 'intelligence is an excellence of mind that is employed within a fairly narrow, immediate and predictable range . . . [with] clearly stated goals' (1974: 25). In this respect, the restrictive nature of question and answer in the quiz show might be seen as more aligned with intelligence rather than intellect (although because their approach was out of step with 'life adjustment education', it is not surprising that critics could be sceptical of their educational value). Nevertheless, it is clear that the reception and circulation of the Big Money shows was inflected by tensions surrounding anti-intellectual attitudes.

For example, in relation to the most popular format, *The $64,000 Question* (and harking back to Fiske's (1987) emphasis on how the quiz show peddles fantasies of equality), there was a popular emphasis on figures such as 'the cop who knew Shakespeare', or the 'cobbler who knew opera' (Anderson 1978: 9). This expressed both an anti-intellectual sentiment (knowledge is suspicious unless 'ordinary' people are involved), as well as an apparent affirmation of the common man as 'basically wise' (ibid.: 39). As the assistant president of CBS observed, 'We're all pretty much alike and we're all smart' (ibid.). In the context of increasing affluence and better standards of living, this chimed with the wider suggestion that mobility was increasing (thus rendering class differences less apparent). But the mythic nature of the 'everybody's equal' ideal is suggested by the fact that some of these 'ordinary folk' (such as the 'cop who knew Shakespeare') had actually enjoyed university educations – information which was often submerged in the show itself (Anderson 1978: 39).

The Big Money shows were seen as promoting consumerism and the American 'good way of life' which communism appeared to threaten (Hoerschelmann 2006: 73). But as Hoerschelmann observes, there were changing attitudes toward both consumerism and education in cultural and governmental discourse as the decade progressed. In facing the threat of the Cold War and recognising the need to compete with the USSR, pundits advised Americans to 'give up their love affair with material goods and strive instead to improve education, science and the quality of national life' (cited in Hoerschelmann 2006: 73). With calls for more engineers and scientists to be produced by the educational system, this context saw increasing criticism of the new progressive life adjustment approach, which was equated with 'mental flabbiness' (ibid.: 74). In this regard, there was an emphasis on the need for a *return* to traditional educational values – a return to the formation of a 'new intellectual elite' which would be morally and intellectually prepared to fight the communist threat. As Hoerschelmann demonstrates, this cultural field also influenced network programming policies on television, as networks such as NBC and CBS responded to the demand to integrate culturally desirable and educational material into their schedules. CBS' *$64,000 Question* and NBC's *Twenty-One* can in fact be linked to the 'enlightenment project' (a point which is especially important given the tendency to link the programmes, following the rigging scandals, purely to corporate greed) (see Chapter 2). The programmes also displayed a clear emphasis on educators (for example, teachers, college/university lecturers) as contestants, and the questions could address particular forms of high cultural capital, such as classical music, literature or European history. It is certainly doubtful that the knowledge demonstrated on quiz shows would be directly useful in the face of the Communist threat. But there is a commonality here as *both* fields expressed an investment in a 'positivist belief in the value of seemingly neutral facts', and the need to invest in areas of 'high cultural distinction' in order to fortify the intelligence of the nation (Hoerschelmann 2006: 75).

As with Whannel's analysis of quiz shows and Thatcherism in the 1980s, the argument here is not that quiz shows simply 'reflected' dominant attitudes toward education and national identity in the 1950s. Rather, this case study indicates how quiz shows can be connected to, and contextualised within, different debates surrounding knowledge and education at this time. In this respect, it is possible to argue that the Big Money quiz shows performed a transitional function – moving between the anti-intellectual strains of the 1950s ('the cobbler who knew opera', 'we're all alike and we're all smart'), and the call for an investment in more elite attitudes toward education as the decade progressed. After all, *Twenty-One's* famous winner, the English professor Charles Van Doren, 'put an all-American face to the university intellectual in an age just getting over its suspicion of subversive "eggheads"' (Doherty 2007).

These case studies provide examples of how knowledge in the quiz show can be read historically. But they also offer examples of method and approach. While 1950s America might be seen to offer a particularly unique and rich opportunity to undertake such contextual analysis, the idea of tapping into the cultural and political field is not specific to this period or case study. Although it is only one way of accessing the social and political contexts of a quiz show, it can be illuminating to examine government discourse on issues such as education or consumerism – something which can be found in history books or media news reports.

Who Wants to Be a Millionaire?: knowledge, class and power

In suggesting that Fiske's approach to knowledge in the quiz show is more useful when contextualised or read historically, the intention is not to imply that we can not see the relevance of his arguments about knowledge/power in modern formats. His argument that 'individuals are constructed as different but equal in opportunity' (1987: 266) remains highly applicable to the globally successful format of *Millionaire*.

When *Millionaire* first emerged in Britain in 1998, it was promoted and discussed as 'the people's show'. The initial opening sequence of the programme features a group of contestants walking toward the illuminated logo, and thus the promise, of the programme, as shafts of green, white and purple light fall across their faces. The group look up, collectively entranced by the beaming title of the show, and the people are clearly intended to represent a plurality of identities. As such, we can refer back to Fiske's point that people are constructed as 'different, but equal in opportunity' (1987: 266). Although *Millionaire* had been in development for many years, it began just after New Labour came to power. In this regard, it chimed with the Blair government's renewed emphasis on the creation of a meritocracy, which nevertheless emerged from an 'equality' of opportunity. New Labour was concerned with 'the cultural bases of capitalist success' (Driver and Martell 1999: 247), insisting 'that what matters is not your background but your talent and your drive' (Freedland 2006).

In the opening sequence of *Millionaire* we see a range of different contestants – black, white, male, female, young and old, while class is also implied by the use of both formal and casual attire. In asking if some contestants are more 'ordinary' than others, Chapter 5 reflects on the dearth of ethnic minority and female contestants on the show as a whole. But it is precisely the presence of these groups in the opening title sequence which offers us an insight into the promise of the programme. One producer described how shows such as *University Challenge* and *Mastermind* were previously 'a forum for people showing off, but the type of questions [on *Millionaire*] now mean the man in the street feels empowered to participate', with the multiple-choice strategy seen as enhancing this impression for both contestants and viewers (Leahy, cited in Thynne 2000). The description of knowledge on the show as 'trivia everyone's got a grasp of' (ibid.) is intended to support this view. But if this is the case, we might ask why it is difficult to conceive of any of the UK contestants who have won the programme's top prize as 'the sort of pub-quiz every-person you could really root for' (Collins 2000: 12).

The first and third top winners on the British version, Judith Keppel and Robert Brydges, were notable for drawing on the codes and connotations of a decidedly upper-class identity. Although presented as a 'gardener from Fulham', Keppel had an explicitly Received Pronunciation (RP) accent, and was later revealed to be distantly related to Camilla, Duchess of Cornwall. Robert Brydges from Hampshire was introduced as an 'aspiring children's novelist', but he had previously been a banker, and he was already a millionaire before going on the show. The other three winners, David Edwards, Patrick Gibson and Ingram Wilcox, had won shows such as *Mastermind* and *Brain of Britain*. With regard to physics teacher David Edwards, for example, *The Guardian* explained how 'Edwards is no ordinary *Who Wants to Be a Millionaire?* contestant – he's a previous winner of *Mastermind* and one-time Mensa Superbrain' (Logan 2001). While discourses of class may not have quite the same currency in the American context, the US version of *Millionaire* has hardly enabled a re-cycling of the emphasis on 'egalitarianism' characteristic of the 1950s: the contestants who were made millionaires in the early years of the show invariably emerged from traditionally middle-class professions, such as teaching and law.

Millionaire primarily trades in a combination of general and academic knowledge. At the most obvious level, questions relating to popular culture are more often, although not always, situated at the lower end of the scale. This is both literally, in terms of monetary reward, and discursively, in terms of cultural value. Such questions are also often equated with the concept of 'the masses' by their frequent connection with the 'Ask the Audience' lifeline, and there is often an implicitly shared agreement between contestant and host that the audience cannot fail to deliver the truth of popular opinion. Equally, we might note Tarrant's exaggerated expression of surprise when the Ask the Audience lifeline is to be used at the top end of the monetary scale, and his playful suggestion that any answer received should be treated with suspicion. As he comments in one edition, 'Anything to do with soaps, celebrity and TV itself has them pressing their keypads with confidence' (11 September 2006). As this quote suggests, knowledge can be seen as gendered as well as classed, and it is impossible to consider the binary of 'high' and 'low' culture without also drawing on discourses of gender.

With regard to hierarchies of knowledge in the format, Amir Hestroni's cross-cultural comparison of *Millionaire* in America, Russia, Poland, Norway, Finland, Israel and Saudi Arabia also concluded that:

> One cannot ignore that [the programme] . . . rewards academic knowledge with more valuable cash rewards than knowledge based on popular topics . . . [T]he elevated knowledge learned in school – science, history, theology, high culture – separates the disconsolate quiz show participant from a bona fide fortune winner. (Hestroni 2004: 152–3)

Hestroni does find that the format is to some degree a 'culture-sensitive mechanism that befits global texts to local preferences' (ibid.: 153), noting how more 'localised' questions and question themes, as well as the use of native MCs and indigenous contestants, all work to nationalise the show in each territory. Hestroni also observes that post-Communist contexts such as Russia and Poland exhibited the lowest investment in popular culture questions, while Saudi Arabia – the most culturally isolated nation in the study – exhibited the lowest number of 'universal questions' (ibid.: 151). Nevertheless, Hestroni concludes that worldwide acceptance of 'Western standards for knowledge hierarchy is another indication of increasing globalization' (ibid.).

This book has outlined how press discourse can be a useful way of accessing the cultural reception of the quiz show at any one time. The knowledge hierarchies in *Millionaire* have not gone unnoticed by press critics in the British context. Euan Ferguson's commentary on Judith Keppel's big win in *The Observer* recalled:

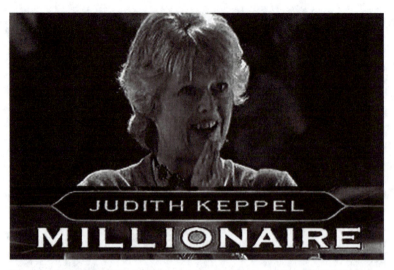

Figure 4.1 The first UK millionaire winner, Judith Keppel (2000). Credit: Rex Features

The wonderful body language as Judith Keppel – gamely trying, like the Queen Mum in the Blitz, to go along with the cattle-class long enough to take their plaudits . . . But this apart, Judith, 'a gardener from Fulham' . . . was sweetly unashamed of her accent, her knowledge, her difference . . . Judith knew about Eleanor of Aquitaine because she's recently visited the grave in France; knew about 'squabs' because she's eaten them in America (which she refrained from calling the New World). If there was any 'fix' going on[8] it was the rather larger one that conspires still to make a private education better than a state one . . . (Ferguson 2000)

Ferguson refers here to some of Keppel's questions (such as her final question: 'Which king was married to Eleanor of Aquitaine?'). But while he nods toward her privileged educational background, Ferguson also foregrounds the more elusive influence of what Pierre Bourdieu (1984) would call cultural capital – the dispositions, knowledges and taste cultures which connect cultural consumption with identity. In capitalist societies, economic capital is able to buy access to cultural and social capital. As such, cultural consumption operates to mark out social distinction, and to sustain social difference – as much as money itself (Storey 1999: 45). In the quote from *The Observer*, Ferguson not only implies that Keppel's penchant for fine foods, travel and history is a mark of social distinction, but he also acknowledges that her access to cultural capital played a role in her progression through the game.

The more recent format *Payday* is specifically organised around playing with this relationship between identity, knowledge and cultural capital. The contestants must work out each other's occupations and salaries and largely base their assessments on the knowledge each competitor displays. This process also attests to the fact that knowledge functions *as* an indicator of cultural capital. As one contestant remarks in *Payday*, 'Sandra knew how much *The Sun* costs, and she answered that question on Majorca. I don't think she is in a highly paid job' (20 June 2007). On another level, however, the fact that the relationship between occupation, identity and cultural capital ('class') is turned into a guessing game here may indicate that the relationship between these spheres is now perceived as more uncertain. Although Bourdieu's concept of cultural capital clearly links class identity to questions of consumption, class has historically been perceived as an occupational identity, particularly within the framework of classic Marxism (Marx 1967). In fact, the relative academic marginalisation of the quiz show – at least in the 1980s and 1990s – may reflect the decline of interest in questions of class (in favour of questions of gender, sexuality or ethnicity), as well as the primary focus on questions of consumption rather than production. Furthermore, since the post-war period, a number of complex social and cultural shifts are seen to have eroded the usefulness of class as a social category, or to have at least led to a concerted discussion about what now constitutes a 'class'. It is argued that changes characteristic of postmodernity (or some may say post-fordist or post-traditional societies) (see Adams 2007) have rendered older categorisations of class outmoded, not least because Western societies have become increasingly affluent since the post-war period. As this suggests, it is the economic and cultural centrality of consumerism which is often foregrounded in debates about the apparent decline of class categories. As Joanne Morreale also comments,

> Choice proliferates and is no longer informed predominantly by status or membership of a particular class but, rather, is based on a fluid and flexible sense of lifestyle. The blurring of boundaries ensues and the social organization of taste by class-differentiated 'habitus' (Bourdieu 1984) becomes problematic because groups can occupy 'contradictory class locations'. (2007: 62)

Morreale's comment here reflects the significance placed on the concept of reflexivity as a key dimension of contemporary identity (Giddens 1991). The contemporary subject is perceived as having a much more uncertain life map (in terms of personal or occupational trajectory) than its predecessors, while various mechanisms of social inclusion (tradition, class affiliation, community, family) are seen to have declined. In this context, the self becomes a 'reflexive project', involving the 'strategic adoption of lifestyle options' (Giddens 1991: 32). As Morreale's comment above suggests, the emphasis is now on lifestyle 'choice' something which the television make-over show both promotes and exploits (see Heller 2007). But the wider point here is that the emphasis is now on types of consumers rather than apparently rigid categories of social class.

In academic work, approaches to consumerism are wide-ranging, moving across a spectrum from classic Marxism's rather 'gloomy' perspective, in which 'consumption provides the motivation for the otherwise immiserated and exploited worker' (Edwards 2000: 17), to poststructural and postmodern perspectives, with the most optimistic model positing a 'self-reflexive and playful identity shopper' (Falk and Campbell 1997: 7). I want to return to the debate about the balance of work and consumer identities below, but these models raise potentially interesting points about the quiz show. If the theoretical emphasis in studies of consumerism is now on the 'use-value' of commodities, precisely because 'the meaningful or cultural aspect of consumption' is seen to reside within how people use the products they consume (Ransome 2005: 5), this aspect of consumption has never been entertained within the generic parameters of the quiz show. In negative accounts of the genre, programmes such as *Sale of the Century*, *The Price is Right* and *Family Fortunes* are seen to promote a slavish devotion to consumer goods (Holbrook 1993). But this impression surely emerges from the fact that we only see the 'ecstatic' encounter between contestant and prize before the programme ends. In other words, the possibility of exploring more complex understandings of consumerism is often circumvented by the nature of the genre itself (which celebrates the act of winning in the here and now).

Second, the fact that commodities have declined as prizes in the quiz and game show further complicates a simple picture of the genre's relations with consumerism. While contemporary shows certainly naturalise, and take for granted, a desire for money, this cannot be directly equated with the promotion of consumerism. To be sure, the fact that the use of commodities as prizes has been subject to decline may reflect back on Morreale's point about consumption and class above. On the one hand, it may indicate the extent to which we still understand commodities to be deeply expressive of class 'taste' (is it possible to offer a prize that is seen as desirable by all?). On the other hand, it may indicate that money is indeed seen as the universal currency through which people can then pursue their own 'flexible' lifestyle choices and identities.

The quiz show emerged on television at the same time that both Britain and America experienced a post-war consumer boom in the 1950s, with an increase in production and better standards of living replacing the greater austerities of wartime. Within this period, what struck British critics (and often attracted their distaste) was the apparently slavish desire for 'new' consumer goods – washing machines, fridges or cookers – which were only just becoming staples of many British homes (Holmes 2008). In the 1970s, the opening sequence of *Sale of the Century* still featured items which, today, would be unlikely to be identified as luxury desirables (it includes televisions, record players and watches cascading 'tantalisingly' across the screen). In fact, it is in part because of apparent consumer saturation that contemporary quiz show contestants are likely to emphasise more eccentric or seemingly individual desires which stand at one remove from the usual system of commodity exchange. On *Millionaire*, while the host may often *confer* consumer identities on contestants (repeatedly emphasising how women 'love to shop') (see Chapter 5), this is not necessarily how contestants articulate their own relations with consumerism. For example, contestant Fiona Wheeler would like to 'travel round Australia with Scottish comedian Billy Connolly', while Geoff Aquatias wants to 'fly a spitfire plane'. Another contestant would like to own his favourite football club, while one participant would like to own a black cab (Holmes 2005a: 166). In this regard, it is not enough to simply accept the argument that a particular show promotes consumerism: we need to examine how it constructs consumer identities in practice. In any case, when compared to the quiz show, a genre such as lifestyle TV – which celebrates the making-over of the self or the home through consumption – is now perhaps a more pertinent genre for discussion where discourses of consumerism are concerned.

As with the quiz show's promise of how 'everyone is equal', we should be wary of suggesting that consumerism has somehow effaced social inequalities. The idea of paying off debt, for example, is not infrequently mentioned in connection with potential winnings on the quiz show, and rising levels of consumer debt have attracted substantial media coverage in recent years. Indeed, one of the critiques of the reflexive model of selfhood discussed above is that it is weak on social structure, giving little consideration to the structural and cultural factors which still regulate the possibilities of 'fashioning' the self (structures of class, ethnicity or gender) (Adams 2007: 50). This is not to argue that class in particular should somehow be reinstated as an essentialist identity. John Frow proposes that in the contemporary climate it is useful to think about 'processes of class formation . . . played out through particular institutional forms and balances of power . . . through desires, and fears, and fantasies' (1995: 111, cited in Skeggs 2003: 117). The discourses that Frow refers to here are the *very stuff* of quiz shows, and when placed within a wider media context, this emphasises how it is crucial to examine how constructions of class circulate at a symbolic and representational level (Skeggs 2003). But in more simple terms, and as the reading of Judith Keppel on *Millionaire* suggests, we *always* make assumptions about people's social status and 'class' (particularly in the UK) when we hear their occupation or voice, or when we survey their body language and attire. After all, for Bourdieu, the habitus, and the cultural capital which emerges from it, is a fundamentally *embodied* phenomenon. It signifies 'a way of walking, a tilt of the head, facial expressions, ways of sitting . . . a tone of voice [and] a style of speech . . .' (Bourdieu 1977: 85, cited in Adams 2007: 146).

With regard to discourses of class in the quiz show, it is not only consumption which is important. If newer models of selfhood seem to position identity as almost 'set adrift from class and occupation' (Ransome 2005: 96), then the quiz show also questions the tendency to play down the significance of work. As Matthew Adams confirms, in the clamour to 'acknowledge . . . the differentiation of [consumer] identities, the continuing salience of "work", however loosely we define it, is often lost' (2007: 35). This is despite the fact the two spheres are obviously inextricably intertwined: if we did not work, we could not consume. The quiz show continues to foreground both 'work' and 'consumer' identities, while also exploring the interaction between them. In fact, it is precisely the importance often placed on work in *Millionaire* which complicates a reading in which it simply endorses traditional class hierarchies (as the discussion of Judith Keppel's appearance might suggest).

In the UK version, it is contestants with low-paid and particularly manual jobs, ranging from refuse collectors, window cleaners and supermarket shelf-stackers to factory workers, who find their work identities most clearly invoked on the show. This is clear in the edition featuring Miles Robson, a yogurt factory worker from Yorkshire (29 September 2001). The initial opening exchange between Tarrant and Robson is as follows:

Chris Tarrant: Miles gets to stare at 10,000 gallons of yogurt per day . . . so you're a factory worker – what would be realistically a nice sum of money for you?

Miles: Well – a thousand pounds would be nice.

Chris Tarrant: Fingers crossed.

Robson's progression through the game demonstrates how the programme measures potential winnings against what Tarrant imagines is the mundanity of his labour in everyday life. Given that one of the most significant shifts in Western labour/consumption has been the shift from the manufacturing to the service industries (Adams 2007: 73), Robson's occupation, combined with his northern accent, makes for a more 'traditional', even old-fashioned, image of labour. At £16,000 Tarrant interjects, 'Now Miles, I won't ask you, but I expect I know how long working in a yogurt factory it would take you to earn £16,000 . . .' Despite this nod to the potentially personal nature of the question, the contestant's financial circumstances become explicitly intertwined with his progression up the scale. When asked the same question again at £32,000, Robson admits that it would take him six years to earn such a figure, and when considering the possibility of £64,000, Tarrant continues the equation by reminding him that it is worth twelve years' labour.

While it is the difference between real work and quiz show 'work' which is being paraded here, it is precisely the real world which must be rendered visible. In offering instant reward, the quiz show has been described as effacing the concept of work from our screens, apparently functioning – in Marxist terms – as a 'typical capitalist text' (Fiske 1987: 275). Yet *Millionaire* might be described as one of few spaces on contemporary television where the emphasis on the 'reality' (for some people) of everyday labour *is* brought into play, however brief and constructed such glimpses may be. In order to play out the idea that 'anyone' can make it, the often less utopian context of the everyday must be acknowledged.

At the same time, this particular example confirms why there has been a shift, both culturally and intellectually, from a work-based to a consumption-based society. Consumption has been viewed as a response to the fact that 'people are becoming less and less willing to accept the limits to identity which the paid occupational role tends to set' (Ransome 2005: 10). To be sure, work does not simply represent 'the grind of necessity', and people invest a great deal of themselves in work as a resource for both personal and social identity (ibid.: 9). But this is not usually rendered visible in the quiz show, precisely because of its desire to provide a space which provides some form of release or escape from the contours of the everyday (see Chapter 3). Nevertheless, while work and consumption, or labour/leisure, are certainly valued and constructed differently within the context of the quiz show, this still questions the simple assertion that quiz shows are a simple conduit for the promotion of consumer discourses.

Cheating, lying, bluffing and 'strategy': is 'merit' under attack?

This chapter will go on to discuss how discourses of work, and work culture, enter the contemporary quiz show in different ways. Given the diversity of programmes within the genre, there is a danger of flattening out differences between formats or sub-groups. While *Millionaire* may draw upon a hierarchical structure which claims that differences of 'natural' ability are discovered, other shows work through different messages about achievement, work, money and success. This in turn suggests a different attitude toward knowledge in the genre.

Chapter 1 referred to the categories of games developed by Roger Caillois in his book *Man, Play and Games* (1961). Caillois uses the term 'Agon' to refer to games in which open competition produces a winner based on merit (the cleverest, the fastest, the strongest). In contrast, the structure of 'Alea' involves games in which winning is the 'result of fate rather than triumphing over adversity' (*alea* is Latin for 'game of dice') (1961: 17). Caillois suggested that, on a social level, these categories are actually complementary. Alea is the natural complement to Agon in so far as 'chance is courted because hard work and personal qualifications are [often] powerless to bring such success about' (1961: 114). In this regard, 'luck' and chance mitigate the harshness of a system based on hierarchies of opportunity (Fiske 1987: 271).

Caillois emphasises how these frameworks can also co-exist in one space, and this is demonstrated by the quiz show. So while the previous discussion of *Millionaire* foregrounded its ethos of Agon (an individual demonstrates knowledge in order to climb up the scale), it also includes small elements of chance within prescribed limits (for example, guessing from multiple-choice options, the use of the 50/50 lifeline). Similarly, a format such as *Wheel of Fortune* combines knowledge of popular phrases or sayings, with the chance-based spinning of the wheel. As Chapter 2 has indicated, regulators also play a role in shaping the relative balance of Agon and Alea in the genre. Whether with regard to the FCC's bid to prevent the radio 'give-aways' in America in the 1930s, the Pilkington Committee's suggestion (1962) that ITV's quiz and game shows should be more 'closely linked to skill and knowledge' (Whannel 1992: 184), or the more recent bid to curb the Call TV Quiz phenomenon (and have the programmes re-classified as lotteries), it is clear that regulators have often preferred quizzes based on the structures of Agon rather than Alea. This pivots on a rather (middle-class) distaste for the circumvention of the protestant work ethic, and the idea of winning 'something for nothing'.

While quizzes always undermine this ethic to some degree (you can win thousands of pounds in seconds or minutes), there may now be good reasons to consider the increased significance of an aleatory culture. As Jon Dovey and Helen W. Kennedy write in their book on computer game culture (quoting Caillois):

> The agonistic subject competes by the rules of the game to become a success; the rules of the game are the social rules of meritocracy, in which the best will be rewarded. The practice of agon presupposes sustained attention, appropriate training . . . and the desire to win . . . The agonistic subject is the preferred subject of Protestant capitalism, competing . . . by the rules . . . The aleatory subject, on the other hand, 'negates work, patience, experience and qualifications' (Caillois 1961: 17). (Dovey and Kennedy 2006: 40)

Dovey and Kennedy discuss how the 'networked societies' and systems characteristic of post-fordism are apparently more subject to chance than the mechanical systems of modernist industrial cultures. For example, when *Millionaire* first emerged, cultural critics linked the thirst to appear on the show to the rise of the dot.com boom – the desire to hit a button and enter the 'strike-it-rich business' (Mahoney 2000).

Deal or No Deal, in which contestants select boxes worth differing prize values, would seem to be a prime example of an aleatory presence in television games. In the UK, the success of the format prompted ITV1 to launch two late afternoon programmes based on chance: *For the Rest of Your Life* (ITV1, 2007), in which couples select cylinders worth different monetary values, and *Golden Balls* (ITV1, 2007) in which contestants are dealt a number of balls from a lottery machine worth different monetary values. But in surveying particular themes and trends in the genre, it is perhaps not so much the emphasis on pure 'chance' which is most apparent, as the presence of the *values* which underpin the aleatory framework. To reiterate Caillois' description above, 'The aleatory subject . . . negates work, patience, experience and qualifications' (1961: 17). How might this structure be applied to examples of the contemporary quiz show?

The Weakest Link: does the 'best' beat the 'rest'?

Invented by the BBC, *The Weakest Link* has had a significant influence on the quiz show, both in terms of tone ('nasty') and game structure. Although received in different ways by different countries (see

Steemers 2004), the show was described in the UK as something of a 'culture shock' when it first emerged.[9] While clearly differing from the extreme tests of physical endurance and punishment associated with Japanese game shows (and which are often held up as spectacles of nationally 'other' television on clip shows such as *Tarrant on TV*), the programme's ritual humiliation of the contestants departed from the social competition of earlier quiz formats. As Chapter 2 acknowledged, the ethos of the show has been seen as evidence of the erosion of public service values (Bourdon 2004: 289).

The Weakest Link drew upon game structures which were already in circulation. The nomination/eviction/voting structure was also being popularised by reality TV, and in the UK, *Big Brother* and *The Weakest Link* emerged in the same year (2000). Bonner observes in her wider discussion of 'ordinary' television how 'the rhetoric of individualism . . . is no longer restrained by social niceties about co-operation and group harmony. Teams become temporary groupings aware that the dominant member will sacrifice them ruthlessly' (Bonner 2003: 168). Although discussing *Big Brother*, John Ellis takes this observation further in his suggestion that the contestants are:

> [t]hrown together by circumstances, they are mutually dependent but in order to survive have to stab each other in the back. The experience is akin to a modern workplace with its project-based impermanence, appraisal processes, and often ruthless corporate management. (2001: 12)

But Ellis's quote only recognises in more explicit terms how work environments are spheres in which people negotiate their identities, operate as individuals and teams, and participate in creating contemporary social conditions.

In so far as *The Weakest Link* pivots on a 'dog-eat-dog' struggle until only one contestant remains, it might actually be related to Caillois' first category of Agon, which he described as being characteristic of competition in society (the 'original brutality' of capitalism) (Caillois 1961: 46). Yet as already outlined, Agon assumes a winner based on open competition and merit. In *The Weakest Link*, the person who wins is *not* necessarily the most intelligent (or the person who triumphs in the general knowledge rounds). In this regard, the outcome of the game does not always reflect the ethos of the show's title. Rather than banishing 'the weakest link', tactical voting can clearly also involve ejecting a strong player. When the host asks contestants why they voted a competitor out of the game, they invariably draw upon discourses of merit ('they got the most questions wrong'). Yet the tendency for contestants to vote off stronger players, especially in the latter stages of the game, has become so commonplace that Robinson emphasises how the *weakest* link should be dismissed in the final vote. Yet as www.UKGame shows.com observes, 'Day in, day out, they ignore her and vote off the strongest link regardless'.[10]

Cheat your way to the top
This questioning of the values of Agon also pervades other formats.UK Gameshows.com refers to *The Weakest Link* as pioneering the 'who can you trust?' format. In terms of surveying wider shifts in the genre, this ethos is particularly apparent in formats which launch an even greater attack on the concept of fair competition and merit: programmes which license cheating, subterfuge and disguise. The format *Beg, Borrow or Steal* (BBC2, 2004), which was invented by the British company 12 Yard productions and made in both Britain and the US, begins with the following address from the host:

> Ever thought you'd never win big money on a quiz show because your general knowledge isn't up to scratch? Well, think again. On this show it doesn't matter if you don't know the answers because you can beg, borrow or steal them from your opponents. You might say it's more about who you know, rather than what you know. Good general knowledge might win you respect, but good strategy will make you rich. (Host Jamie Theakston, 25 October 2004)

Beg, Borrow or Steal was not the first (or only) format to incorporate cheating and subterfuge. Other examples are the British formats *The Enemy Within* (BBC1, 2002), *Traitor* (BBC2, 2004), and the American-invented format *Dirty Rotten Cheater* (Pax, 2003, beginning in the UK in 2007). (With varying degrees of success, *Dirty Rotten Cheater* has since been sold to Britain, Italy, France and Japan.) These formats also share clear similarities with the Belgian-invented reality format of *The Mole*, which was first launched in 1999. As the title suggests, one of the contestants is a 'mole' who has been hired by producers to sabotage the efforts of the rest of the group, as they perform a combination of mental, physical and psychological tests. In the quiz formats, however, the aim of the infiltrator is less to bring the group down, than to win the game without being detected as the cheat.

In *The Enemy Within* (see also Chapter 3), one of the contestants has been sent the answers a week in advance. If, throughout various general knowledge rounds, the other contestants can pinpoint the 'enemy' (and it is clearly in his/her interest not to answer every question correctly lest that attract suspicion), then they share out the money. If they fail to locate the cheater, then that person scoops the cash. Transparent screens and personal surveillance cameras encourage us to contemplate host Nigel Lythgoe's suggestion that 'cleverness is not what it seems' and, like the contestants, the home and studio audience is given the opportunity to vote on who they think the 'faker' is. Although the cheating contestant is stigmatised by the use of words such as 'dirty rotten', 'enemy' and 'traitor', the game structure is clearly willing to validate them. As Lythgoe tells 'cheating' contestant Malcolm when he successfully elides detection in *The Enemy Within*: 'Congratulations, you outwitted them. You *deserve* their money, and get all their winnings. It proves that cheats can prosper on *The Enemy Within* [my emphasis]' (21 August 2002).

Referring back to the anthropological studies of games by Huizinga and Caillois (see Chapter 3), the cheating formats demonstrate the argument that a cheat's 'dishonesty does not destroy the game', essentially because they still give the impressing of playing it (Caillois 1961: 7, see also Huizinga 1970: 10). In contrast, the 'spoilsport', who abandons the game and refuses to play, is a far greater threat, as he or she shatters 'the play-world itself' (Huizinga 1970: 30). It is precisely the cheat's ability to pass through the game structure which is rewarded by *The Enemy Within* (and which is then aligned with playing a 'good game'). But it is important to add a note of qualification here. Programmes such as *The Enemy Within*, *Traitor* and *Dirty Rotten Cheater* actively license cheating. When cheating occurs in the 'real' world of quiz show competition, such as when Major Charles Ingram cheated his way to the top prize on the British version of *Millionaire* (2003), the results are rather different. The British courts found Ingram guilty of intent to defraud (he received a suspended sentence), and while he later became a minor celebrity in the UK, he has repeatedly claimed to be on the receiving end of death threats and verbal abuse. In this regard, and returning to Chapter 3's conception of the game space as both separate from, yet invested in, the regulations of the everyday, we might ask whether the cheating formats function as 'safety valves' – allowing for the expression of anti-social impulses which are still seen as immoral in the context of the everyday.

It would be misleading to foreground only reassurance or containment here. The term 'the enemy within' has been used at various historical junctures (including the period of McCarthyism discussed earlier in this chapter), and it has also been used as the title of numerous books, plays and documentaries. But in the current political climate, the term immediately resonates with the global threat of terrorism. It was explicitly invoked with regard to 9/11, and then later in connection with the 7 July (2005) London bombings (Rice-Oxley 2005). The use of this phrase also indicates how recent years have seen a shift in social conceptions of terrorism in the Western world. Rather than terrorism being an identifiable threat from 'without', Jean Baudrillard describes how recent social constructions suggest that 'terrorism, like a virus, is everywhere. Immersed globally, terrorism, like the shadow of any system of domination, is ready everywhere to emerge as a double agent' (2002: 14). While again seeking to avoid a crude analysis in which quiz shows are seen to 'reflect' particular political contexts, it is possible to suggest that the formats above take on a new resonance within this climate.

On one level, these formats address what is assumed to be an increasingly vigilant populace, and the host of *The Enemy Within*, Nigel Lythgoe, signs off by saying: 'Remember, keep your friends close and your enemies closer – when you spot them'. The programme might be seen as offering a 'safe' space for the dramatisation of fears which, in reality, have no simple resolution. Yet as Lythgoe's comment also hints, the programme's rhetoric of surveillance and suspicion is more complex than this suggests. Not only does the 'enemy' frequently go undetected, but there is the suggestion that suspicion is not only confined to the competitors *in* the game. When the studio audience is asked to vote on the identity of the 'enemy', the image of the studio audience is saturated by a grey/blue wash, covered with superimposed images of Lythgoe's face. Eyes narrowed, Lythgoe appears to be casting his gaze across the studio audience rather than the contestants. The music also becomes increasingly dramatic, and with a rapid onrushing of shots, we see reams of data scrolling across the screen – iconography which might be associated with national security or policing. Just as Baudrillard describes the 'virus' of terrorism as 'everywhere', so the programme dramatises the anxiety that the 'double agent' (Baudrillard 2002: 14) could be spatially, and socially, pervasive.

Yet the power of ideology often also resides in the *not* said. While the shows imagine the infiltrator as quite literally invisible, someone who can slip through unnoticed, many of the Western fears surrounding terrorism have been racially, and thus visibly, marked. In UK media discourse, the term the 'enemy within' in 2005 was specifically used in relation to British Muslims (resulting in the stigmatisation and marginalisation of this community) (Rice-Oxley 2005). Furthermore, as Chapter 5 goes on to explore, there is a double displacement at work here given that quiz contestants, and quiz cultures, still remain predominantly white.

Bluffing the self

Programmes need not include a cheat to represent some form of assault on the traditional structures of Agon. Other formats take the concept of bluffing and combine it with the display of general knowledge (*Pokerface*), or the hand of chance (*Golden Balls*). The prime-time Saturday evening offering of *Pokerface* is hosted in the UK by Ant and Dec, and it offers a £1 million prize. *Pokerface* is also an international format, in so far as it has been sold to territories such as Sweden, Norway, Poland, Mexico and Australia. (The Mexican version is called *Doble Cara* (*Double Face*), while the Australian version was re-titled *The Con Test*.) Although drawing on the bluffing element of poker, *Pokerface* is actually a general knowledge game, with the twist that the contestants cannot see each other's scores. During each round, the on-screen graphics indicate how a contestant is really performing (they receive a tick or a cross for each question they answer), while we witness them bragging and bluffing about their score. Although the figure of the host has traditionally mediated between contestants in the quiz show, in *Pokerface* this structure notably encourages a good deal of interaction between players as they try to catch each other out:

> Dominic: I'm feeling very confident about my score thanks – I did really well in that last round. But I don't think Richard did well – Richard how did you do?

> Richard: Probably better than you.

> Dominic: So what was the answer to the question about the solar system?

> Richard: If you got it right you already know the answer.

> Dominic: Yes I do, and clearly you don't! (*Pokerface*, 10 March 2007)

The objective of this bluffing banter is to get someone else to fold because they think they have the lowest score. There is an incentive to fold if you think you might be losing, as if you *are* at the bottom of the scoreboard and do not fold, then you lose the money you have accrued. *Golden Balls* draws on a similar structure as contestants bluff about the value of their 'hand' (the value of the balls they have been dealt). What these programmes have in common with the cheating formats is that it is less ability, than a convincing presentation of the self, which can win you the game.

Such structures of selfhood chime with postmodern and poststructural strands of thought which have made a 'depth' model of the self unfashionable. In the words of Douglas Kellner, they have problematised the very 'notion of identity, claiming that it is a myth, an illusion' (1992: 143). Pre-modern and modern conceptions of selfhood were more invested in the idea of an inner 'core', while postmodern conceptions have embraced the idea of identity as a shifting surface, a mediatised 'theatrical play with identity' in which the self can be produced and reproduced to suit the demands of the context (ibid.: 174). (This also chimes in with the socio-logical emphasis on reflexive models of selfhood mentioned earlier in this chapter.) With regard to television, these discourses have been dis-cussed in relation to reality TV, a form which encourages self-reflexive discussion about 'who is being themselves' and who is 'performing for the camera' as a matter of course (see Holmes 2004a). Yet when it comes to conceptions of selfhood, the discourse of a programme like *Big Brother* is more conservative than this model might imply. *Big Brother*, and reality TV as a whole, encourages us to look for moments when people are '"really" themselves in an unreal environment' (Hill 2002: 324), and reality formats often validate people who appear to have been 'them-selves', and who display consistent and reassuring models of selfhood. In this regard, it seems pertinent to note that the quiz formats discussed above offer no such reassurance: indeed they reward contestants who can project selves which have little to do with their 'real' identity, occupation or level of intelligence.

One the one hand (and as the discussion of reality TV implies), cap-italism remains invested in the concept of the individual as a 'major moving force' (Dyer 1986: 10). Yet at the same time, and to return to the analogy with contemporary work environments, workers are trained to work together in temporary groupings, 'to enhance their personal communicative skills', and to be increasingly 'nomadic, self-reflexive, and flexible', adapting themselves to new contexts, and to social and technological change in the workplace (Bratich 2007: 11; Ransome 2005). Following on from this, there emerges an interesting paradox. The formats which most circumvent the discipline and 'hard work' associated with agonistic games nevertheless appear to take the politics of *work cultures* as their playpen of choice.

In terms of relating this section back to the previous discussion of merit-based formats, as well as the relationship between knowledge and power, a number of points and questions arise. First, we might ask whether these formats are more 'democratic' than those discussed earlier in the chapter. To some extent, it is possible to argue that they are. Rather than being rooted in the structure of the education system in Western societies ('All are equal in front of the examination paper') (Fiske 1987: 266), there has been a shift toward the validation of other skills and values: the 'gift of the gab', guesswork, confidence and subterfuge. But it is also worth sounding a note of caution here. As in reality shows, participants are explicitly abstracted from their wider social, cultural and familial contexts in order to place the focus on the internal politics of the game. As such, the implication might be that, when it comes to competition, these contexts no longer matter. Furthermore, game structures are never innocent of power. If the newer formats are more 'ruthless' and 'aggressive' in their values, this raises (for example) questions of gender, given that these attributes are more associated with, and expected from, men. In fact, according to Bonner, *The Weakest Link* mirrors the 'masculine dominance of public space' (2003: 169).

Second, it is perhaps less the case that aspects of Alea have overtaken the values of Agon, and more that these structures co-exist in the same space. After all, even if it is in the context of a 'deepening consumption-identity', 'we are even more workerly than we were before' (Ransome 2005: 189). As Caillois' original argument pointed out, the structures of Agon and Alea can be complementary, not least of all because games drawing on an aleatory element compensate for the hierarchical ethos of agonistic games. In this respect, whether these newer formats represent a 'safety' valve in this respect is open to debate.

Thirdly, the 'who can you trust' formats have enjoyed – at best – varying degrees of success. While *The Weakest Link* has garnered an international reputation, and *Pokerface* has enjoyed moderate success, the cheating formats have often been short-lived in both the UK and US contexts. As Chapter 6 outlines, quiz show viewers take pleasure in competing with on-screen contestants, or in admiring demonstrations of knowledge. In this regard, the cheating formats must offer quite different forms of engagement, frustrating what have traditionally been deemed as one of the generic pleasures of quiz shows.

Conclusion

It has become commonplace to observe that knowledge is power, and this chapter has aimed to examine the various ways in which this might be applied to the quiz show. Categorisations of knowledge can be used to examine how quiz shows perpetuate, work through or expose existing social hierarchies (for example, class). Knowledge is also a way of contextualising and historicising quiz shows – a means of relating them to the various social and political contexts in which they were produced. This chapter has also demonstrated how anthropological theories of play, especially Caillois' categories of Agon and Alea, can be applied to any quiz show in order to critically examine the relative balance of merit and chance.

The next chapter further considers how games are both 'identity producing and culture making' (Dovey and Kenney 2006: 32). But in order to do so, it examines the construction of 'ordinary' people as contestants in the quiz show.

Notes

1. We might also note the historical link with comedy: a number of quiz and game show hosts emerged from variety and stand-up comedy – spheres which are also gendered male.
2. Audience research report, *Ask the Family*, 23 August 1967 (WAC).
3. Audience research report, *What Do You Know?*, 2 August 1953 (WAC).
4. 'Too much quiz?', *Birmingham Mail*, 15 October 1946.
5. 'Parlour games and quizzes on radio and television', *Glasgow Herald*, 4 November 1953.
6. 'Mylene', http://www.iqagb.co.uk/ trivia/ viewtopic.php?t=4370 [accessed 11 June 2007].
7. Originally associated with the political actions of US Senator Joseph McCarthy, McCarthyism subsequently took on a wider meaning, referring to the period of anti-Communist feeling/suspicion in American from the late 1940s to the late 1950s.
8. The reference to a 'fix' in many of the press reports referred to the (unfounded) speculation that ITV had 'fixed' the big win in order to compete with the last ever episode of a popular sitcom on BBC1.
9. http://www.ukgameshows.com/page/index.php/The_Weakest_Link [accessed 1 July 2007].
10. As above.

5 The Quiz Show and 'Ordinary' People as Television Performers

> Ordinariness is not much in demand [on television] any more. Even reality TV shows claiming to explore the lives of the unfamous turn their subjects into stars, [producing] . . . fodder for *heat* magazine. The genuinely ordinary – the sort of people who might wear skirts with elasticated waists, eat fish fingers for tea and worry vaguely about fungal infections on their feet . . . are beneath general notice. (Bell 2004: 15)

Geraldine Bell's description of 'ordinary' people in *The Guardian* indicates how responses to 'ordinary' people on television are often couched within discourses of (class) taste. The references to 'elasticated waists' (*read* unfashionable, cheap clothes) and 'fish fingers for tea' (*read* unfashionable, cheap food) are far from neutral. But Bell is also pointing to what she sees as the disappearance of the 'ordinary' on television. Reality TV has developed an appetite for the type of 'ordinary' people that can guarantee something close to a semi-professional performance. As press critic Ian Parker puts it, 'the real person who cannot rustle up a heightened TV persona is asked to step aside' (cited in Piper 2004: 282). But the fact that television's portrayal of 'ordinariness' may differ across genres, or that it appears to be changing over time, usefully foregrounds its status as a cultural construction – something which is brought into being *by* television. It is this process of constructing the 'ordinary' which is the focus of this chapter.

The media/ordinary hierarchy

Given that the very 'category of "ordinariness" is . . . produced within discourse', we can examine how 'ordinariness' is constructed on television, and how 'ordinary' identities on television are brought into being (Teurlings 2001: 261). The use of inverted commas around the term 'ordinary' acknowledges this process of construction, while it also reminds us that the term cannot be taken at face value. As Jane Root observed in 1986, television employs people '*to be* ordinary [my emphasis]', and part of 'the real person's job is to be just like those watching, to act as viewers momentarily whisked to the other side of the screen' (1986: 97).

Just why this is the job of the 'ordinary' person on television is illuminated by Nick Couldry's emphasis on a distinction between a media and ordinary worlds – a distinction which is central to the media's symbolic power. We often accept without question that to step into television is to enter a form of privileged reality, a 'special space' (Couldry 2000: 47), and this is what Couldry calls the pervasive acceptance of the media/ordinary hierarchy. The idea of a boundary between media and 'ordinary' worlds is ultimately illusory: the 'media world' is *not* separate from 'our world'; it is part of the same world dedicated to mediating it (ibid.). Yet we nevertheless take these distinctions for granted – as is demonstrated by the discursive categorisation of people on screen. The media categorises social subjects as either 'media people' (celebrities) or 'non-media people' ('ordinary' people). As Couldry summarises, it seems ' "common sense" that the "media world" is somehow better, more intense than "ordinary" life, and that "media people" are somehow special' (ibid.: 44). But this is not the whole story, as in order to claim a privileged access to 'reality', the media must *also* appear to offer a shared space which matters to 'us'. In other words, it also has to make a claim to the 'everyday' and the 'ordinary': enter the significance of 'ordinary' people as performers (ibid.: 47).

'Being on TV': ordinary or extraordinary?

Quiz and game shows invite 'ordinary' people into the apparently special space of television. As such, they have historically been a key television space in which the ritual meeting of media and ordinary worlds occurs. The sense of a hierarchy here is clear in that, despite the perception that 'the contestant is everything' (Hutchinson 2006), 'ordinary' people go unpaid and uncredited for their appearance on a quiz or game show (Root 1986: 95). This is precisely because the real prize is perceived to be the contestants' 'fifteen minutes of fame' – a conception which further shores up the privileged status of the television frame.

Yet it has also been suggested that this attitude, and our cultural perception of television, has changed over time. Writing in 1998, a critic in *The Guardian* reflected on the historical tendency to give smaller prizes on British quiz shows, and how this seemed to be changing in the wake of *Millionaire*. He also observed how 'free-gift' shows have:

> [S]uffered from a historical shift . . . a decline in the novelty of appearing on television. The earlier programmes could get away with lesser [prizes] . . . because being screened into your neighbour's living room was part of the prize. These days, most potential contestants will have a fly-on-the-wall documentary team in their workplace, their holiday resort and their shopping centre.[1]

Written when the docusoap was enjoying considerable popularity on British television in the late 1990s, the critic foregrounds the pervasive mediation of everyday life, and its impact on how people conceptualise their relationship with the 'media' world.

It is true that we may perceive the media world to be increasingly accessible. With the advent of websites such as 'beonscreen.com' or 'StarNow.co.uk', you can shop for opportunities to appear on television online – much like shopping for ordinary commodities such as music, DVDs, clothes or groceries. *Broadcast* magazine also reflected on this shift when it asked 'Where Did All the Contestants Go?' (2006):

> Years ago, people were clamouring to get on TV and quiz show researchers had easy jobs . . . Yet now TV production companies have found that these heady days of contestant enthusiasm are long gone. Of course, there are exceptions to this rule – like *The Weakest Link*, which relies on a cult following, and *Millionaire*, which lures people in with the promise of large prizes, but in general, quiz shows are really struggling to find participants . . . It simply doesn't make sense when quizzes are so hugely popular in the UK.[2]

The article goes on to explain how 'TV is no longer shrouded in mystery nor is it the big draw it once was, so production companies simply need to work harder to find contestants' (ibid.).

Gary Carter from Endemol describes how the public attitude to television has changed over the last two generations, 'from accepting the medium as an unquestioned source of authority, to a more critical and savvy engagement . . . Today, the man on television is just another voice amid the hubbub of a high-tech multimedia age' (cited in Cummings 2002: xiv). Reality TV has been cited as the most obvious example of this shift. From *Big Brother*, *Pop Idol*, *The Apprentice* to *Wife Swap*, reality TV is eager to find 'ordinary' people who embrace mediation, and who are only too willing to meet the camera's gaze head on. Far from accepting the medium as an 'unquestioned source of authority', many no longer feel that they are 'too ordinary' to take part.

Furthermore, reality TV offers its participants a greater 'scope of action' when compared to the traditional quiz and game show (although that is not to suggest that the participants simply get to represent 'themselves') (Haralovich and Trossett 2004: 78). But it is important to stress here that simply because reality TV participants adopt a more 'savvy' attitude toward appearing on television, this does not in itself challenge the idea of a symbolic hierarchy between media/ordinary worlds. In fact, reality TV has clearly shored up the belief that television is the *ultimate* space in which to validate the self, and it is only because this cultural myth has become so pervasive that the desire to appear on television seems more 'ordinary', and reachable, than ever before.

When compared to the more youth-orientated ('cool') connotations of reality formats, quiz shows do not necessarily solicit a 'savvy' approach to television mediation. Indeed, quiz and game shows are more likely to foreground 'ordinary' people temporarily touching the media world, and this often involves signalling that contestants are also viewers. On *Millionaire*, contestants are frequently asked how they 'do when playing along at home' (a question which also advertises the popularity of the show itself). As Michael Clarke observes, coming across as 'quintessentially ordinary' on a quiz show often involves the 'expression of 'some awe and nervousness [about] . . . being on television' (1987: 53). Contestants are also asked how they are feeling ('Are you nervous?), or if they want to wave to someone 'back at home'. An interesting question here, and one which is implicitly explored throughout the chapter, is whether quiz shows still demand more traditional representations of television 'ordinariness'.

Managing rituals of exchange

As the discussion so far suggests, any examination of how 'ordinary' people are constructed as performers is also an examination of agency and power. In this regard, this chapter works from a negotiated perspective which recognises that, in the words of Jan Teurlings, while 'people who appear on television are not freely expressing their true selves', neither 'are they the helpless objects of exploitative broadcasters' (2001: 259). As Teurlings argues in her analysis of 'Producing the Ordinary: Institutions, Discourses and Practices in Love Game Shows', it is crucial to recognise that participants play a role in producing 'constructions of the "ordinary" *themselves*' [original emphasis] (ibid.: 256), even if they do not do so on an equal terrain. Teurlings draws attention to the importance of what she calls the 'structured and managed setting' in which 'ordinary' people perform. This setting includes:

> Strategies of selection (through which the production crew aim to find the 'right' participants for the show); strategies of form (aimed at directing the 'communicative' behaviour of the participants); and strategies of content (intended to enhance the production of desirable discourses and performance of identities). (ibid.: 253)

Teurlings is drawing our attention here to the relationship between performance and power. Much attention has been focused on the concept of performance in television, media and cultural studies, although it is difficult to offer a neat definition of what performance actually means. Everyday life has long since been understood as demanding a particular 'presentation of the self' (Goffman 1972), but as Myra Macdonald explains, when the notion of everyday performance 'is transferred to the public arena of television . . . more explicitly performative abilities come into play' (2003: 82). 'Ordinary' people become social actors, and they enter into rituals of exchange which shape the presentation of the self (ibid.).

The allocation of social roles in the genre (what Teurlings above would position as 'strategies of form') clearly shape the quiz show's rituals of exchange. 'Ordinary' people are often encouraged to display their personalities while acting as the straight man or woman to the host (Whannel 1992: 193). In the first televised version of ITV's *Double Your Money* in 1955, the host Hughie Greene introduces the section of the show in which a husband and wife team compete together. Mr and Mrs Wally are an elderly couple who have been married for fifty-three years, and when Greene asks Mr Wally how they met, the contestant says, 'I asked her if she'd like to go for a drink'. Greene turns to the camera and the studio audience and rolls his eyes before quipping, 'Geez, it's been a *long* drink, hasn't it?' (26 September 1955). As this suggests, in entering into rituals of exchange, 'ordinary' people are required to occupy roles, especially gender roles, which they may not wish to inhabit (Whannel 1992: 193). A number of British hosts in the 1950s brought comedic talents from variety theatre. Furthermore, the very concept of 'television' – not only appearing on it but also watching it – was still new (and Mr and Mrs Wally blink warily under the studio lights). In this respect, the power imbalance between host and contestant seems particularly apparent in this early period. Yet the notion of the 'ordinary' person providing material for the 'spontaneous' comedy of the host has clearly continued beyond this time, from

The Price is Right and *Strike it Lucky* (ITV, 1986–99 [intermittent]) to *Millionaire*.

Rituals of exchange usually involve contestants telling stories about themselves, although this varies between programmes. Different shows require and shape different constructions of 'ordinariness'. As one executive producer explains:

> The stories, the experiences, people's hopes and . . . dreams, are all grist to the mill to finding good contestants . . . But what makes a 'good' contestant changes from programme to programme. With the *Price is Right*, for example, you want somebody who is going to be . . . presentable, who is going to react well, and who is going to be able to play the game. But 'excite-ability' is not important for *Mastermind*. (Greenstone 2006)

Furthermore, the 'meaner' formats discussed in Chapter 4, from *The Weakest Link* and *Pokerface* to *The Enemy Within*, are less likely to include an emphasis on contestant stories. The sentiments of these anecdotes – 'warm', amusing and eager to please – do not sit easily with the more ruthless values of these shows. Mike Beale was part of the initial creative team which worked on *The Weakest Link*, and he recalls the emphasis on how 'we don't care about these people – roll them in and get them out, that was part of the charm' (Beale 2006).

However, it would be misleading to suggest that the use of contestant stories is outmoded. Despite having little or nothing to do with the game, they remain important in establishing the people *as* 'ordinary', in suggesting a 'shared' culture, and in facilitating identification between contestant and viewer. In the UK version of *Supermarket Sweep*, we learn a little more about the contestants after the first round of questions. Vicky and Jean from Glasgow are pair number three, and host Dale Winton explains:

> Dale: So Vicky made a mistake when she started working in the hospital, as she washed ten male patients using a commode rather than a washbasin – is that right? [Looking at Jean]
>
> Jean: Yes, she'd just started – I told her to get the basin, but she went and got the commode. [The studio audience laughs]
>
> Dale: Have I got this right? Oh no! Oh how funny – those poor men! Still, we've all made mistakes on the first day of a new job right? (4 April 2006)

Indicating the importance of 'strategies of selection' (Teurlings 2001: 253), a 'story' can also emerge from discussions of how people will spend their winnings. Mike Beale from 12Yard Productions explains how 'good stories' are important:

> We don't want everyone to come and say they will spend the money on a shopping spree in Harrods, it is not a great story. But 'I am going to buy my mum new teeth' is funny – it's a good story. (Beale 2006)

In light of this comment, it is not difficult to see that the 'ordinary' quickly becomes the 'extraordinary'. After all, it is more 'ordinary' to aspire to a shopping spree in Harrods than it is to dream about purchasing false dentures for your Mum. Indeed, the entertainment demands of television mean that the 'ordinary' is often 'brightened up' a little, indicative of the extent to which the truly 'ordinary' is perhaps not so interesting after all. As Bonner observes in her book *Ordinary Television*, the fact that some are more 'usefully ordinary than others should put a dampener on any temptation to perceive ordinary television as necessarily a democratising force' (2003: 52).

The scandal of it! Approaching 'authenticity' – are 'real' people really 'real'?

The debate about democratisation further suggests how television's construction of the 'ordinary' takes place within relations of power. In this respect, press criticism of quiz and game shows has historically perpetuated an image of 'ordinary' people as manipulated and duped – subject to the exploitative demands of entertainment television. In 1950s Britain, quiz and game shows were debated by critics as the television equivalent of 'man-baiting', and were discussed as a mechanism of 'torture' (see Holmes 2008). Furthermore, even the most cursory survey of headlines across the decades ('Swapping Your Dignity for a Moment of Fame' on *The Price is Right*, receiving 'Physical Trauma and Public Humiliation' with the advent of *The Chair*) reveals a distaste for the apparently desperate desire for fame, and the extent to which this is exploited by ratings-hungry broadcasters. This chapter has indicated how academic approaches adopt a more nuanced view of power, yet the press criticisms nevertheless speak to what Karen Lury has described as our 'uneasy ambivalence' in our appreciation of the 'ordinary' performer: we may 'empathise uncomfortably' if we perceive the person to lack control, or we may occupy a sadistic position, hoping that they may be 'punished or humiliated for [their] . . . "unseemly" desire to perform' (1995: 126).

Lury's paradigm reflects back on the convention of contestant stories discussed above. When watching quiz and game shows, we have all experienced the slightly uncomfortable experience of seeing 'ordinary' people tell 'amusing' anecdotes about their wedding day, holiday or first day at work, and this uneasiness also reflects the extent to which we recognise these stories to be *rehearsed*. This brings into view a key concept which has long since structured discussions of 'ordinary' people as performers on television: the concept of authenticity.

Quiz and game shows offer highly artificial settings, but through their use of 'ordinary' people, they also make a claim to the real. 'Ordinary' people on television have historically been valued for their spontaneity, realness and difference from a learned or professional performance. But as Root observes, in reality, 'no-one in television wants real people to behave like the amateurs they are . . . [D]irectors pray for "naturals": individuals who . . . can . . . conjure up skills that professionals spend years perfecting' (1986: 95). This contradiction, in which the 'ordinary' can quickly become the 'extraordinary', and the amateur can become the professional, is captured by a comment from a BBC producer in the 1980s: 'People can become professionals very quickly. Ironically, that "party piece" approach can undermine the credibility of what they are saying' (cited in Root 1986: 97). This is why a certain 'roughness around the edges' – such as colourful clothes, odd hair or glasses, or a regional accent – can be important in ensuring that real people look 'real' (ibid.). The anxiety here about 'ordinary' people being 'real' reinforces Lury's wider point that 'the otherwise accepted duality of character and actor is made problematic when we witness real people perform. For if real people convincingly "put on an act" where can sincerity, authenticity and real emotion be located with any conviction?' (1995: 126).

It is now difficult to read this comment without thinking of reality TV, as the debate about whether 'ordinary' people are really 'real' has frequently attended its circulation. But while reality TV may have crystallised concerns about 'ordinary' people and authenticity, these debates are not new. A famous precursor in this regard is represented by the American Big Money shows of the 1950s – programmes which found themselves at the centre of the quiz show scandals (see Chapter 2). Contestants were trained as 'actors', and required to perform roles within a pre-planned (rigged) narrative outcome. The first show to be placed under investigation in 1958 was *Dotto*, and one contestant made a clear connection with fiction when he explained to a British journalist how:

You'd think I was Marlon Brando. I was told how to bite my lips, clench my fists and look agonized as I supposedly struggled to find the answers. They even told me how, at the last moment, to make my face light up as if the answer had suddenly come to me. It made the whole thing very dramatic.[3]

The concept of casting was also important here. The producer of the American show *Twenty-One* had dressed contestant Herbert Stempel in a frayed shirt and an ill-fitting suit (the 'penniless ex-GI'), and the fact that Stempel's wife was from a relatively wealthy family was not disclosed (see Anderson 1978: 49).

Yet rather than suggest that the American producers misunderstood the status of the quiz shows as fiction, failing to grasp their dual appeal of both 'reality' *and* 'drama' (Cooper-Chen 1994: 18), it is more appropriate to argue that while the quiz show was understood to be an 'uncontrolled and unpredictable contest . . . between non-actors, producers were sensitive to their affinities with traditional dramatic forms' (Boddy 1990: 104). Notably, it seems that this 'affinity' was recognised as more important where television was concerned (with its emphasis on the visual). Peter Conrad effectively makes this point when he suggests that we can actually describe the 'corrupt' American producers as pioneers:

> Though the medium reviled them, they were actually doing its work, turning the quiz show from an aural examination into a visual spectacle . . . Was this malpractice, or was it merely the medium's early, astute recognition that whatever happens on it must be a performance, and therefore a simulation? (1982: 91)

This usefully points to the possibility that the scandals offered an exaggerated example of the 'structured and managed setting' (Teurlings 2001: 253) which *always* shape the televisual contexts in which 'ordinary' people perform. The strategies used above, from 'casting' and directing the visual expressions of the contestants, to choreographing the outcome of the game, all represent very heightened examples of the strategies of 'selection', 'form' and 'content' which always shape television's construction of 'ordinary' identities.

There is a long history of quiz and game shows insisting upon their authenticity, as well as the spontaneous and authentic nature of the contestant performances – even when there is no suggestion of malpractice at all. We might note, for example, how each contestant on *The Price is Right* is asked to confirm that they 'didn't have the slightest idea' they would be picked to 'Come on down'. Equally, we can observe Tom McGregor's suggestion in the behind-the-scenes book on *Millionaire* that:

Anyone who saw [the first female contestant in 1998] ... will remember her shaking with nerves, unable even to hold a glass of water, providing the most riveting piece of drama that no actress, however well rehearsed, could even begin to equal. (1999: 17)

The anxiety surrounding the authenticity of the quiz show, and especially the authenticity of its performers, speaks to a number of tensions which structure its generic form. The genre offers a tightly formatted arena which aims to guarantee certain entertainment values, but its very appeal is also based on a claim to the 'unwritten' and the 'real' (see also Chapter 2). Furthermore, while the 'presentation' of the self in everyday life may require elements of performance, we have seen how more explicitly 'performative abilities come into play' when 'ordinary' people become 'social actors' on television (Macdonald 2003: 82).

Disorderly 'ordinariness'?: keeping 'ordinary' people under control

This chapter began by acknowledging the importance of a negotiated perspective which does not simply see the contestants as 'passive' pawns, at the mercy of quiz show producers and hosts. Chapter 6 engages with how *contestants* conceptualise the construction of the 'ordinary' in the quiz show, something which often involves a self-reflexive and critical attitude toward the performative demands at stake. But programmes themselves can also complicate a picture in which 'ordinary' people are 'slotted' into the genre as interchangeable subjects.

As indicated earlier in the chapter, it may be that changing conceptions of appearing on television, with people no longer feeling that they are too 'ordinary' to take part, have begun to renegotiate the boundaries of interaction here. In a number of modern formats, the contestant is likely to retort to jokes made by the host, or to give the impression of a greater ownership of the game space. In *Deal or No Deal* the games are explicitly named after their players ('Becky's game'), providing the context for a more confident encounter between contestant, host and invisible banker. In fact, contestants regularly gesture to the studio audience to support or applaud their actions ('Come on!') – something which was traditionally the preserve of the host. Just as the *Deal or No Deal* contestants engage in feisty bargaining with the banker, or the contestants on *The Chair* enter into verbal sparring with John McEnroe, so contestants on *The Weakest Link* articulate one-liners in response to the criticisms and put-downs from the host. When Anne Robinson asks a middle-aged female contestant, 'Do you do your hair yourself? [It is a bit] old fashioned isn't it?', the contestant bluntly responds: 'But Anne your [hairstyle] . . . looks like a dead ferret' (13 April 2005). As a member of the production team explains, the contestants have become Robinson's comedy 'sidekicks – it's as much their show as hers'.[4] But such behaviour is licensed by the game itself. When the qualities that make 'ordinary' people 'real' *genuinely* make 'them more difficult to manage in routine ways' (Grindstaff, cited in Macdonald 2003: 80), it is quickly apparent.

The BBC's *The National Lottery Jet Set* is one of the quiz programmes screened as part of the Saturday night lottery draw. A studio contestant plays to take the jet-set lifestyle away from the current champion, who is living the luxury jet-set life abroad. They thus aim to exchange their general knowledge for the chance to go on 'the trip of a lifetime'. In a 2006 edition, a middle-aged man from Newcastle, Allan Flanagan, is the contestant in the studio (30 March 2006). From the start, Allan displays a heightened emotional investment in the game. When thinking or answering, he closes his eyes and clenches his fists, punching the air when he gives a correct answer. In this regard, Allan seems utterly focused on the game, talking to himself in such a way which seeks to build, while also express, his inner confidence. He repeatedly shouts 'It's my day, it's my day – come on!', and after the host, Eamon Holmes, repeatedly tells the contestant to 'calm down', he comments with a wry smile: 'Your day, Allan? Well, let's see if it is'. When Allan wins the game and finds out that he will be living the jet-set lifestyle in Mexico for a week, he leaps from his chair and launches himself at the host, cutting Holmes's lip in the process. Through a clenched smile and gritted teeth, Holmes waves goodbye to the camera as the credits roll. When a studio contestant called Laura ends Allan's jet-set lifestyle the following week, Holmes is visibly pleased with the result.

The fact that Allan's performance represents a source of tension here is interesting in at least two ways. First, with his dramatic and intense expressions, Allan in many ways displays a 'good' television performance. But he also fits awkwardly into *Jet Set* because he perhaps wants to win *too much*. Television trades to a large degree on its sociability (Scannell 1996), but rather than reflecting the public conventions of how to appear sociable and personable on television, Allan is resolutely invested in the private ambition of winning. To be sure, Chapter 4 outlined how the 'meaner' formats, from *The Weakest Link* and *Beg, Borrow or Steal* to *Pokerface*, positively encourage ruthlessness, foregrounding the unsocial aspects of competition with glee. This confirms the extent to which different shows offer different roles to their contestants (and thus demand different constructions of ordinariness). But as with the verbal sparring on *The Weakest Link*, those formats license such behaviour as *part* of a 'good' performance. When it is not acknowl-edged to be part of the theatrics and rules of the game, as in *Jet Set*, such behaviour is clearly less acceptable. Allan also disrupts the regulation of roles in the genre: he quite literally invades the host's space, actually causing Holmes minor injury in the process.

Jet Set is broadcast live, so there was no second take here. But it is instructive to observe that such transgressions are rarely seen in the programmes themselves – they usually emerge in out-take pro-grammes, or in shows which pivot on moments when things go wrong (for example, *It Shouldn't Happen to a Quiz Show Host* (ITV1, 14 April 2005). More recently, these moments may appear on the internet site Youtube.com. Viewers upload, share and discuss clips of interesting or amusing quiz show performances, including those which effectively transgress the accepted codes of conduct in the genre. You can view a man activating his buzzer with his head on an Australian edition of *Sale of the Century*,[5] or you can witness the highly excitable Tom Spencer on the American version of *Millionaire* demanding to hear the music ('dedeludelude') which accompanies the moment when the lights go down and the contestant sits in the hot seat. Tom explains to the host, Meredith Vieira, that he never heard the music at the end of his last appearance when they 'ran out of time'. (The absence of music is cus-tomary in these instances, as the lights go up and a horn sounds to signal the end of that edition, and the interruption of the contestant's game.) Tom asks for two rounds of the music as compensation, and, while visibly amused, Vieira exerts control over this 'loose cannon' with a firm but fair 'Tom, you will get *one* dedeludelude' – a move which the studio audience applauds.[6] The framing and selection of these clips (the Tom Spencer clip is captioned as 'Open and Weird Guy on *Millionaire*') shows how viewers also play a role in perpetuating perceptions of appropriate contestant behaviour. Indeed, these moments are only seen as interesting and humorous *because* they disrupt or challenge the cul-tural rules of the game space. But in the context of this chapter, they are interesting because they effectively push at the boundaries of the 'structured and managed setting' (Teurlings 2001: 253) in which 'ordin-ary' people always perform. In doing so, they momentarily accentuate the constraints of this framework, while simultaneously attesting to the always unstable nature of agency and power.

Celebrity games

It is worth pausing here to acknowledge that not all formats pivot on the spectacle of 'ordinary' people under pressure. There have long since been formats which deliberately mix celebrities and 'ordinary' people, for example *Celebrity Squares* (initially ITV, 1975–9, and called *Hollywood Squares* in America), *Blankety Blank*, and *The Big Call* (ITV1, 2005). In each of these examples, celebrities are there to 'help' 'ordinary' people win a prize. But there are also occasions when celebrities enter formats originally designed for members of the public, as is the case with the UK versions of *The Weakest Link*, *Millionaire* and *Mastermind*. While this may have become more common, it is by no means a new innovation. The appeal of inserting famous faces into existing formats was already apparent in the 1950s. As DeLong describes when discussing the American Big Money shows, with the choice of 'uniquely interesting candidates off the street somewhat diminished and ratings a bit sluggish, why not regularly bring on a famous individual with specialized knowledge of a subject, preferably outside of his [sic] professional field?' (1991: 204). *The $64,000 Challenge* pitched Edward G. Robinson against fellow actor Vincent Price. Both were art experts and collectors, and after they had made six appearances on the show, a tie was declared and the prize split (ibid.). As DeLong's comment suggests, inserting celebrities into an existing format designed for 'ordinary' people is a way of providing regulated difference within a programme – something which aims to prevent audience interest from waning. *Millionaire* clearly adopted this strategy, asking celebrities, from sports men and women to singers and television entertainers, to compete in pairs. *The Weakest Link* has also exploited celebrity editions, sometimes involving a television theme (for example, an edition with soap stars, or an edition with actors and actresses from medical dramas). When British television launched *The Gameshow Marathon* in 2005 (it was also adapted in America and Germany), celebrities competed in 'classic' formats such as *The Price is Right*, *Play Your Cards Right* and *The Golden Shot*. While this often involved a heavy dose of irony about the perceived 'naffness' of the games, the programme was hugely popular, and led (in the UK) to a re-launching of older formats such as *The Price is Right* on daytime TV.

The fact that celebrities must play for charity in these formats is interesting in itself. Celebrity is ultimately a hierarchical phenomenon which, like capitalism, enables a relatively small number of people to become wealthy at the expense of others. As such, it does not sit easily with a genre which pivots on discourses of 'egalitarian' opportunity (and the concept of a 'shared' culture). Furthermore, just as 'ordinary' contestants are not invited to dwell on real poverty or hardship, so celebrities are not encouraged to discuss their relative wealth. The rise in celebrity quiz editions certainly reflects our increasing cultural fascination with the famous. But the submerging of wealth also points to a more ambivalent attitude toward celebrities. Magazines such as *heat* and *Now* evince a punitive attitude toward celebrity status, gleefully 'papping' them sporting sweat patches, spots or fashion *faux pas*, while celebrity reality formats, from *I'm a Celebrity . . . Get me Out of Here!* to *Celebrity Big Brother*, aim to strip away the celebrity façade, exploiting viewers' hunger for seeing famous faces outside their usual media roles. Although the spatial, aesthetic and ideological context of the studio quiz/game show does not make a similar claim to the 'real', it can still cater to the 'vicarious pleasure in seeing celebrities undone' (Greenstone 2006). Indeed, in light of the decline of meritocratic ideologies of fame (see Gamson 2001), it is certainly not expected that celebrities will display startling intellect on television (and 'serious' quizzers often resent the inclusion of celebrities in general knowledge formats).[7] We can watch celebrities being anxious and nervous on *Millionaire*, and we may even be invited to consider how 'celebrity X is a complete dunce' (Greenstone 2006). But while such editions may be positioned as part of a broader desire to render celebrities more 'ordinary' and 'accessible' (more 'like us'), we should be wary of celebrating it as a boisterously democratic move. Celebrities may increasingly occupy television spaces originally designed for 'ordinary' people, but this does not diminish or alter the economic and cultural hierarchies on which the phenomenon of celebrity is based.

'A natural reluctance to be competitive?': 'it's not very feminine, is it?'

This chapter has drawn attention to ways of conceptualising a 'good' television performance within the context of the quiz show – good in the sense of abiding by the genre's rules, and good in the sense of being (tele)visual. But whether implicitly or explicitly, these conceptions are often also shaped by wider frameworks of identity, such as gender and class. With regard to gender in the UK version of *Millionaire*, it was suggested that women make better contestants – with their apparent proclivity to be 'more emotional, more responsive [and] ready to scream with excitement' (Barber 2000: 33). This preference for female contestants is ironic given that women have long since been more reluctant to enter the quiz show space. This gender imbalance is related to, but cannot be collapsed with, the relative invisibility of the female host (Chapter 4).

When *Millionaire* emerged in Britain, and then later in the US, there was considerable discussion about the numerical dominance of male contestants. *Guardian* critic Anita Chaudhuri asked in 1999: 'What is the last bastion of male supremacy on our TV screens . . .? The answer is – and you'll kick yourself when you hear it – TV quiz shows' (1999: 6). Chaudhuri notes that, after one year of *Millionaire*, only 20 per cent of the 'Fastest Finger First' contestants had been female. As a result of this ratio, women were understandably making infrequent appearances in the hot seat. Around the same time, the American host, Regis Philbin, openly enquired in one edition: 'Why is it that nearly all of our contestants are white men? . . . We really would like a little more diversity! . . . Everyone out there . . . who isn't a white male – dial that . . . number and let's get into the game' (Cohn 2000: 12). The image of diversity, in terms of both gender and ethnicity, is crucial to the apparently egalitarian promise of the show. In fact, at a time when reality and makeover TV have displayed a 'pluralling up' of the identities that can be seen as 'ordinary' on television (Brunsdon 2003: 17, cited in Redden 2007: 152), quiz shows appear stubbornly traditional.

With respect to gender, the predominance of male contestants is not specific to *Millionaire*. A 2006 survey by Quizzing.co.uk revealed that only about 25 per cent of all applicants for British quiz shows were women.[8] The imbalance has a long history. In the 1950s, Big Money American shows such as *The $64,000 Question* and *Twenty-One* were already witnessing a relative dearth of female contestants (Anderson 1978: 106). While producers sent out talent scouts to locate female contestants, professors and critics aimed to offer explanations for the gender imbalance. Some pinpointed the role of knowledge (women tend to have fewer hobbies and therefore 'less vocational knowledge' than men), while others claimed that women were simply 'less tolerant of that nonsense . . .' (ibid.: 107). Similar discussion was going on in Britain. In 1957, the host of the British *Double Your Money*, Hughie Greene, emphasised how only 15 per cent of the show's applicants were women, and he commented that, 'Women are always crying out for equality. But I say that the reason we don't have many . . . is that they just haven't got the courage to come along and compete like the men . . .'.[9]

Perhaps the BBC held a similar view. The first ever script for *Mastermind* (written in September 1972), explains how 'one of these [competitors] will emerge as Mastermind'.[10] Although the title of the show is itself gendered, the script originally read 'He or she' ('He or she will emerge as the winner of . . .'). Yet the word 'she' was scored out with a pencil before broadcast. This may have simply reflected the gender composition of the contestants in the first edition. But the 'correction' seems to have a far greater significance when considered in relation to the longer history of competitors on the programme. In 2006 the (second) *Mastermind* host, John Humphrys, wrote an article for *The Daily Mail* about the lack of female applicants and winners on the programme, a disparity which is more apparent now than in the early years of the show. Humphrys quotes the view of an early female winner, Anne Ashurst, who observes (much like Hughie Green above) how: 'Women just aren't as competitive as men. You don't see as many women on programmes like *Who Wants To Be A Millionaire*. Why? Because they just don't apply' (Humphrys 2006). When writing about *Millionaire*, Chaudhuri (1999) indeed highlighted how more 'serious' general knowledge programmes had often struggled to recruit female contestants, although this had not been a problem for shows such as *Family Fortunes* and *The Price is Right*. These are formats which pivot on the more culturally female domains of shopping, consumerism and family (and they are also shows which are more likely to attract derision than prestige).

This comparison gives further pause for thought when we survey the discourses on gender which circulate across contemporary television programming. British and American reality formats, such as *Big Brother*, *Wife Swap*, *America's Next Top Model* and *The Bachelor*, regularly position women as intrinsically competitive, but only when the other competitors are *women*. This seems to suggest that women don't 'naturally' involve themselves in competition unless the rewards fall within spheres traditionally prescribed as feminine (home, marriage, romance, fashion). Nor do these formats require intelligence – at least as this might be traditionally conceived of – in the manner of the quiz show.[11]

In this regard, explanations of the gender imbalance in the quiz show shift between biological and cultural explanations of gender. The emphasis on women's 'natural reluctance to be competitive', or the suggestion that men might be quicker at reflex actions while women are better at problems which involve 'working through' (Brownlow, Whitener and Rupert 1998), make recourse to innate, apparently biological, differences between men and women. Yet these discussions are also based on cultural perceptions of gender (constructions of masculinity and femininity). Men are *expected* to be individualist, aggressive and competitive – as emerging from their association with the workplace – while women have traditionally been associated with nurturing, and conceived in terms of communal relations. As Chapter 4 has outlined, quiz formats have increasingly licensed ruthless behaviour from all contestants. But while this may mean that they are less invested in merit (knowledge), the emphasis on gender here may complicate the bid to label them as more democratic.

The quantitative study ' "I'll Take Gender Differences for $1,000!":
Domain-Specific Intellectual Success on "Jeopardy"', by Brownlow,
Whitener and Rupert (1998) also observed that women displayed a
greater tendency to underestimate their intelligence, while men were
more likely to overestimate theirs. Yet again, this seems to represent
less a reflection of biological differences, than a reflection of the roles
traditionally allotted to men and women in society. Historically, men
have been more likely to occupy high-status occupations which encourage them to display their 'competence and intellect' more often (1998:
271). This also relates to what might be called the cultural appropri-
ateness of women demonstrating intellect. As Cynthia W. Walker and
Amy H. Sturgis observe, 'Even with wider opportunities available to
women, the classic stereotype of intelligence – the "nerd" – remains
essentially male' (forthcoming). In confirming the polarisation of looks
or brains (body or mind), they go on to observe how:

> Women who are timid, wall-flowerish, and unusually smart have
> always managed to occupy a more acceptable place in the social
> order. In fact, the mousy, unattractive woman (usually a librarian)
> who takes off her spectacles and lets down her hair to reveal a stun-
> ning beauty is a common cliché in popular culture. (forthcoming)

The popular phrase 'Men don't make passes at girls who wear glasses'
nods to a dichotomy (as discussed in Chapter 4 with respect to the
female host) in which women are valued for their looks, rather than
their intelligence. The phrase also implies that intelligence is incompatible with female beauty, and that women's intelligence is threaten-
ing to men (doubly so if combined with sexual power). In contrast, it is
apparently far more acceptable for men to combine these qualities, and
the concept of 'the sexy male nerd' has a more visible presence in
popular cultural representations (see ibid.).

Daphne Fowler, a veteran TV quiz show contestant in Britain, confirms that:

> It's a very male culture and you have to enjoy the limelight; you can
> feel very exposed. Even now, after twenty years of competing, I still
> stutter and pretend I am guessing . . . even though I know the answer
> is right . . . I still feel a bit embarrassed . . . about being seen to know
> more than men. It's not very feminine, is it? (Fowler, cited in
> Chaudhuri 1999: 6)

This suggests how cultural constructions of masculinity and femininity
play a role in shaping the actual lived experience of gender (and
should not be dismissed as simply stereotypes). Fowler's quote also

demonstrates how performativity is central to the construction of gender identity – it is something we *do* (Butler 1990). In this regard, Fowler indicates how an appearance on television might be seen as magnifying the conventions of self-presentation which already structure everyday life (Goffman 1972), including the conventions of gender presentation.

It is not only constructions of intelligence which may be salient where the relationship between femininity and the quiz show is concerned. Both gambling and bread-winning have traditionally been seen as male preserves. On *Millionaire*, the UK host Chris Tarrant frequently naturalises a relationship between competing, winning and 'bringing home the bacon'. A typical comment would be: 'So you've got a wife up there in the audience and two kids, what would be a serious amount of money for you to take home?' (14 January 2001). In contrast, women, whether in the hot seat or present as the supportive partner or spouse, are invariably constructed as consumers. Tarrant regularly comments, 'Don't turn around and look at . . . she's spent it already', or 'They do that, girls – she's thinking about shoes, holiday, shopping in that order' (9 February 2001) (and we might note the diminutive reference to 'girls') (Holmes 2005b). Whether constructed as a voracious consumer or the 'good wife' at home, these images seem striking when compared to the presence of economically independent career women found in other television genres (for example, crime drama, hospital drama, comedy).

The emphasis on the male breadwinner forms part of what Wayne calls the programme's 'fantastic emphasis on the family' (2000: 215). According to Wayne, this relates to the capitalist ethos of the quiz show and its relations with consumption, while – with respect to *Millionaire* – it also deflects associations of individual greed (ibid.). In this regard, *Millionaire* is evidence of how 'ordinary' television has historically offered conservative and traditional conceptions of the family. As Bonner describes, 'The trajectory of the ordinary life [is] . . . one in which romance, marriage children and grandchildren follow inevitably' (2003: 110).

This is also illustrated by how little visibility gay identity is permitted in the genre, especially when compared to other genres such as reality TV. To be sure, in casting gay men, reality TV has often drawn upon the stereotypical expectation that such participants will be naturally dramatic and/or entertaining. Gay identity is also visible in such contexts precisely because there is a bid to cast an array of diverse characters, out of which the producers hope to elicit conflict and drama. But with regard to reality TV, it would be a mistake to paint these relations in purely reductive terms: participants may have more agency than their fictional counterparts to problematise existing stereotypical representations, and reality TV has done much to render a broader array of gay identities visible and knowable. The quiz show differs markedly in this regard, in so far as it barely acknowledges gay identity at all.

In the UK, it seems that it is only in the context of a format which essentially satirises the quiz show that gay identity can be openly acknowledged. Often 'called "the next Kenneth Williams" due to his self-consciously camp performing style, acerbic wit and waspish persona',[12] Julian Clary hosted the suggestively titled *Sticky Moments with Julian Clary* (C4, 1985–9). The questions and games were saturated with references to sexuality, both gay and straight: (Q: ' "What M melts in your mouth and not in your hand?" A: "M and Ms?" Q: "No, Mel Gibson, sorry!" ').[13] When Clary later hosted the BBC's *Come and Have a Go . . .* (BBC1, 2004–5), the format of the show was more traditional, but Clary retained the bid to poke fun at the existing conventions of the genre. Rather than politely eliciting contestant's 'funny' stories, Clary cuts them off ('I'm really not that interested in this toilet paper story . . .'), or mocks conventions of quiz show sociability ('Have you had a "lovely day?" '). It is notably only in this context that contestants can be acknowledged as gay.

In one edition Clary introduces Tom and David, before turning to the camera to add, 'They're a gay couple and they don't care *who* knows it!'. Here, Clary acknowledges the dominance of a heterosexual culture which makes this statement a revelation (or a 'confession'), while he also pokes fun at its repressive ideals. But in a space which relies on the traditional family unit for its image of 'ordinariness', and which often assumes a familial address, it is notable that gay identity is still not really seen as 'ordinary' at all. Lesbian identity, as is often the case with a wide range of cultural representations, is even more invisible in the genre (and lesbian identity clearly conflicts with the wider emphasis that quiz and game shows have placed on women as objects of exchange within a heterosexual, capitalist economy). In other words, while it would be a mistake to homogenise perceptions of how the quiz show mediates discourses of consumerism (Chapter 4), the traditional nuclear family is still imagined as the basis for capitalist 'reproduction' and consumption in the genre.

This is certainly the case on *Millionaire*, and while women may be a more exceptional sight in the hot seat itself (Tarrant exclaims, 'It's a woman!' when a female contestant gets into the chair), they are still included within constructions of the 'ordinary'. As in advertising, the focus on gender here springs from its 'signifying power' – it can be communicated in an instant and it is heteronormatively assumed that it addresses us all (Jhally 1990: 136). In a bid to get more women on air, Celador produced a burst of *Millionaire* programmes in 2001 entitled 'Women's Specials'. But it would be literally *unthinkable* to turn this same approach to questions of ethnicity, despite the fact that the paucity of black or Asian contestants is surely the most striking disparity of all.

Quiz shows – a 'white culture'?

DeLong comments with regard to the American television quizzes in the mid 1950s that there was 'a concerted effort to bring blacks to the forefront as contestants', and he notes that not all 'big-money winners' were white (1991: 246). But he also explains that it was not really until the 1970s that the doors opened wider to black contestants and indeed to all members of ethnic-minority groups (ibid.). In 1950s Britain, this 'concerted effort' is evident in early ITV shows (for example, *Double Your Money* and *The 64,000 Question*). This was a time when Britain witnessed a sharp rise in immigration from India and Africa, and gradually became a more multi-ethnic population. But since this period, the quiz show has intermittently been highlighted as one of the most 'white' genres on British television (Whannel 1992: 195). In a survey of 1,500 competitors across British quiz and game shows in 1976, *Time Out* reported that only four were black, and one producer justifiably commented that there 'was actually more ethnic diversity . . . in the days of *Double Your Money*'.[14]

Knowledge on quiz shows is not simply classed (and gendered) (see Holmes 2005a), but also racialised. Whannel has observed how the apparently 'shared culture' of quiz shows is often in fact a largely white culture which trades in references to a distinctly 'white past' (1992: 197). But the issue with *Millionaire* was not about achievement or success, but the fact that largely white contestants were applying in the first place (and in percentages which did not reflect the ethnic ratio of Britain as a whole). Other shows which exercise more control over contestant selection do display more ethnic diversity, although this is only a matter of degree.

Quiz show producers are certainly aware of this issue, and while some are at a loss to explain it, others draw upon problematic stereotypes of ethnic identity (for example, the absence of black viewers might be linked to the fact that 'quiz shows are not seen as "cool"' (Beale 2006)). As with the discussion of gender, it is difficult to disentangle cultural myths and ideologies from the lived experience of identity here. But in terms of Asian identity, and a discussion emerging from a thread on the British website 'Asians in the Media',[15] there was at least the suggestion that there may be a feeling of 'added' pressure when it comes to performing on a quiz show as a member of an ethnic-minority group: while white people are seen as just representing 'themselves', Asian contestants represent 'Asian' identity – precisely because whiteness is seen as a dominant and 'invisible' ethnicity (Awan 2007). The possibility of 'failure' also had a resonance in other ways, and one Asian contestant pointed to the significance of 'izzat' (family honour) which might conflict with the bid to be 'out there and showy with what you can do' (ibid.). To be sure, there is clearly a danger here of subscribing to a logic of homogenisation: after all, we do not speculate as to why white viewers do or do not choose to apply. Furthermore, there are also wider issues which seem pertinent, but almost intangible (for example, cultural perceptions of the relationship between wealth and ethnicity, the relationship between ethnicity and stereotypes of intelligence).

What *can* be observed is that the ethnic imbalance in the genre may be self-perpetuating. If, according to Root, part of 'the real person's job is to be just like those watching, to act as viewers momentarily whisked to the other side of the screen' (1986: 97), this propensity for 'reflection' clearly depends on who you are. White faces can become as much a part of the visual imagery of the genre as the set, the studio audience or the host. While contemporary shows may be keen to foster an image of diversity in the genre, quiz shows have historically presented a cultural and television space which has been 'shared' in particular ways (Whannel 1992: 195).

This chapter has explored how 'ordinary' people are *constructed* as 'ordinary' within the context of the quiz show. In doing so, it has also argued for a negotiated perspective which understands that, while 'ordinary' people are required to adopt particular roles within the genre, and to enter into certain rituals of exchange, they are not simply the passive pawns of the producers or hosts. As the chapter has aimed to make clear, questions surrounding performance and authenticity frequently attend the discussion of 'ordinary' people on television, and the quiz show makes for a fruitful comparison with reality TV. But discussion should not *start* with reality TV in this respect: the often ignored history of 'ordinary' people as performers in the quiz and game show, one of few entertainment spaces where 'ordinary' people appeared as a matter of course, offers crucial insights into the historical, conceptual and theoretical debates which now attend this sphere. When 'ordinary' people appear on television, discussions about performance and 'acting up' usually take on a negative tone (see Hill 2005). But this need not be the case and, as Macdonald observes, we should recognise that individuals cannot merely take their 'pre-packaged, supposedly "authentic" selves for an outing on television' (2003: 82). In this regard, a simple duality between performance and authenticity is not always helpful.

Contestants are obviously central to the quiz show format, and without them the game could not take place. In this respect, the issues discussed in this chapter cannot neatly be separated from other chapters in the book. Given that the genre literally encourages us to 'jump into the tube' (Cooper-Chen 1994: 87), any discussion of contestants is also a discussion of the audience. This is the focus of the next chapter.

Notes

1. 'Come on down?', *The Guardian*, 5 September 1998. BFI Press clippings folder on quiz shows.
2. Written for *Broadcast*, but reproduced at http://www.iqagb.co.uk/trivia/viewtopic.php?t=1230 [accessed 20 December 2006].
3. 'US Inquiry into Quiz Shows', *The Times*, 28 August 1958, p. 7.
4. *The Weakest Link: The Story So Far* (tx 7 January 2007, BBC2).
5. http://www.youtube.com/watch?v=dvyH8wUoXV0 [accessed 18 March 2007].
6. http://www.youtube.com/watch?v=hOc_itwNt4A [accessed 18 March 2007].
7. http://www.iqagb.co.uk/trivia/viewtopic.php?t=4370 [accessed 7 June 2007].
8. http://www.iqagb.co.uk/trivia/viewtopic.php?t=1230 [accessed 20 December 2006].
9. 'How the *Double Your Money* contestants are chosen', *TV Times*, 22 February 1957, p. 6.
10. *Mastermind*, script one, 6 September 1972, T14/3,354/1 (WAC).
11. Thanks to Shelley Cobb at UEA for discussing this matter with me.
12. http://www.screenonline.org.uk/people/id/517266/index.html [accessed 21 June 2007].
13. http://www.ukgameshows.com/page/index.php/Sticky_Moments [accessed 21 June 2007].
14. 'Generation Gap', *Time Out*, 17 September 1976, p. 23.
15. http://www.asiansinmedia.org/.

6 'Asking the Audience': Quiz Shows and Their Viewers

Intelligent without being too highbrow; stimulating because one can try to answer questions; instructive when one can't. (BBC viewer talking about *What Do You Know?*, 1959)[1]

A good quiz compere will manage to get some personal info [about a contestant] that is interesting to all out in the public domain. Aligned with a good programme editor, you will get [aspects of] . . . personal 'colour' which paints the canvas of the quiz. (Posted by mquiz, quizzing.co.uk, 2002)[2]

It's those Most Embarrassing Moment stories that . . . get on my nerves. I reckon a good proportion of them are fictitious – mine was. Anyone else like to come clean? (Posted by kvm irving, quizzing.co.uk, 2005)[3]

These responses offer fleeting insights into audience, as well as contestant, relationships with quiz shows. Although academics and press critics also provide evidence of quiz show 'reception', audience responses have been all but invisible in academic work on the genre. This is despite the fact that quiz shows might be described as one of the more obvious sites for audience research. Many shows are designed to encourage us to 'play along' while viewing, and quiz formats often encode the participatory presence of the viewer into the text itself. Furthermore, in sometimes appearing as contestants and players, quiz show viewers can be visible on screen. The idea of audience visibility has also taken on new connotations with the advent of the internet. The growth of the internet has challenged the boundaries of public/private where television 'audiencing' is concerned, generating highly visible and participatory fan cultures across genres. The evidence offered by fan sites on the internet demands careful gathering, synthesis and analysis, but one of the key implications of the internet where fan studies are concerned is the relative democratisation of fan research. Fan cultures can be accessed and analysed as part of the study of any television genre – including the genre of the quiz show.

There are a number of different ways in which the relationship between quiz shows and their audiences might be approached. We can think about the 'subject position' offered to the viewer by the programme text; we can examine traces of historical reception (for example, BBC Audience Research reports, letters to the press or magazines); or we can conduct empirical audience research (for example, focus groups, online fan cultures). As such, this chapter cannot claim to be definitive or exhaustive, and a key part of its analysis is based on quiz show fandom on the internet. The chapter aims to use this evidence to respond to key topics and debates raised earlier in the book. Audiences play a role in constructing genre boundaries (Chapter 1), assessing the 'commercialisation' of quizzes (Chapter 2), debating the role of knowledge in the genre (Chapter 4), and interrogating the power relations between contestant and show (Chapter 5).

Audience participation

Whether based on the concept of a hypothetical subject position, or empirical responses from real viewers, television studies has expressed an ongoing interest in the relative 'activity' or 'passivity' of the television audience. Although this binary has since been perceived as rather reductive, the terms of debate have equally been challenged by our changing media environment. The growth of digital culture and 'new' media has prompted renewed debate about the approaches and theories used to study media audiences (including television). Jon Dovey and Helen W. Kennedy offer a useful illustration of this changing context in the following chart (2006: 3):[4]

Media studies	New media studies
Active audiences	Interactive users
Interpretation	Experience
Spectatorship	Immersion
Representation	Simulation
Centralized media	Ubiquitous media
Consumer	Participant/co-creator

Given that the quiz show has long since addressed a participative audience, it offers a particularly interesting site through which to assess these shifts.

There are many different ways of thinking about the participative nature of quiz shows – from the bid to recruit the contestants from the studio or home audience, to encouraging the viewer to play along as the programme unfolds. With regard to the early history of the genre on radio in the 1930s and 1940s, one of the most important channels of audience participation was the encouragement to listeners to send in questions for the shows (that is, the questions actually used in the programmes themselves). This strategy was apparent in both Britain and America. But participation is not the whole story here, as eliciting audience feedback can also be understood as a form of control (Ang 1991). Not only does it seek to construct a loyal and close relationship between programme and listener, but it also provides information about the audience which can then be sold to advertisers (Hoerschelmann 2006: 52). In this respect, there is a clear link here between 'old' and 'new' media contexts. The internet and interactive television both offer forms of participation which make viewers – and knowledge about them – more accessible and visible to producers, corporations and broadcasters. In the 1940s, the BBC represented a public service monopoly which had no need to compete (and certainly no need to sell audiences to advertisers). Yet its strategies still suggest a desire to win and hold listeners, and to 'know' what Ien Ang (1991) has referred to as an essentially 'unknowable' broadcast audience.

Radio established broadcasting as a mass medium, and as Hoerschelmann observes, once the quiz show moves to television, the visual representation of the studio audience *on screen* replaces the direct involvement solicited by radio. As he outlines, 'integrating a visual representation of the audience in quiz shows in the mid 1950s . . . serve[s] as a surrogate for the close text-audience relationship from the earlier history of the genre' (2006: 64). That is not to suggest that the genre was no longer participatory. But as a visual medium, television began to develop its own aesthetic which would enable the viewer to 'enter' into the game. In other words, audience participation becomes a central part of quiz show aesthetics, whether we refer to the on-screen interface which spells out the questions to viewer, or the choreographing of shots allowing us to shift between 'player', studio audience and observer. The extent to which programmes encode viewer participation into their textual form varies between formats (for example, the graphic interface on *Millionaire* beckons us to play along, while *Mastermind* makes no such 'concession'). Nevertheless, Fiske asserts that with their 'unwritten' narratives and participatory address, quiz shows might be seen as producing particularly 'active' viewers (1987: 272).

Interactive intentions

What exactly 'active' means here is no simple matter, and this question now seems even more urgent given that the beckon to participate has increased with the advent of new media technologies. To be sure, quiz and game shows have long since been multi-textual entities, with books and board games addressing the audience as viewers-turned-participants. These have now been joined by PC games and DVDs (and as discussed below, online games). In economic terms, the success of these products should not be underestimated. The first *Millionaire* PC game sold 1.3 million units in its first year, making it the fastest-selling PC game ever.[5] Along with *The Weakest Link*, *Millionaire* has also enjoyed success as a mobile phone game, with SMS and WAP technology launching the game in over thirty territories (to over 400 million subscribers).[6] In the UK, *Millionaire* later integrated mobile phone use into the programme itself with the 'Walkaway Game'. (A contestant is asked a question prior to a commercial break, and viewers at home are invited to text the answer during this slot. If correct, the viewer is entered into a draw the next working day, with the chance of winning £1,000.) By 2001, four versions of an on-line game had also increased ITV's web traffic by 800 per cent, making itv.com one of the most popular internet sites in the UK.[7]

Interactive options have also supplemented the possibilities of existing shows. Although *Millionaire* is only one example among many (and Challenge TV offers interactive options with most of its shows), it launched as interactive in 2001, with the interactive version initially available on ITV2 (the digital sister channel of terrestrial ITV1). After paying an entry fee, viewers are able to register their answers by pressing buttons on their remote control, and points are awarded for correct answers and speed. The highest scores are later entered on a leader board, creating a weekly league of the best 'armchair' contestants.

These are not really examples of the much-touted concept of 'media convergence'. Rather, they indicate media forms being used in a parallel manner. This 'multi-platform context' also plays out a shift from the traditional category of 'the audience' to the new media category of 'user' (Marshall 2004: 11). Yet television scholars (and as we shall see later in the chapter, viewers) have also been critical of the political economy of multi-platform television. As Janet Jones observes, the key to making money in the multi-platform media age is to 'encourage us all to participate in the "return-path" economy. Revenue is collected by convincing audiences – or more appropriately, *interactive consumers*, to respond to a variety of stimuli [original emphasis]' (2004: 212). Colman Hutchinson, one of the executive producers of *Millionaire*, freely admits that the 'Walkaway' texting game was only introduced when the revenue from the premium contestant phone-line went into decline. Rather than an enhancement of the format, the game was purely envisaged as a means to generate money for the overall prize fund – as paid for by the audience (Hutchinson 2006).

There is also a question as to whether a multi-platform text should necessarily be labelled 'interactive'. Although associated with new communication technologies and the move away from transmissional (one-way) models of communication, definitions of interactivity have been both various and ambiguous. Interactivity has been used to describe the context in which messages are exchanged, a property of the technology itself, or even a perception in users' minds (Kiousis 2002: 356). The concept of 'feedback', 'the ability for message receivers to respond to message senders' (ibid.: 359), initially emerged as an important point of discussion here. But even this seems weak if we are aiming to investigate a potential shift in media culture: 'feedback' must include telephone participation, and this been part of the radio quiz since the 1930s and the television quiz since the 1950s (see Chapter 2).

Frustrated with the liberal use of the term 'interactive', scholars studying computer games have aimed to make the concept more specific. As Dovey and Kennedy observe, the term 'configuration' has emerged as a 'description which makes a distinction between "push-button" interactivity and the productive processes of gameplay' (2006: 6). Configuration describes a context in which the user makes 'significant interventions' in a game which then have 'dynamic effects throughout its system' (ibid.). Computer games (which can be based on quizzes) still offer a limited number of gaming paths, but it seems doubtful that Dovey and Kennedy would conceive of the multi-platform quiz text as evidence of 'configuration'. Whether playing on the internet, interactive TV or a mobile phone, people *do* determine the outcome of their own game, and participation is no longer represented by the chance to play along as *the* game unfolds on your television screen. But this participation clearly takes place within prescribed limits, and the dominant mode of interaction here pivots on the concept of multiple choice. It should also be noted that advertisers, broadcasters and producers *want* an engaged and 'participatory' audience, hence the increased beckoning to enter into the game.

Playing on the internet

The offer to play internet versions of television quizzes on-line is another example of this participatory culture. Yet although not necessarily differing in the degree of agency which is offered to the audience, these games deserve further mention as part of the expanded media context for quiz shows. When compared to interactive television (which has not been the runaway success the industry had hoped for), the internet has emerged as the more popular 'new' media interface where quiz and game show culture is concerned. The internet has also emerged as a gaming medium in its own right, not simply with the use of computer games and puzzles, but with the popularity of on-line gambling (that is, poker).

Entertainment Weekly was already commenting in the late 1990s on how quiz games have helped build audiences for 'new' media in the three eras of the radio, the television and the internet.[8] Just as television quiz shows adapted radio successes, so the internet has capitalised on hit television quizzes and games, adapting them for web use. Positioned in a more ambiguous space where the 'return-path' economy is concerned, internet games based on television quizzes do not all represent a direct revenue stream. Although some award cash prizes or commodities, many do not, and as a consequence, they are often free to play. When compared to their television counterparts, these games are also cheap to run, with no overheads for 'talent' or on-screen production each time a contestant plays.

Certainly, the sites may still perform an economic function. They maintain interest in the programme brand, while also acting as a recruitment device for the television show. For those that do not ultimately enter the television space, they might be seen as a democratising force. ABC's 'enhanced TV' site based on *Millionaire* uses a 360-degree rotating image of the studio. With sound and visuals replicating the aesthetic construction of the game space, it enables us to 'experience' what it would look like to be sat opposite the host.[9] As June Deery observes, 'web technology thus offers a simulated experience to all of something ordinarily enjoyed by a few' (2003: 29).

Not all formats are suited to on-line transference, and this may in turn point to some of the social and technological differences between television and the internet. While formats such as *Jeopardy!*, *Wheel of Fortune*, *Millionaire*, *The Weakest Link*, *Deal or No Deal*, *Mastermind* and even *Family Feud* can be played on-line, formats such as *Supermarket Sweep* cannot. The more participatory environment of *The Price is Right*, which affords a central role to the studio audience, also struggles to capitalise on a web identity. Individual games from the show are abstracted for use on the web, but there is no bid to replicate the actual structure of the show.[10] In fact, this particular example may be a stark reminder of the extent to which the promise of an 'interactive use

culture' – with the user replacing the viewer – is increasingly individu-
alised. The community promised by the television version of *The Price
is Right* is not 'real' in any social sense. But the shift from the noisy ebul-
lience of the studio to the silent pricing options of 'Jackpot Joy' on the
web, mark out a rather individualising trajectory.

This comparison may actually point to the 'divergence' (rather than
convergence) of television and the internet. While the phone-in has
long since been used as part of the quiz/game show, the Call TV
Quiz services which have proliferated in recent years have made this
the primary feature (and function) of the show (see Chapter 2).
Exemplifying the barest logic of transactional TV, programmes such as
Quizmania, *The Mint* and *Glitterball* make money by encouraging individual viewers – *en masse* – to call up and interface with the game (you
phone in to solve the puzzle on screen). This ideal of 'one on one' play
is a great success on the more narrowcast address of the web. In contrast, while the Call TV Quiz shows began on niche channels, the controversy they generated spoke to the fact that television remains
wedded to a broadcast model. In addition to concerns about how these
programmes were regulated, debate also circled around their apparent
lack of programme 'value'. If you are not inclined to ring up yourself,
watching a host filling in large gaps of time while urging people to call
can be a strange and awkward viewing experience indeed. This is not
so much indicative of the internet replacing television as a space for
quizzing, as it points to the different ways in which the media articulate the concept of a quiz. The reactions to the Call TV Quiz phenomenon may suggest that television quizzes best address us as
participant-observers – the shift ushered in by television in the 1950s,
and described at the start of this chapter.

This section began with Fiske's suggestion that quiz shows presup-
pose particularly 'active' viewers (1987: 273). But Fiske does admit that
the emphasis on an 'unwritten' narrative and a participatory form of
address does not in itself provide evidence of a critical engagement with
the genre's meanings. 'Active' in television, media and cultural studies
traditionally meant how the audience responded to the meanings of the
text. The changing media environment (and the shift from viewer to
user) has put pressure on the parameters of these debates, and this has
in turn raised questions about whether 'active' should be conflated with
'interactive'. After all, responding to the discourses in a text does not in
itself have a direct relationship with shouting at your screen, playing on
your mobile, or pressing 'your red button now' to select an answer.
This point resonates with broader scepticism about the amount
of viewer 'power' actually offered by multi-platform/interactive TV

(Holmes 2004b). But it may also reflect back on the specificity of the quiz show. The rules of a game are specifically intended to shape and limit the scope of participant action, and on a wider level, rules determine what 'holds' in the temporary world of play (Huizinga 1970: 30). As such, there is a wider question as to how much scope, agency and flexibility we might expect 'interactivity' to offer where the quiz show is concerned.

This chapter has so far suggested that recent technological and social shifts have beckoned us to immerse ourselves further *in* the game. Yet there are also spaces (which sit alongside the internet games) that encourage an immersive investment in the genre *as well* a critical reflection on its possibilities. I refer here to internet fan cultures. Rather than the atomised internet player clicking up points on-line, internet fan cultures attest to the fact that we are always watching, and playing along, with identifiable others.

Fan cultures on the internet

Quiz show internet sites can be genre-based, as with UKGameshows. com, the forums on Challenge TV,[11] or quizzing.co.uk. They can also be programme-based (taking in both official and unofficial sites). In undertaking the research for this chapter, I largely observed interaction, focusing on what Virginia Nightingale calls 'the performance of the audience' (1996: 95) in naturally occurring sites. But on quizzing.co.uk (contextualised below), I also entered into the fan dialogue, asking participants why they 'watched and entered' quizzes.[12] This question/post prompted a substantial debate which took on a life of its own, and I draw on the resulting evidence in this chapter.

Long-running American formats such as *Jeopardy* and *Wheel of Fortune* have a clear online presence (especially *Wheel*), although many sites devoted to individual shows focus on programmes which have emerged since the internet developed (*The Weakest Link, Millionaire, Deal or no Deal, Are you Smarter than a Fifth Grader*). Earlier formats such as *The Price is Right* and *Family Fortunes/Feud* have an on-line circulation, but they do not attract such active online communities. The more 'serious' programmes such as *Mastermind* and *University Challenge* do not appear to attract fan sites as such, although these programmes are commented on in generic quiz sites. Fan sites can also focus on personality, with the likes of Pat Sajak and Vanna White (host and hostess of the US *Wheel of Fortune*), Anne Robinson (UK and US *The Weakest Link*), and Bruce Forsyth (*Play Your Cards Right, Bruce's The Price is Right*) all the subjects of on-line fan celebration.

Popular media images of fandom have historically pivoted on a number of unflattering social stereotypes, ranging across the 'brainless consumer', the 'geeky nerd', the 'social misfit' and the 'psychotic loner'. Many of these types assume that the fan is unable to separate fantasy from 'reality' (Jenkins 1992: 10). Academic work on fandom has challenged such caricatures, arguing for fandom as an active cultural practice which blurs the boundaries between production and consumption. Henry Jenkins famously argued in his 1992 book *Textual Poachers* that while fans operate from a position of 'cultural marginality and weakness', they also emerge as 'selective users of a vast media culture whose treasures . . . hold wealth that can be mined and refined for alternative uses' (1992: 27). Jenkins described these 'alternative uses' as a form of 'poaching', a term which 'forcefully reminds us of the potentially conflicting interests of producers and consumers, writers and readers' (ibid.: 32). From this perspective, fans may be stigmatised or ridiculed in part *because* they challenge attempts to regulate the circulation of popular meanings.

But the explosion of internet culture has put pressure on such arguments in at least two ways. First, although not everyone participates in programme fan cultures on the internet, the internet has 'mainstreamed' fandom, replacing the concept of the 'fringe obsessive' with the image of an 'average web user' (Pullen 2000: 56). Second, and related to this, if the bid to involve viewers in a pervasive intertextuality is now encouraged (targeted) as part of the mainstream viewing experience, this complicates Jenkins's image of a 'grass-roots' form of fan resistance (Brooker 2004). At the same time, it would be rash to suggest that the internet has rendered Jenkins's conception of fandom outmoded, and it would be more appropriate to argue that the internet has had contradictory implications for the cultural construction of fandom. It offers a more direct dialogue between fans and producers, and makes fans more available (vulnerable) to corporate marketing and policing, while also offering a space in which collective and alternative interpretations can actively proliferate (McCracken 2003: 137).

Quiz sites: differences and debates

This chapter aims to demonstrate how Jenkins's (1992) emphasis on a power struggle between producers and viewers remains apposite. But it also argues that it is useful to be more specific about questions of genre when we think about the scope of fan activity, and its relationship with the academic approaches outlined so far. Jenkins's conception of poaching, and the wider field of work which has been influenced by it, privileges fictional texts as the objects of fan interest (and considerable attention has been directed at fantasy/sci-fi programmes which are more likely to emerge as 'Cult TV'). The emphasis on 'poaching' largely assumes a fan culture which produces fiction/slash fiction, extending and/or reinterpreting the fictional universe seen on screen. In contrast, quizzes offer non-fictional worlds which the viewer encounters in relatively discreet (formatted) units – making the kind of activity described above rather unlikely.

Quiz fans produce internet discourse in a range of different ways, but general examples include discussions of contestant performances ('Cameron was a great contestant', 'I couldn't believe Lorana said 'D' [in the] . . . prize puzzle'),[13] discussing the host (and news items relating to them), speculation about game outcomes (relevant to shows which are not played out in one edition), recording factual details from game outcomes ('Round four: scores at this point . . .'), and entering into debate about how *they* would have played the game ('Go on, who would have gone for the final offer?').[14] In addition, discussion is also generated by the activity of moving into the television space: online participants share audition stories, swap audition advice and discuss the experience of 'actually' being on TV.

It is crucial to stress that, across these spheres of discussion, fans express critical, as well as celebratory attitudes toward the shows. Quizzing.co.uk specifically solicits people to post a messages if they wish to 'critique . . . a particular TV quiz show'. At the same time, and despite the emphasis (see Chapter 3) on how ludic cultures appear to sit 'outside' the world of the everyday, fans engage with the programmes *as they are*. This is certainly not to imply that they do not debate how the programmes might be better. But it does indicate a difference from forms of fictional fandom (particularly fantasy-based fiction). Yet to suggest that these differences make quiz fan cultures less 'active' is to replicate the cultural judgements which have lead to the marginalisation of the genre in academic criticism. Quiz show fan cultures can certainly be conceived as 'semi-structured spaces' where competing 'interpretations and evaluations of common texts are proposed, debated and negotiated and where readers speculate about the nature of the mass media and their own relationship to [them]' (Jenkins 1992: 86). In this regard, Jenkins remains useful. But the particular concept of 'poaching' should not be used as a yardstick to evaluate and analyse quiz show fandom. Quiz shows thus raise wider debates about whether different television genres demand *different* inflections in fan 'theory'.

In the context of this study, it was less the distinction between 'official' and 'unofficial' sites which emerged as significant, than the distinction between genre-based and programme-based sites. While genre-based sites are just as open to observation and monitoring by quiz show producers (Colman Hutchinson, one of the executive producers of *Millionaire*, was very well-versed in the debates found at quizzing.co.uk) (Hutchinson 2006), sites such as quizzing.co.uk and UKGameshows.com do not function to brand particular shows. Yet it should be acknowledged that quizzing.co.uk, which is by far the most active site in terms of the volume of internet chat, has an ambiguous identity as a 'fan' site. The site explains how 'Quizzing.co.uk [the UK arm of the International Quizzing Assoc.] is the largest quiz organisation in the UK with nearly 30,000 members', and it offers a range of professional services which include question-writing and consultancy services, fund-raising and PR, and contestant calls. It also includes on-line games, news of quiz events, quiz rankings, contestant profiles, and a range of busy discussion forums. Television quizzes remain a central focus on the site, but quizzing.co.uk also attests to the popularity of quizzes as a cultural practice, with news and discussion including references to pub quizzes and other tournaments.

In this regard, while all sites play out the blurring of the line between contestant and viewer, this is particularly apparent on quizzing.co.uk, and the site attracts a good deal of people who would be classified as 'professional quizzers' by the television companies. This raises questions as to whether the term 'fan' is entirely appropriate here, as well as questions about the typicality of the responses. Yet it could also be argued that the site is revealing precisely *because* it gives us access to people who are passionately involved with quizzing, while the presence of 'professional' quizzers offers a unique insight into television's demands and expectations concerning contestant performers (see Chapter 5). Furthermore, in other respects, the site redresses some of the disparities and inequities which permeate the genre on-screen. Over 60 per cent of the site's members are women, and my research into the internet sites more generally often suggested a clear female presence.

This may suggest that quizzing as a cultural practice is not as male-dominated as quizzing on TV. It may also suggest something about gender and contemporary internet use. While earlier studies of internet culture emphasised men's greater access to the medium, and explored how gender inequities of face-to-face interaction could be perpetuated online (Herring 1996), the mass proliferation of the medium – and particularly its domestication – now asks questions about these arguments. With regard to the quiz show, it would be easy to suggest that the concept of a more community-based ethos on-line differs from the more competitive and individualist ethos on-screen (which has been seen as pivoting on 'male' values, and as creating an uneasy space for women) (see Chapter 5). At the same time, it is important to acknowledge that fan communities are far from simply utopian spaces. Much like quiz shows, fan cultures are what Hills calls 'social hierarchies' where people compete to display knowledge of the object in hand. In this regard, Hills suggests that it is possible to describe fans as 'players' (2002: 46).

This is especially resonant where the quiz show is concerned: fans/participants compete by expressing knowledge about the fan object (that is, a programme) while also competing in terms of the display of knowledge itself (that is, their status as quiz show competitors *and* viewers). Furthermore, quiz shows represent a particularly interesting genre where social constructions of fandom are concerned: certain social stereotypes of fandom, such as the 'nerd' or the 'geek', resonate with stereotypes of intelligence, which are in turn associated with avid quiz participants or viewers. At the same time, this again raises questions about generic specificity. Given the nature of the genre, markers of intelligence can also be promoted and celebrated (as suggested by the use of name domains such as 'wiseoldowls' or 'boffin444').[15]

Why watch quiz shows?

Before television studies was established, there were two social-science studies which took an interest in why people enjoy quiz shows: Herta Herzog's (1940) study of quiz programmes on 1940s American radio, and Denis McQuail, Jay G. Blumler and J. R. Brown's (1972) uses and gratifications study of three British shows of the 1970s – *University Challenge*, *Ask the Family* and *Brain of Britain*. Herzog's study found that listeners gained pleasure from 'improving their imagined position' within a cultural/educational hierarchy (Hoerschelmann 2006: 61). McQuail, Blumler and Brown (writing about the more class-delineated context of Britain) found that viewers from middle-class groups used the shows in question to check and test their own 'academic' knowledge, while viewers from lower socio-economic groups used the shows to 'prove' to themselves that they are intelligent, and that their school-assessed performance is not a true measure of their ability (Fiske 1987: 274). In this regard, the researchers stressed what we might call the 'self-rating' appeal of the genre (McQuail, Blumler and Brown 1972: 150).

Although depending on the nature of the format in hand, these interpretative frameworks are still important today. On quizzing.co.uk (and after I specifically asked the question as to why people watched quizzes), a number of viewers admitted that it was to 'feel superior to the contestants'. As one poster pointed out, if many people do watch in order to boost their self-rating appeal, 'this all utterly demands [quizzing] . . . as a sport when contrasted with athletics . . . where people like to admire those who are better than themselves'.[16] But the pleasure of self-rating clearly had its limits, as many on quizzing.co.uk said that they did not enjoy shows when contestants were revealed to be consistently 'poor'. This does not appear to be the case on Youtube.com, which has developed a particular strand of clips devoted to 'shaming' apparently 'idiotic' quiz show contestants from around the globe (for example, 'Who wants to be a Stupidaire?' (Croatia), 'Who Wants to be a Millionaire in France – Stupidity', 'Millionaire – Third UK loser').[17] This rather punitive discourse, which does not appear to be specific to American 'anti-intellectualism' (see Chapter 4), is not as apparent on quiz-orientated internet sites. The users of Youtube.com are, of course, not necessarily 'fans' of quiz shows or quiz show contestants at all.

On quizzing.co.uk, others disagreed that self-rating was the key viewing motivation in the first place, making such comments as 'I watch TV quiz shows to see folk display their erudition and to be awed by them'. These attitudes are not mutually exclusive however, as self-rating, admiring and learning ('filling in the gaps in my own general knowledge' (*Mastermind, University Challenge*)) were often intertwined in the same response.[18] To be sure, the decontextualised nature of internet responses, as well as the complexity of defining the concept of class, makes it difficult to relate these responses back to the earlier studies of quiz audiences mentioned above, but evidence suggests that the users of quizzing.co.uk have a range of occupations, and identify themselves as belonging to a range of class backgrounds.[19]

Yet given the extent to which quiz shows, especially in terms of knowledge, may play a role in perpetuating ideologies of class (see Chapter 4), a key question is how knowledge is evaluated and discussed by viewers/participants. While many sites adopt a critical attitude toward the use of knowledge across shows, often interrogating how questions are ranked in terms of monetary value ('That question was never worth £32,000!'), this is not the same as interrogating the very status of knowledge in the genre itself. At least on quizzing.co.uk, a number of participants did not perceive that socio-economic background/educational opportunity played a role in shaping quiz success. As 'davey boy', a past contestant from *Millionaire*, insisted, 'I think that the profile of a . . . successful TV quiz contestant has nothing to do with class issues . . .'.[20] The emphasis on 'natural' ability and/or 'luck' would seem to suggest the ('invisible') power of the ideology described by Fiske: that the programmes function as an 'enactment of capitalist ideology', claiming that individuals are different, but 'equal in opportunity' (1987: 266). Yet others were more ready to note that opportunity was indeed a social construction, scrutinising the questions answered by the first UK millionaire winner, Judith Keppel, and quoting press articles ('Class divide hits learning by age of three') that related quizzes to wider social and political contexts.[21] However, given the differences between sites, and the specificity of quizzing.co.uk, it should be noted that this was unique to this particular site. In contrast, the spectacles of 'stupidity' on Youtube provide the least critical (and perhaps the most asocial) response to the genre's political construction of knowledge.

The reference to class implies that viewers, and not just academics, understand quiz shows to be political (structured by relations of power). Given that women appear to have a greater presence in on-line quiz cultures than on screen, it does not seem surprising that gendered participation is itself an object of debate. Given that women represent 60 per cent of quizzing.co.uk members, topics such as 'Pub quizzes – a man's domain?' or 'The gender barrier in quiz' are not infrequent.[22] The discussion may parallel the wider media debate surrounding gender disparities in quiz show participation (see Chapter 5), but the difference here is that women themselves play a more active and vocal role in assessing their own relations with quiz cultures.

Despite the popular claim that quiz shows do not display or test 'real' intelligence, it is clear from some of the responses that they are perceived as educational. But as this book has outlined, much of the critical distaste directed at the genre has circled around the apparent investment in greed. This topic may well provide evidence of the limits of engaging with fan discourse. We might ask, for example, how greed as a motivation for viewing or even participating could be 'measured'. Furthermore, while viewers were quick to emphasise how they found quiz shows educational, the concept of greed has socially undesirable connotations, meaning that it is less likely to be openly expressed as a motivation for viewing. But in terms of the discourse on the internet (and the limited scope of the study undertaken here), it is at least possible to observe that there was very little focus on prizes or winnings. This may attest to Clarke's earlier speculation that interest in the genre is more invested in the *process* of winning, and how the contestant responds to 'wealth, loss, acquisition and denial' (1987: 43).

The only clear emphasis on monetary reward was found on the official (Sony) American *Wheel of Fortune* site. Here, a board member called Andy keeps a rolling total of the season's winnings, including the name of the contestant, the theme and date of the show (for example, 'Hawaii Week'), and the amount won ('Great job guys! We've just passed the $2 million mark!').[23] As this comment implies, this is about people participating in the show as contestants ('Hopefully Linda will make $100K when she tapes this Friday . . .'). But what is striking here is the extent to which, much like the internal dynamic of *Millionaire* with its 'Ask the Audience' and 'Phone a Friend' lifelines, the emphasis on individualism is mitigated by the idea of a community or 'team' effort ('us' taking money from Sony). Although the money is not being pooled, the emphasis on contributing to the cumulative total is part of belonging to the participative dynamic of the site. As one participant comments, 'You can add my total from Monday, even though I wasn't a big winner!'.[24] This suggests how quiz sites play a role in framing the social meanings of the money won (which offers a more complex insight into the genre than the emphasis on vicarious or actual 'greed').

Call TV Quiz: 'No "respectable" quizzers have admitted to using them . . .'

The first section of this chapter focused on the subject position(s) offered to the viewer in the context of the multi-platform media environment. The concept of the subject position, based on a hypothetical, homogenous idea of the viewer/user, has traditionally been linked to ideas about a 'passive' response, while empirical research (with 'real' viewers) has often been linked to 'active' modes of reception. This is indicative of how different methodologies produce different results, and it is certainly true that viewers on-line are highly critical of the 'return-path' economy which seeks to position them as interactive consumers. The notion of 'interactive' or 'participative' television often appears in inverted commas on-line (' "Text to vote" has become a way of life now'),[25] and this inserts a level of distance between viewer and text. Given the huge press and media attention devoted to 'rip-off' phone-line participation in British television in 2006–7, these critical attitudes do not seem that surprising. With regard to Call TV Quiz, posts on quizzing.co.uk frequently included articles from the press (for example, *The Times, The Guardian*) which framed these programmes as 'a phenomenon of the digital age: the equivalent of fairground stalls that invite passers-by to try their luck against the clock at superficially easy games . . .'.[26] Fans on-line also remained critical of the extent to which live viewer competitions now take up considerable space in 'proper' TV quizzes (for example, *Millionaire, Brainteaser*).

In this respect, such responses are to some degree shaped by the press discourse, showing how available 'reading formations' (the extratextual relations within and around texts) (Bennett 1985), shape the interpretative frameworks used by viewers. Indeed, quizzers variously refer to 'the fools that phone in and take part in these programmes', and the 'vulnerable viewer' who calls up 'hundreds of times'[27] – mirroring the attitudes displayed by both press critics and regulators. Given that audience judgements also play a role in shaping the construction of generic categories (Mittell 2004a: Chapter 1), these debates play a role in defining and delineating the 'proper' boundaries of the site's attention. This is made explicitly clear when 'cjdemooi' posts: 'I notice no "respectable" quizzers have admitted to using [Call TV Quiz services], so who is? I think we should be told'.[28]

As Hills aptly reminds us, 'fans may secure a form of cultural power by opposing themselves to the bad subject of "the consumer"', building up their own identities in relation to perceptions of other audience groups (2002: 44). This indicates how fans police the boundaries of their own communities, while it also suggests the attempt to construct hierarchies between groups. Programmes such as the Call TV Quiz show *Glitterball* do in fact have their own fan sites,[29] although these can be niche (twenty-three members), and are primarily organised around interest in the young presenters of the shows. On more general chat forums, such as digitalspy.co.uk and tvforum.co.uk, viewers engage in heated debates about these programmes, variously defending their legitimacy, or claiming to view them in a distanced and ironic manner: 'so bad it's good', 'I only watch with dark glasses on as far away from the screen as possible . . .'.[30] But while none of these people seem to be the 'vulnerable fools' imagined by press critics and quizzing.co.uk, it is difficult to find threads in which the posters actually 'admit' to their own use of these phone lines. In this regard, the self-accepted stigmatised identity of the Call TV Quiz viewer reminds us of Hills's point that 'fans seek to value their own activities' in ways which are inevitably shaped by wider discourses of value and meaning (2002: 43).

'Be yourself. If that's still possible': contestants and constructions of the 'ordinary'

Finally, even the most cursory glance at quiz fan cultures on the internet attests to the fact that the genre encourages us to 'jump into the tube' (Cooper-Chen 1994: 87). The quiz cultures on many sites are primarily made up of people who are also actively involved in the genre as contestants (something less true of reality TV, perhaps because the latter has more of a mass appeal). As a result, such sites offer a unique insight into how contestants conceptualise the institutional and cultural experience of being on television, and how they comprehend the performative demands at stake. Chapter 5 emphasised Teurlings's argument that 'ordinary' people are not free to express their 'true selves' on television, but nor are they 'the helpless objects of exploitative broadcasters' (2001: 259). While applicable to the analysis of the contestant on screen, this dialectic is particularly evident when we assess the 'behind-the-scenes' discourse produced by the contestants (or would-be contestants) on-line.

Chapter Five drew attention to how the quiz show naturalises what Couldry (2000) calls the media/ordinary hierarchy, in which television is seen as a 'higher reality', a special space which confers cultural (as well as economic) capital on anyone who enters it. Quiz internet sites are awash with excited comments about 'getting the letter!' (which may offer confirmation of an audition, or make the offer to actually appear on a show). Even quizzing.co.uk, which is less likely to acknowledge 'being on television' as a primary motive for applying, has a forum devoted to the subject of 'Quizzers on the telly', where people can announce their appearance on television and discuss their experience. All of this suggests an acceptance of the prestige and status which is imbued by a television appearance.

Yet the reference to a 'behind-the-scenes' perspective (above) reflects the extent to which there is also an emphasis on disappointment and dissatisfaction, as well as the mundanity of the process through which people seek to gain access to television space. Internet sites tell of the long waits for letters, emails and phone calls, people repeatedly attending auditions and not getting through, expenses not being paid, and people appearing in editions which do not ultimately get screened. As one participant puts it, contestants are just treated as ' "Fodder" for [a] . . . programme, they don't matter . . .',[31] and quizzing.co.uk also launched an internet questionnaire which asked, 'Are we sick of being treated badly by TV companies?'[32] Of course, the fact that so many people are willing to put up with the process may confirm the coveted nature of television visibility, but such discussion threads nevertheless attest to the fact that this is no utopian experience. They also offer insight into the mechanics of a process which, as far as the wider audience is concerned, simply results in the contestant displaying a personable identity on screen.

If this suggests a certain distance between on/off-screen identity where contestants are concerned, then it seems problematic to envisage a context in which people are simply 'slotted' into the genre's generic conventions with little awareness of the performative codes required. In reality TV, participants speak routinely of how to provide 'good TV', demonstrating a 'savvy' knowledge of generic context in which they are placed. Yet quiz shows are not as self-reflexive in this respect, and this makes their on-line discourse all the more revealing and significant.

Notable in this regard is the advice featured in the on-line 'Good Game Guide'.[33] Based on the experience of auditioning for quiz/ game shows, and written by student Tom Scott, the guide has been reproduced in the advice on 'Auditioning for game shows' on UKGameshows.com.[34] The guide attests to the fact that contestants fashion discourses of 'ordinariness' as much as producers. While initially giving advice on choosing a show ('Pick desperate shows', 'Work out the odds of winning'), it focuses on the application form and the audition. Scott recognises the importance of providing 'plenty of fodder for the pre-game interview', and acknowledges that this information makes the contestant both accessible and 'ordinary' ('What are your ambitions? 'Do you have any embarrassing stories?'). But what is particularly interesting here is his discussion of the audition itself. This is quite clearly set out as a performance which, complete with advice on costume, facial expressions and dialogue, aims to meet the requirements of 'ordinariness' utilised by contestant researchers/producers. Reflecting Clarke's argument that, in terms of contestant identification, the ideal contestant is 'neither too rich nor too poor . . .' (1987: 53), prospective quizzers are advised to go 'for a happy medium . . . not the suit and tie, excessively smart look, but don't go in with clothes that say "impoverished student"'. Scott goes on to emphasise how the 'personality test', rather than the knowledge test, is the most important part of the audition, and there is a clear recognition of the need to be personable and sociable. The guide ends by advising, 'Oh, yes, and be yourself. If that's still possible'.

As this last comment reminds us, the concept of 'performance' need not be seen as inauthentic, dishonest or calculated (unless this is of course actively licensed by the game) (see Chapter 4). It is more appropriate to suggest that the television quiz/game show demands a particular presentation of the self (see Chapter 5), and Tom Scott's guide suggests that this is recognised as an implicit 'contract' between producers, contestant researchers and contestants. To be sure, the contestants are not setting the agenda of this contract, and they enter into it because it may bring them what they want: an appearance on a television quiz show. But it does complicate the perception that the contestants function as passive 'pawns'. Participants produce discourses of 'ordinariness' *themselves* – albeit in a managed setting (Teurlings 2001: 26).

This 'contract', and the question of an 'authentic' performance, is pushed to its limit where the concept of the professional quizzer is concerned. Colman Hutchinson, one of the executive producers of *Millionaire*, describes how the 'professional quizzer' represents a 'problem' for the show:

> We have contestants who genuinely want to win, but give nothing. We call them . . . 'professional quizzers'. They see [the show] . . . as a means of making money . . . [and they tend to be] middle-aged men – the 'grey brigade': fifty years of age, they are greying and they are dull . . . They are not there to have a great day out . . . The best sort of quiz or game show contestant is someone who thinks, 'This is just going to be a great experience. I hope I win some money. Even if I don't it will be a fascinating experience', and we do go out of our way to look after [such] people as best we can . . . (Hutchinson 2006)

This description brings together what Chapter 5 outlined as the criteria for a 'good' televisual performance. We see the importance of being from the 'ordinary' world (excited about, and unversed in, the concept of appearing on TV), of being personable and sociable (a 'good sport'), of being accessible (someone with whom the audience can identify), and of producing 'good' (dramatic) television. Professional quizzers, who are more likely to be found on quizzing.co.uk, are the furthest away from this idea of a 'good' contestant. They are possibly more experienced in the business of appearing on TV, are looking to improve their quiz ranking, and may steam through the questions without much struggle or anxiety.[35]

Indeed, quizzing.co.uk expresses frustration at how producers and contestant researchers use these criteria to gate keep access to television's quizzing space. The site is also revealing in indicating just what people are asked to do at quiz show auditions. 'Peterzed' discusses his failed audition for BBC1's *In It to Win It* (which periodically forms part of the National Lottery draw), expressing frustration at the aesthetic/dramatic demands of the genre:

> I was invited to a second audition. This time we just played the game but were videoed as we played and . . . had to pretend that we had won big. I didn't get [through] . . . I attribute my failure to the fact that I am more introvert than extravert and have to force myself to go through all the punching of the air and orgasmic behaviour that modern shows seem to require of their winners.[36]

Furthermore, the advice routinely circulated on quizzing.co.uk includes such comments as, 'As with all TV [quiz] auditions – don't mention you are a Quizzer – and waffle on about something/anything totally inane',[37] or, 'If you put *Mastermind* or similar on your application form you can kiss goodbye to getting on most shows . . .'.[38] This ongoing topic of discussion was also represented by a lengthy thread on the 'Ethics of entering quiz shows': should quizzers lie about their previous experience in order to get on a show?[39]

It is in the best interest of the programmes if their aims are presented as being congruent with those of the contestant, and the notion of an imagined 'contract' (above) seeks to marshal these interests into a seamless whole. Yet the discussion in this section suggests that, rather than a top-down assertion of power, this 'contract' represents a highly contested terrain. The fact that this is most apparent *off*-screen, and within the busy circuits of internet communication, may well suggest the institutional power of television to regulate its constructions of the 'ordinary'. But in our expanded media environment, internet discourse represents *part* of the quiz show 'text' (and indeed another form of quiz show 'performance'). In this regard, it may lead us to the conclusion that viewers and contestants increasingly see the provision of a 'good' televisual performance as part of the 'game' itself.

Conclusion

The analysis of the quiz show should not begin and end with the programmes themselves. This chapter has aimed to suggest ways in which the relationship between quiz shows and their audiences might be approached, and the themes which might be examined within this sphere. Whether we are analysing the hypothetical concept of the subject position, looking at letters in magazines, or examining fan interaction on the internet, assumptions and judgements about audience response need to be treated with care. When it comes to accessing 'real' responses, it is also important to note that ' "asking the audience" cannot act as a guarantee of knowledge' where exploring a genre's reception is concerned (Hills 2002: 66).

The internet has offered a new public visibility to fan cultures, and 'for the archivist and the academic as well as the fan, the . . . web makes accessible a degree of information and a variety of points of view that is unprecedented' (McCracken 2003: 138). In the study of the quiz show, there is no longer any excuse for audience responses to remain invisible. We can all explore the relationship between fan theory and quiz show scholarship in order to better understand the cultural circulation of the genre. Hills comments that, 'The battle to place fandom on the cultural studies agenda has long since been won' (2002: 183). But not all genres are equal in this regard. It is hoped that this chapter has suggested why quiz shows deserve a place on this agenda in the horizons of future research.

Notes

1. BBC Audience Research Report, *What Do You Know?*, 15 January 1959, R19/1970/1 (WAC).
2. Quizzing.co.uk forum, http://www.iqagb.co.uk/trivia/viewtopic. php?t=3688 [accessed 7 June 2007].
3. 'Do we need to know about contestants?', 31 May 2005, http:// www.iqagb.co.uk/trivia/viewtopic.php?t=3688 [accessed 7 June 2007].
4. The chart is only reproduced in part here.
5. http://millionaire.itv.com/millionaire/tvshow [accessed 11 June 2007].
6. http://news.softpedia.com/ news [accessed 11 June 2007].
7. http://news.bbc.co.uk/1/hi/entertainment/new_media/1332056. stm [accessed 11 June 2007].
8. *Entertainment Weekly*, 13 November, 1998. http://www.ew.com/ ew/article/0,,285668,00.html [accessed 10 April 2007].
9. http://abc.go.com/games/millionairetv/game [accessed 11 June 2007].
10. http://www.gamesys.co.uk/marketinglive/TPIR/Jackpotjoy.html [accessed 12 June 2007].
11. http://www.challenge.co.uk/forums/ [accessed 12 June 2007].
12. In both cases I made clear that I was researching an academic book on quiz shows.
13. *Wheel of Fortune* Sony Pictures message board, http://boards. sonypictures.com/boards/showthread.php?t=3044 [accessed 11 June 2007].
14. *Deal or No Deal* message board, Channel 4 http://community. channel4.com/eve/forums/a/tpc [accessed 6 June 2007].
15. Quizzing.co.uk
16. http://www.iqagb.co.uk/trivia/viewtopic.php?t=6261 [accessed 11 June 2007].
17. http://www.youtube.com [accessed 16 June 2007].
18. All responses from the thread http://www.iqagb.co.uk/trivia/ viewtopic.php?t=6261 [accessed 11 June 2007].
19. See the thread above.

20. As above.
21. Wiseoldowls, 11 June, 2007, http://www.iqagb.co.uk/trivia/viewtopic.php?t=6261.
22. http://www.iqagb.co.uk/ trivia/ viewtopic.php?=5972, 3 October 2003, http://www.iqagb.co.uk/ trivia/ viewtopic.php?=3243, 22 January 2005, [accessed 7 June 2007].
23. http://boards.sonypictures.com/boards/showthread [accessed 11 June 2007].
24. http://boards.sonypictures.com/boards/showthread [accessed 11 June 2007].
25. 'Roll up, roll up for multichannel television's latest money-spinner', *The Guardian*, 28 November 2005, posted on quizzing.co.uk by 'Sequin', 28 November 2005 [accessed 7 June 2007].
26. As above.
27. 'Quiz rip-off channels', quizzing.co.uk, 28 November 2005.
28. 'Satellite TV quiz channels', 24 June 2005, http://www.iqagb.co.uk/trivia/viewtopic.php?t=3785 [accessed 7 June 2007].
29. http://www.groups.myspace.com/theglitterballfansite.
30. http://www.digitalspy.co.uk/forums/printthread.php?t=360273&page=120&pp=25, 21 June 2006 [accessed 15 June 2007].
31. 'Channel 4 DER BRAINS!!!!!', 16 November 2004, http://www.iqagb.co.uk/trivia/viewtopic.php?t=4212 [accessed 7 June 2007].
32. 'Are we sick of being treated badly by TV companies?', 11 June 2006, http://www.iqagb.co.uk/trivia/viewtopic.php?t=5015 [accessed 7 June 2007].
33. http://www.thomasscott.net/gameshow/ [accessed 30 July 2007].
34. http://www.ukgameshows.com/page/index.php/Auditioning_For_Game_Shows.
35. Although Hutchinson is right to indicate that the professional quizzer is more likely to be male, quizzing.co.uk suggests that a number of women also place themselves in this category.
36. 'In It to Win It', 24 November 2003, http://www.iqagb.co.uk/trivia/viewtopic.php?t=968 [accessed 3 June 2007].
37. 'Countdown audition', 17 July 2006, http://www.iqagb.co.uk/trivia/viewtopic.php?t=5826 [accessed 7 June 2007].
38. 'Ethics of entering quiz shows', 26 March 2004. http://www.iqagb.co.uk/trivia/viewtopic.php?t=1698 [accessed 7 June 2007].
39. As above.

Conclusion:
'Not the Final Answer . . .'

Despite its enduring popularity with audiences, the quiz show continues to have an uneasy place in television studies. It has been the intention of this book to offer an introduction to the study of the quiz show, while also contributing to the scholarly visibility of the genre. Furthermore, the book has also aimed to reflect back on the *study of television* itself. Whether with regard to television history, issues of institutional regulation, television aesthetics, the circulation of programme formats or fan research, the quiz show has much to teach us about television as an object of study.

Skovmand (2000) is right to point out that a range of factors have contributed to the critical marginalisation of the genre, ranging from the apparent difficulty of approaching quiz shows as 'texts for analysis', to judgements of cultural value. In this regard, I have to admit that there was something deliciously strange about viewing extant archival copies of quiz and game shows at the British Film Institute in London. Sandwiched in between two students watching silent film classics, the images playing on my monitor (of pairs attempting to make wedding cakes on a 1973 edition of *The Generation Game*, or of the bespectacled 'Norma' who was called by the host to 'Come on down!' in a 1984 edition of *The Price is Right*) suddenly seemed conspicuous in their difference and their frivolity – apparently out of place in the more 'serious' atmosphere of an academic context.

This is not so much a point about the study of popular television versus film – television studies has long since invested its energies in the study of popular television forms. But it is a point about studying the quiz show. It is in part because the genre is seen as one of television's most ephemeral forms that the experience of viewing archival quiz shows (where they actually exist) is rendered 'strange'. But the curious experience of viewing these programmes also attests to the fact that while quiz shows themselves 'may fluidly cross . . . the boundar[y] between highbrow and lowbrow' (Mittell 2007), the genre challenges

aspects of television studies itself, asking questions about the boundaries of the popular, and its own judgements of 'quality' and value.
Furthermore, unlike fiction or documentary, quiz shows do not sit still
for aesthetic or cultural analysis: games are not static media texts – they
are also activities (Dovey and Kennedy 2006: 23). This is made especially clear by the discussion of the audience (Chapter 6), and more
work in this sphere may offer fresh insights into the genre's cultural
politics, pleasures and possibilities for future research.

In the wake of reality TV, it is important to see studio-based quizzes
and games as rather more than simply the 'earlier generation of game
shows' (Bratich 2007: 13), as this denies these programmes their own
cultural and critical history. At the same time, it is perhaps the case that
the rise of reality TV, and television's accelerated appetite for games, has
made the history of the quiz show of even greater interest in the present
moment. Television may well have 'entered the age of the "ordinary"'
(Teurlings 2001: 249), but quiz and game shows have historically been
one of few broadcast genres to showcase 'ordinary' people as a matter
of course. As Chapter 5 has made clear, there is much to be gained in
this respect from a historical and theoretical comparison between quiz
shows and reality TV (and debates which seem 'new' or contemporary
clearly have a history). In this respect, we can point to John Corner's
wider observation about television history – that an 'enriched sense of
"then" produces, in its differences and commonalities combined, a
stronger and more imaginative sense of "now"' (2003: 275).

Chapter 2 quoted Boddy's observation that the quiz show has
endured long periods of 'critical disdain and indifference, interrupted
by infrequent moments of . . . often hyperbolic reaction to the spectacular success of a specific show or format . . .' (2001: 79). While
not entirely misleading, this view of quiz show history has meant that
certain key moments or programmes are fetishised by critics and scholars. We might point to the notorious American quiz show scandals of
the 1950s, the birth of commercial television in Britain (1955), or the
global success of *Millionaire*. But this 'spotlighting' approach can also
skew the historical picture of the genre (Mittell 2004a: 54), thus leaving
its 'everyday' existence rather ignored. The very idea of what constitutes a key juncture or programme should be up for discussion, and in
line with revisionist approaches to history, this book has approached
history less as immovable 'fact' than as a process of textual interpretation which is open to contest, re-fashioning and debate. For example,
it has questioned the tendency to make generalising contrasts about
'British' and 'American' attitudes toward the genre. Of course, greater
contrasts could likely be found in comparisons of more divergent

national contexts (and whether such differences *are* being eroded by the increasingly global flow of television formats remains open to debate). But with regard to the quiz show, it seems useful to keep a contradictory conception in play. While it is problematic to see 'the DNA of formats' as being intrinsically rooted in particular cultural values (they are designed to 'travel well') (Waisbord 2004: 368), formats can also operate as 'culture-sensitive mechanism[s] that [link] . . . global texts to local preferences' (Hestroni 2004: 153). When it comes to national differences, comparisons have largely focused on national adaptations of the same format (Moran 1998; Skovmand 2000; Hestroni 2004). But there are also wider questions to be explored here which ask questions about how the quiz show has developed in different national contexts. Each nation clearly has its own history to tell where the quiz show is concerned, and with the increasing turn to history in television studies, there is a wider picture of the quiz show waiting to be reconstructed, debated and explored.

The book has also placed an emphasis on the relationship between quiz shows and power – foregrounding theories and perspectives which emphasise the uneven nature of ideological production. From the perspective of these models, it is quite possible to draw different conclusions about different aspects of the genre, or about different shows. Thus, the mediation of gender politics in the quiz show may well be seen as regressive (Chapter 4/5), while constructions of class (Chapter 4), or audience relations with the genre (Chapter 6) may emerge as more contradictory. Furthermore, concepts such as capitalism, work and consumerism do not represent homogenous or unchanging discourses in the quiz show. Rather, they need to be explored in relation to particular shows at specific junctures.

The book has drawn attention to change and development in the quiz show, while also emphasising the remarkably enduring nature of particular themes, debates and concerns. A linear model of generic history is problematic, not least because it seeks to impose a sleek and ordered trajectory on what is a more unruly set of textual relations and developments. Such a model may also pose particular problems when it comes to the study of formatted television, and the quiz show in particular. Newer shifts or programmes do not simply consign earlier examples to quiz show 'history', in part because earlier formats continue to circulate as part of the genre. This can be applied to other genres to some degree: 'classic' sitcoms, for example, are repeated alongside newer interventions, and a particular series can continue to be made for many years, changing and developing over time. But this is not directly comparable to the production of formatted television.

A quiz format may have emerged from a particular set of institutional, industrial, cultural or political contexts. Yet it can continue to be re-made, whether in the same form, or with minor tweaks and adjustments (such as a new host or 'look') for many years.

As such, there remain further questions to be posed about the study of the quiz show. What happens to the initial contexts of a format (in creating and contextualising its meanings) when it later re-appears? Do we need to look for a different set of contexts? How do we begin to explain the enduring appeal of certain formats over decades? How do national variations factor into this historical trajectory, not simply in terms of national adaptations of the same format, but with regard to the different periods in which formats are taken up and enjoyed? As these questions suggest, this book is clearly not the 'final answer' where the study of the quiz show is concerned.

Bibliography

Adams, Matthew (2007), *Self and Social Change*, London: Sage.

Addison, Paul (1985), *Now the War is Over: A Social History of Britain 1945–51*, London: BBC/Jonathan Cape.

Allen, Jane (2007), [director of Quizzing.co.uk] personal email correspondence with author.

Altman, Rick (1999), *Film/Genre*, London: BFI.

Anant, Victor (1955), 'The "Give-Away" Shows – Who is Really Paying?', *Picture Post*, 10 December, p. 27.

Anderson, Kent (1978), *Television Fraud: The History and Implications of the Quiz Show Scandals*, Connecticut: Greenwood Press.

Ang, Ien (1991), *Desperately Seeking the Audience*, London: Routledge.

Awan, Fatimah (2007), [contributor to 'Asians in the media' forum, http://www.asiansinmedia.org/] personal email correspondence with author.

Bakhtin, Mikhail (1993 [1941]), *Rabelais and His World*, trans. Hélène Iswolsky, Bloomington: Indiana University Press.

Barber, Lynn (2000), 'The Successful Format', *The Observer*, 2 April, p. 33.

Baudrillard, Jean (1994), *Simulacra and Simulation*, trans. Sheila Faria Glaser, Ann Arbor: University of Michigan Press.

Baudrillard, Jean (2002), 'L'espirit du terrorisme', trans. Donovan Hohn, *Harper's*, 18 February, pp. 13–18.

Beale, Mike (2006), [deputy managing director of 12yard Productions] telephone interview with author, 27 November.

Bell, Philip and Theo Van Leuwen (1994), *The Media Interview: Confession, Contest and Conversation*, Sydney: New South Wales Press.

Bell, Geraldine (2004), 'Fiction: Very Ordinary People', *The Observer*, 28 March, p. 15.

Bennett, Tony (1980), 'Popular Culture: A Teaching Object', *Screen Education* 34, Spring, pp. 17–30.

Bennett, Tony (1985), 'Texts in History: The Determinations of Readings and Their Texts', *Journal of Midwest Modern Language Association* 18 (1): 1–16.

Bird, S. Elizabeth (2003), *The Audience in Everyday Life: Living in a Media World*, London: Routledge.

Boddy, William (1990), *Fifties Television: The Industry and Its Critics*, Urbana: University of Illinois Press.

Boddy, William (2001), 'Quiz Shows', in Glen Creeber (ed.), *The Television Genre Book*, London: BFI, pp. 79–81.

Bodycombe, David (2003), *How to Devise a Game Show*, found at http://www.ukgameshows.com/prizepound/gameshowbook/GameShowTrial.pdf [accessed 16 June 2007].

Bonner, Frances (2003), *Ordinary Television*, London: Sage.

Bourdieu, Pierre (1977), *Outline of a Theory of Practice*, Cambridge: Cambridge University Press.

Bourdieu, Pierre (1984), *Distinction: A Social Critique of the Judgment of Taste*, London: Routledge.

Bourdon, Jerome (2004), 'Old and New Ghosts: Public Service Television and the Popular – a History', *European Journal of Cultural Studies* 7 (3): 283–304.

Bratich, Jack Z. (2007), 'Programming Reality: Control Societies, New Subjects and the Powers of Transformation', in Dana Heller (ed.), *Make-over Television: Realities Remodelled*, London: I.B. Tauris, pp. 6–22.

Brayfield, Celia (1976), 'Secrets of the Master Race', *Evening Standard*, 26 October (BBC press cuttings on *Mastermind*).

Brooker, Will (2004), 'Living on Dawson's Creek', in Robert Allen and Annette Hill (eds), *The Television Studies Reader*, pp. 569–81.

Brownlow, Sheila, Rebecca Whitener and Janet M. Rupert (1998), 'I'll Take Gender Differences for $1,000!: Domain-Specific Intellectual Success on "Jeopardy" ', *Sex Roles* 38 (3–4): 269–85.

Brunner, Rob (1999a), 'Let the Games Begin', *Entertainment Weekly*, 15 October, found at http://www.ew.com/ew/article/0,272183,00.html [accessed 18 March 2007].

Brunner, Rob (1999b), 'The Con Game', *Entertainment Weekly*, 29 October 1999, found at http://www.ew.com/ew/article/0,271317,00.html [accessed 18 March 2007].

Brunsdon, Charlotte (2003), 'Lifestyling Britain: The 8–9 Slot on British Television', *International Journal of Cultural Studies* 4 (1): 5–23.

Butler, Jeremy (2002), *Television: Critical Methods and Applications*, London: Lawrence Erlbaum.

Caillois, Roger (1961), *Man, Play and Games*, trans. Meyer Barash, New York: The Free Press.

Cannadine, David (1998), *Class in Britain*, London: Penguin.

Casey, Emma (2003), 'Gambling and Consumption: Working-class Women and UK National Lottery Play', *Journal of Consumer Culture* 3 (2): 245–63.

Cassidy, Marsha F. (2005), *What Women Watched: Daytime Television in the 1950s*, Austin: University of Texas Press.

Chaudhuri, Anita (1999), 'Women: Who Wants to be a Quiz Show Contestant?', *The Guardian*, 29 November, p. 6.

Clarke, Michael (1987), 'Quiz and Game Shows', in Michael Clarke, *Teaching Popular Television*, London: Methuen, pp. 49–61.

Cohn, Edward (2000), 'Are Men's Fingers Fastest?', *The American Prospect* 11 (11), 24 April, p. 12.

Collins, Andrew (2000), 'A Big Fix?', *The Observer*, 26 November, p. 12.

Conrad, Peter (1982), *Television: The Medium and its Manners*, London: Routledge & Kegan Paul.

Cooper-Chen, Anne (1994), *Games in the Global Village: A 50-Nation Study of Entertainment Television*, Ohio: Bowling Green State University Popular Press.

Corner, John (2003), 'Finding Data, Reading Patterns, Telling Stories: Issues in the Historiography of Television', *Media, Culture and Society* 25: 273–80.

Couldry, Nick (2000), *The Place of Media Power: Pilgrims and Witnesses of the Media Age*, London: Routledge.

Cowdery, Ron and Keith Selby (1995), *How to Study Television*, Basingstoke: Macmillan.

Creeber, Glen (2004), '*Who Wants to be a Millionaire?*', in Glen Creeber (ed.), *Fifty Key Television Programmes*, London: Arnold, pp. 232–6.

Crisell, Andrew (2001), *An Introductory History of British Broadcasting* (2nd edn), London: Routledge.

Cummings, Dolan (2002), 'Introduction', in Dolan Cummings (ed.), *Reality TV: How Real is Real?*, London: Hodder & Stoughton, pp. x–xvii.

Deery, June (2003), 'TV.com: Participatory Viewing on the Web', *Journal of Popular Culture* 27 (2): 161–83.

DeLong, Thomas A. (1991), *Quiz Craze: America's Infatuation with Game Shows*, New York: Praeger.

Derrida, Jacques (1992), 'The Law of the Genre', in Jacques Derrida, *Acts of Literature*, New York: Routledge, pp. 23–31.

Doherty, Thomas (2007), 'Quiz Show Scandals', found at www.museum.tv/archives/etv/Q/htmlQ/quizshowsca/quizshowsca.htm [accessed 16 June 2007].

Dovey, Jon and Helen W. Kennedy (2006), *Game Cultures: Computer Games as New Media*, Berkshire: Open University Press.

Driver, Stephen and Luke Martell (1999), 'New Labour: Culture and Economy', in Larry Ray and Andrew Sayer (eds), *Culture and Economy after the Cultural Turn*, London: Sage, pp. 246–69.

Du Gay, Paul (1996), *Consumption and Identity at Work*, London: Sage.

Dyer, Richard (1977), 'Entertainment and Utopia', *Movie* 24, Spring, pp. 2–13 (reprinted in *Only Entertainment* below).

Dyer, Richard (1986), *Heavenly Bodies: Film Stars and Society*, Basingstoke: Macmillan.

Dyer, Richard (1992), 'Entertainment and utopia', in Richard Dyer, *Only Entertainment*, London: Routledge, pp. 17–34.

Edwards, Timothy (2000), *Contradictions of Consumption: Concepts, Practices and Policies in Consumer Society*, Buckingham: Open University Press.

Ellis, John [1982] (1992), *Visible Fictions: Cinema, Television, Video* (2nd edn), London: Routledge.

Ellis, John (2000), *Seeing Things: Television in the Age of Uncertainty*, London: I. B. Tauris.

Ellis, John (2001), 'Mirror, Mirror', *Sight and Sound* 11 (7): 12.

Falk, Pasi and Colin Campbell (1997), 'Introduction', in Pasi Falk and Colin Campbell (eds), *The Shopping Experience*, London: Sage, pp. 1–13.

Ferguson, Euan (2000), 'One Foot in the Gravy', *The Observer*, 26 November, found at http://observer.guardian.co.uk/ [accessed 1 March 2001].

Feuer, Jane (1992), 'Genre Studies and Television', in Robert C. Allen (ed.), *Channels of Discourse: Reassembled*, Carolina: University of North Carolina Press, pp. 138–61.

Fiske, John (1987), *Television Culture*, London: Routledge.

Fiske, John (1990), 'Women and Quiz Shows: Consumerism, Patriarchy and Resisting Pleasures', in Mary Ellen Brown (ed.), *Television and Women's Culture: The Politics of the Popular*, London: Sage, pp. 131–43.

Fiske, John and John Hartley (1978), *Reading Television*, London: Methuen.

Foucault, Michel (1980), *Power/Knowledge: Selected Interviews and other Writings*, ed. and trans. Colin Gordon, Brighton: Harvester Press.

Foucault, Michel (1990), *The Will to Knowledge: The History of Sexuality*, vol. 1, London: Vintage.

Freedland, Jonathan (2006), 'What *The Apprentice* says about Blair's Britain: Only Profit Matters', *The Guardian*, 3 May, found at http://www.business. guardian.co.uk [accessed 5 May 2006].

Frow, John (1995), *Cultural Studies and Cultural Value*, Oxford: Oxford University Press.

Gamson, Joshua (2001), 'The Assembly Line of Greatness: Celebrity in Twentieth-Century America', in C. Lee Harrington and Denise D. Bielby (eds), *Popular Culture: Production and Consumption*, Oxford: Blackwell, pp. 259–82.

Giddens, Anthony (1991), *Modernity and Self-Identity*, Cambridge: Polity.

Goffman, Erving (1972), *The Presentation of the Self in Everyday Life*, London: Pelican.

Gramsci, Antonio (1998), 'Hegemony, Intellectuals, and the State', in John Storey (ed.), *Cultural Theory and Popular Culture*, Hemel Hempstead: Prentice Hall, pp. 206–19.

Greenstone, Danny (2006), [executive producer, Entertainment, Talkback Thames] telephone interview with author, 13 December.

Haralovich, Mary Beth and Michael W. Trossett (2004), ' "Expect the Unexpected": Narrative Pleasure and Uncertainty Due to Chance in *Survivor*', in Susan Murray and Laurie Ouellette (eds), *Reality TV: Re-making Television Culture*, New York: New York University Press, pp. 75–96.

Heller, Dana (ed.) (2007), *Make-over Television: Realities Remodelled*, London: I. B. Tauris.

Herring, S. (1996), 'Posting in a Different Voice: Gender and Ethics in Computer-mediated Communication', in C. Ess (ed.), *Philosophical Approaches to Computer-mediated Communication*, Albany: State University of New York Press, pp. 115–45.

Herzog, Herta (1940), 'Professor Quiz – A Gratification Study', in Paul F. Lazarsfeld (ed.), *Radio and the Printed Page*, New York: Duell, Sloan and Pearce, pp. 27–41.

Hestroni, Amir (2004), 'The Millionaire Project: A Cross-Cultural Analysis of Quiz Shows from the United States, Russia, Poland, Norway, Finland, Israel, and Saudi Arabia', *Mass Communication and Society* 7 (2): 133–56.

Hill, Amelia (2000), 'Why do we love quizzes?', *The Observer*, 5 November, p. 23.

Hill, Annette (2002), 'Big Brother: The real audience', *Television and New Media* 3 (3): 323–41.

Hill, Annette (2005), *Reality TV: Audiences and Popular Factual Television*, London: Routledge.

Hills, Matt (2002), *Fan Cultures*, London: Routledge.

Hills, Matt (2005), 'Who Wants to Be a Fan of *Who Wants to Be a Millionaire?*: Scholarly Television Criticism, "Popular Aesthetics" and Academic Tastes', in Catherine Johnson and Rob Turnock (eds), *ITV Cultures: Independent Television Over Fifty Years*, Berkshire: Open University Press, pp. 177–95.

Hoerschelmann, Olaf (2006), *Rules of the Game: Quiz Shows and American Culture*, New York: State University of New York Press.

Hofstadter, Richard [1963] (1974), *Anti-Intellectualism in American Life*, New York: Alfred Knopf.

Hoggart, Richard (1958), *The Uses of Literacy*, London: Penguin.

Holbrook, Morris. B (1993), *Daytime Television Gameshows and the Celebration of Merchandise*, New York: Bowling Green State Popular Press.

Holderman, Lisa (ed.) (2008), *Common Sense: Intelligence as Presented on Popular Television*, Lexington Books.

Holland, Patricia (1987), 'When a Woman Reads the News', in Gillian Dyer and Helen Baehr (eds), *Boxed in: Women and Television*, London: Pandora Press, pp. 121–37.

Holmes, Su (2004a), ' "All you've got to worry about is the task, having a cup of tea, and what you're going to eat for dinner": Approaching Celebrity in *Big Brother*', in Su Holmes and Deborah Jermyn (eds), *Understanding Reality Television*, London: Routledge, pp. 111–35.

Holmes, Su (2004b), 'But This Time *You* Choose!: Approaching the Interactive Audience of Reality TV', *International Journal of Cultural Studies* 7 (2): 213–31.

Holmes, Su (2005a), ' "It's a woman!": The Question of Gender in *Who Wants to be a Millionaire*', *Screen* 46 (2), Summer, pp. 155–73.

Holmes, Su (2005b), ' "Not the final answer" ': *Who Wants to be a Millionaire* and Revisiting Critical Approaches to the Quiz Show', *European Journal of Cultural Studies* 8 (4): 483–503.

Holmes, Su (2008), *Entertaining TV: The BBC and Popular Television Culture in the 1950s*, Manchester: Manchester University Press.

Hughes, Scott (1998), 'Will You Watch If the Price is Right?', *Independent*, 4 May, p. 12.

Huizinga, Johan [1938] (1970), *Homo Ludens: A Study of the Play Element in our Culture*, London: Temple Smith.

Humphrys, John (2006), 'Why Don't Women Ever Win *Mastermind*?', *The Daily Mail*, 6 December, found at www.dailymail.co.uk [accessed 19 June 2007].

Hutchinson, Colman (2006), [executive producer of *Who Wants to Be a Millionaire*, UK] telephone interview with author, 10 November.

Jacobs, A. J. (1996), 'Games People Play', *Entertainment Weekly*, found at http://www.ew.com/article/0,292650,00.00.html [accessed 18 March 2007].

Jenkins, Henry (1992), *Textual Poachers: Television Fans and Participatory Culture*, New York: Routledge.

Jhally, Sut (1990), *The Codes of Advertising*, London: Routledge.

Jones, Janet (2004), 'Emerging Platform Identities: Big Brother UK and Interactive Multi-platform Usage', in Ernest Mathijs and Janet Jones (eds), *Big Brother International: Formats, Critics and Publics*, London: Wallflower, pp. 210–31.

Kavanagh, Dennis (1987), *Thatcherism and British Politics*, Oxford: Oxford University Press.

Kellner, Douglas (1992), 'Popular Culture and the Construction of Postmodern Identities', in Scott Lash and Jonathan Friedman (eds), *Modernity and Identity*, Oxford: Blackwell, pp. 141–77.

Kiousis, Spiro (2002), 'Interactivity: A Concept Explication', *New Media and Society* 4 (3): 17–32.

Lacey, Nick (2000), *Narrative and Genre: Key Concepts in Media Studies*, Basingstoke: Macmillan.

Lewis, Bill (1984), 'TV Games: People as Performers', in Len Masterman (ed.), *Television Mythologies*, London: Comedia, pp. 42–6.

Logan, Brian (2001), 'How I Made a Million', 24 April, found at http://www.MediaGuardian.co.uk [accessed 16 June 2007].

Lury, Karen (1995), 'Television Performance: Being, Acting and "Corpsing"', *New Formations* 26: 114–27.

Lury, Karen (2005), *Interpreting Television*, London: Arnold.

Lusted, David (1998), 'The Popular Culture Debate and Light Entertainment on Television', in Christine Geraghty and David Lusted (eds), *The Television Studies Book*, London: Arnold, pp. 175–97.

McCracken, Allison (2003), 'Audiences and the Internet', in Michele Hilmes (ed.), *The Television History Book*, London: BFI, pp. 137–40.

Macdonald, Myra (2003), *Exploring Media Discourse*, London: Arnold.

McGregor, Tom (1999), *Behind the Scenes on Who Wants to be a Millionaire*, Basingstoke: Boxtree.

McGuigan, Jim (1992), *Cultural Populism*, London: Routledge.

McQuail, Denis, Jay G. Blumler and J. R. Brown (1972), 'The Television Audience: A Revised Perspective', in Denis McQuail (ed.), *Sociology of Mass Communications*, Middlesex: Penguin, pp. 135–65.

Mahoney, Bridget (2000), 'A Million Dollars? Yes, Please!', *Observer* on-line, 10 March, found at http://www.nd.edu/~observer/03102000/Scene/0.html [accessed 18 March 2007].

Marshall, P. David (2004), *New Media Cultures*, London: Arnold.

Marx, Karl (1967), *Das Kapital*, London: Penguin.

Marx, Karl and Frederick Engels (1968), *The German Ideology*, trans. S. Ryazanskayal, Moscow: Progress Publishing.

Metham, Wesley (2006), 'Games of Sociality and Their Soft Seduction', in David Escoffrey (ed.), *Essays on Truth and Representation: How Real is Reality TV?*, North Carolina: McFarland and Company, pp. 231–41.

Mills, Adam and Phil Rice (1982), 'Quizzing the Popular', *Screen Education* 41, Winter/Spring, pp. 15–25.

Mills, Sara (2003), *Gender and Politeness*, Cambridge: Cambridge University Press.

Missen, James (2001), 'Who Wants Us to Be Millionaires?': The Culture of Trivial Intellect in the Contemporary Game Show', in Murray Pomerance and John Sakeris (eds), *Closely Watched Brains*, Boston: Pearson Education, pp. 143–52.

Mittell, Jason (2002), 'Before the Scandals: The Radio Precedents of the Quiz Show Genre', in Michele Hilmes and Jason Loviglio (eds), *Radio Reader: Essays in the Cultural History of Radio*, London: Routledge, pp. 319–42.

Mittell, Jason (2003), 'Quiz and Audience Participation Programs', in Christopher Sterling and Michael Keith (eds), *The Encyclopaedia of Radio*, New York: Fitzroy Dearborn, pp. 34–6.

Mittell, Jason (2004a), *Television and Genre: From Cop Shows to Cartoons*, London: Routledge.

Mittell, Jason (2004b), 'A Cultural Approach to Television Genre Theory', in Robert C. Allen and Annette Hill (eds), *The Television Studies Reader*, London: Routledge, pp. 171–81.

Mittell, Jason (2007), personal correspondence with author.

Moran, Albert (1998), *Copycat TV: Globalisation, Program Formats and Cultural Identity*, Luton: University of Luton Press.

Moran, Albert and Justin Malbon (2006), *Understanding The Global TV Format*, Bristol: Intellect.

Morreale, Joanne (2007), '*Faking It* and the Transformation of Identity', in Dana Heller (ed.), *Make-over Television: Realities Remodelled*, London: I. B. Tauris, pp. 95–6.

Neale, Steve (1990), 'Questions of Genre', *Screen* 31 (1): 45–66.

Neale, Steve (2001), 'Genre and Television', in Glen Creeber (ed.), *The Television Genre Book*, London: BFI, pp. 3–4.

Nightingale, Virginia (1996), *Studying Audiences: The Shock of the Real*, London: Routledge.

Pfeffer, Wendy (1989), 'Intellectuals Are More Popular in France: The Case of French and American Game Shows', in Roger B. Rollin (ed.), *The Americanization of the Global Village*, Ohio: Bowling Green State University Popular Press, pp. 24–32.

Pilkington Report (1962), *Report of the Committee on Broadcasting, 1960*, Cmnd paper, 1753, London: HMSO.

Piper, Helen (2004), 'Reality TV, *Wife Swap* and the Drama of Banality', *Screen* 45 (4), Winter, pp. 273–86.

Pullen, Kirsten (2000), 'I-Love-Xena.Com: Creating Online Fan Communities', in David Gauntlett (ed.), *Web.Studies: Rewiring Media Studies for the Digital Age*, London: Arnold, pp. 52–63.

Ransome, Paul (2005), *Work, Consumption and Culture: Affluence and Social Change in the Twenty-first Century*, London: Sage.

Redden, Guy (2007), 'Makeover Morality and Consumer Culture', in Dana Heller (ed.), *Make-over Television: Realities Remodelled*, London: I. B. Tauris, pp. 150–64.

Rice, Lynette and Dan Snierson (2001), 'On the Air', *Entertainment Weekly*, 25 May, found at http://www.ew.com/ew/article/0,256487,00.html [accessed 18 March 2007].

Rice-Oxley, Mark (2005), 'Britain Faces "the Enemy Within" ', *The Christian Science Monitor*, 14 July, found at http://www.csmonitor.com/2005/0714/p06s02-woeu.html [accessed 2 July 2007].

Robins, Jane (2000), 'Quiz Shows: Naff Old Men in Sparkly Jackets?', *Independent*, 3 November, p. 23.

Robinson, Anne (2001), *Memoirs of an Unfit Mother*, London: Simon & Schuster Inc.

Root, Jane (1986), *Open the Box: About Television*, London: Comedia.

Scannell, Paddy (1990), 'Public Service Broadcasting: the History of a Concept', in Andrew Goodwin and Garry Whannel (eds), *Understanding Television*, London: Routledge, pp. 11–29.

Scannell, Paddy (1991), 'Introduction: The Relevance of Talk', in Scannell (ed.), *Broadcast Talk*, London: Sage, pp. 1–13.

Scannell, Paddy (1996), *Radio, Television and Modern Life: A Phenomenological Approach*, Oxford: Blackwell.

Sendall, Bernard (1982), *Independent Television in Britain: Origin and Foundation: 1946–62*, London: Macmillan.

Skeggs, Beverley (2003), *Class, Self, Culture*, London: Routledge.

Skovmand, Michael (2000), 'Barbarous TV: Syndicated Wheels of Fortune', in Horace Newcomb (ed.), *Television: The Critical View* (6th edn), Oxford: Oxford University Press, pp. 367–82.

Steemers, Jeanette (2004), *Selling Television: British Television in the Global Marketplace*, London: BFI.

Storey, John (1999), *Cultural Consumption and Everyday Life*, London: Arnold.

Storey, John (2001), *Cultural Theory and Popular Culture: An Introduction* (3rd edn), London: Prentice Hall.

Sutcliffe, Thomas (2000), 'Welcome to Planet Quiz', *The Independent* 28 December, found at findarticles.com/p/articles/mi_qn4158/is_20001228/ai_n14347772 [accessed 16 June 2007].

Taylor, Celia (2007), [deputy controller of Challenge TV] telephone interview with author, 14 January.

Teurlings, Jan (2001), 'Producing the Ordinary: Institutions, Discourses and Practices in Love Game Shows', *Continuum: Journal of Media & Cultural Studies* 15 (2): 249–63.

Thynne, Jane (2000), 'The Appetite for Quizzes', *Independent*, 18 July 2000, p. 22.

Tucker, Ken (2001), 'The Strong Survive', *Entertainment Weekly*, 20 April, found at http://www.ew.com/ew/article/0,106574,00.html [accessed 10 June 2007].

Tulloch, John (1976), 'Gradgrind's Heirs: the Presentation of "Knowledge" in British Quiz Shows', *Screen Education* Summer, pp. 3–13.

Turner, Graeme (1996), *British Cultural Studies: An Introduction*, London: Routledge.

Turner, Graeme (2001a), 'The Uses and Limitations of Genre', in Glen Creeber (ed.), *The Television Genre Book*, London: BFI, pp. 4–5.

Turner, Graeme (2001b), 'Genre, Format and "Live" Television', in Glen Creeber (ed.), *The Television Genre Book*, London: BFI, pp. 6–8.

Venanzi, Katie (1997), 'An Examination of Television Quiz Show Scandals of the 1950s', found at http://www.honors.umd.edu/HONR269J/projects/venanzi.html [accessed 16 June 2007].

Waisbord, Silvio (2004), 'McTV: Understanding the Global Popularity of Television Formats', *Television and New Media* 5 (4): 359–83.

Walker, Cynthia. W and Amy H. Sturgis (2008), 'Sexy Nerds: Illya Kuryakin, Mr Spock, and the Image of the Cerebral Hero in Television Drama', in Lisa Holderman (ed.), *Common Sense: Intelligence as Presented on Popular Television*, Lexington Books.

Wayne, Mike (2000), 'Who Wants To Be a Millionaire?: Contextual Analysis and the Endgame of Public Service Television', in Dan Fleming (ed.), *Formations: A 21st Century Media Studies Textbook*, Manchester: Manchester University Press, pp. 196–216.

Whannel, Garry (1992), 'The Price is Right but the Moments are Sticky: Television, Quiz and Games Shows and Popular Culture', in Dominic Strinati and Stephen Wagg (eds), *Come On Down: Popular Culture in Post-War Britain*, London: Routledge, pp. 179–201.

Index

ABC Spelling Bee, 39
Adams, Kay, 88
Adams, Matthew, 105, 106, 107
Amazing Race, The, 24, 25
American quiz shows
  comparison with the British
    context, 43, 44, 50–1, 55, 96,
    163; *see also* BBC
  early development of quiz, 36, 42
  quiz show 'scandals', 46–51
  see also scandal, American quiz shows
America's Next Top Model, 133
Anderson, Kent, 48, 49, 95, 97, 126,
  132
Ang, Ien, 142
Anti-intellectualism, 95–9, 152; *see*
  also knowledge
Apprentice, The, 14, 25, 27, 28, 96, 120
Are You Smarter than a Fifth Grader?,
  55, 65, 92, 96, 147
Are You Smarter than a Ten Year Old?, 55
Ask Me Another, 40, 41
Ask the Family, 51
Audience, and the quiz show,
  140–61; *see also* fandom
Awan, Fatimah, 138

Bachelor, The, 133
Bakhtin, Mikhail, 77
Barber, Lynne, 131
Barker, Bob, 91
Baudrillard, 63, 113
Beale, Mike, 4, 73, 89, 123, 124, 137
Beat the Clock, 44

Beg, Borrow or Steal, 111, 128
Bell, Geraldine, 118
Bell, Philip, 87
Bennett, Tony, 60, 84, 155
Big Brother, 1, 4, 14, 18, 21, 25, 27,
  28, 29, 88, 110, 115, 120, 133
Big Call, The, 32, 130
Big Surprise, The, 46
Biggest Game in Town, The, 32
Black, Cilla, 88
Blankety Blank, 24, 41, 68, 95, 130
Blind Date, 14
'Bluffing', in the quiz show, 114–15
Blumler, Jay, 151
Boddy, William, 33, 46, 49, 70, 126,
  163
Bodycombe, David J., 14, 74
Bonner, Frances, 23, 62, 68, 72, 84,
  94, 116, 124
Bourdieu, Pierre, 102, 106
Bourdon, Jerome, 52, 110
Brains Trust, The, 39, 43
Brainteaser, 12, 88, 154
Bratich, Jack Z., 26, 82, 115, 163
British Broadcasting Corporation
  (BBC), 31
  'ban' on prizes, 38; *see also* prizes
  BBC Worldwide, 19
  early origins of quiz show in radio
    and television, 36–43
  early comparison with ITV, 44
  perception of American quiz/game
    shows, 41–2
  public service, 35, 52

Brooker, Will, 148
Brown, J. R., 151
Brownlow, Sheila, 133, 134
Brunsdon, Charlotte, 132
Bullseye, 24
Butler, Jeremy, 5

Caillois, Roger, 16, 58, 76, 84,
    108–9, 110, 112, 116
'Call TV Quiz' services, 25, 53–4,
    88, 108, 146, 154–5
Cameron, Rhona, 88
Campbell, Colin, 104
Card Sharks, 33
Carter, Gary, 120
Cash Cab, 12, 13, 21, 77, 81–2
Celebrities, on quiz shows, 129–31
Celebrity Big Brother, 131
Celebrity Squares, 130
Chair, The, 32, 66–7, 71, 73, 124, 127
Challenge TV, 4, 23–4, 143, 147
Chamber, The, 66
Changing Rooms, 4
Channel Four, 52, 53
Charlie Chester Show, The, 40, 41–2, 45
Chaudhuri, Anita, 132, 134
'Cheating', on quiz shows, 111
Chester, Charlie, 41
Clarke, Michael, 121, 153, 157
Clary, Julian, 136
Cohn, Edward, 132
Cold War, the, 95, 98
Collins, Andrew, 100
Come and Have a Go…, 136
Communism, 97–8
Competition, ideologies of, 93–4
Conrad, Peter, 126
Consumerism, and the quiz show,
    45, 76–81, 94–5, 98, 103–5, 106,
    135
Contestants, 118–39, 154–9; *see also*
    'ordinary' people
Cooper-Chen, Anne, 5, 7, 51, 126,
    139, 155
Corner, John, 163
Couldry, Nick, 119, 156

Countdown, 62, 89
Cowan, Louis G., 46
Cowdery, Ron, 33
Creeber, Glen, 6, 67, 68, 69
Crowther, Leslie, 80
Crystal Maze, The, 14, 24, 52
Cultural capital, 102–4; *see also*
    Bourdieu
Cultural value and the quiz/game
    show, 4, 162
    and aesthetics, 72–5
    in the television industry, 4
Cummings, Dolan, 120

Deal or no Deal, 14, 16, 55, 109, 127,
    145
Deery, June, 145
DeLong, Thomas, 34, 49, 130, 137
Dennis, Les, 70
Derrida, Jacques, 13
Dickson, Chris M., 74
Dirty Rotten Cheater, 74, 111, 112
Dr I.Q., 42
Dog Eat Dog, 19
Doherty, Thomas, 48, 99
Don't Call Me Stupid, 29–30
Don't Try This at Home, 23
Dotto, 46, 125
Double Your Money, 18, 44, 45, 122,
    132, 137
Dovey, Jon, 77, 80, 109, 117, 141,
    144, 163
Driver, Stephen, 94, 100
Dyer, Richard, 77, 79, 80–2, 84, 115

Edwards, Tim, 60, 104
Eggheads, 70, 73
Ellis, John, 51, 110
Enemy Within, The, 32, 66, 111–13,
    123
Engels, Frederic, 59
Enright, Dan, 47
Ethnicity, and the quiz show, 113,
    132, 137–8; *see also* hosts;
    'ordinary' people
Every Second Counts, 62

Falk, Pasi, 104
Family Feud, 33, 92, 145, 147
Family Fortunes, 15, 16, 24, 69, 70, 92, 95, 104, 133, 147
Fandom
  and gender, 150
  on-line fandom (quiz show), 147–61
  and 'poaching', 148–9; *see also* Jenkins
  stereotypes of fandom, 148
Fear Factor, 24, 25
Federal Communications Commission (FCC), regulation of quiz/game show, 37, 108
Ferguson, Euan, 101–2
Feuer, Jane, 13
Fifteen-to-One, 18, 65, 70
Fiske, John, 15, 61, 62, 63, 65, 70, 71, 78, 92–3, 94, 95, 97, 99, 107, 115, 142, 146, 151
For the Rest of Your Life, 18, 109
Formats, 16–22
  adaptation of, 20, 164–5
  definition of, 17
  economic value for broadcasters, 19
  European trade in, 21
  'glocalization', 20
  relationship with genre, 17–18
Forsyth, Bruce, 70, 91, 147
Foucault, Michel, 86
Fowler, Daphne, 134
Foxworthy, Jeff, 65
Francis, Arlene, 88
Freedland, Jonathan, 100
French quiz shows, 96
Friends Like These, 19
Frow, John, 106

Game show, difference from quiz show, 14–16, 23
Game space, analysis of, 63–70; *see also* set design
Games, The, 27
Gameshow Marathon, The, 130

Gamson, Joshua, 131
Gascoigne, Bamber, 71
Gay identity, and the quiz show, 135–6
Gender in the quiz show, 116
  competition and gender, 131–5, 153
  host, 87–91; *see also* host
  intelligence and gender, 89
  sexuality, 89–91, 134
Generation Game, The, 51, 52, 162
Genre, 11, 12
  and the quiz/game show, 11–16
  discursive approaches to, 22–6
  see also Mittell
Giddens, Anthony, 103–4
Glitterball, 53, 146, 155
Goffman, Erving, 122, 135
Golden Balls, 109, 114
Golden Shot, The, 68, 130
Goodman, Mark, 24
Gramsci, Antonio, 60
Greed, 153, 154
Greed, 32
Greene, Hughie, 44, 122, 132
Greenstone, Danny, 4, 16, 73, 123, 131
Grindstaff, Laura, 2, 86, 128
Grisewood, Freddie, 39
GSN: The Network for Games, 23–4
Guru-Murthy, Krishan, 90

Haralovich, Mary Beth, 26, 27, 47, 121
Hartley, John, 70, 71
Have a Go!, 39–40, 41, 52
Herzog, Herta, 151
Hestroni, Amir, 101, 164
Hill, Amelia, 92
Hill, Annette, 115, 138
Hills, Matt, 53, 60, 74, 151, 155, 159, 160
Hobley, MacDonald, 40
Hoerschelmann, Olaf, 13, 15, 28, 36, 39, 50, 61–2, 95, 98, 142

Hofstadter, Richard, 95–6, 97
Holbrook, Morris B., 3, 104
Holderman, Lisa, 92, 96
Holland, Patricia, 89
Holmes, Eamon, 128–9
Holmes, Su, 45, 50, 72, 105, 115,
      124, 135, 147
Hosts
   ethnicity of, 91
   gender of, 87–91
   role of, 70–1
   sexuality of, 136
Huizinga, Johan, 8, 58, 62, 63, 75–6,
      80, 83, 112, 147
Humphrys, John, 90, 133
Hutchinson, Colman, 4, 22, 69, 88,
      90, 119, 150, 158

I'm a Celebrity… Get Me Out of Here!,
      4, 131
In it to Win it, 158
Independent Committee for the
   Supervision of Standards of
   Telephone Information Services
   (ICTSTIS), 25
Independent Television (ITV)
   and 'Americanisation', 44
   early involvement with the
   quiz/game show, 44–6
Independent Broadcasting
   Authority (IBA), 52
Independent Television Authority
   (ITA), 50
Independent Television
   Commission (ITC), 52
ITV Play, 25, 53
   see also Call TV Quiz services
Information Please!, 39; *see also The*
   Brains Trust
Ingram, Major Charles, 112
Intelligence, stereotypes of, 151; *see*
   also gender
Interactivity, 143–7
Internet
   impact on fan research, 140–1
   quiz games on-line, 144–7

Inter-regional Spelling Competition, 39
It's a Knockout, 52

Jenkins, Henry, 148, 149
Jeopardy!, 5, 14, 32, 145, 147
Jhally, Sut, 137
Jones, Janet, 143

Kaleidoscope, 40
Kavanagh, Dennis, 94
Kellner, Douglas, 114
Kennedy, Helen W., 77, 80, 109,
      117, 141, 144, 163
Keppel, Judith, 32, 100, 101–2, 106,
      153
Kiousis, Spiro, 144
Know Your Partner, 40
Knowledge
   categories of, 15, 92–3; *see also*
      Fiske
   class and knowledge, 93–4, 153
   gender and knowledge, 78
   in the quiz/game show, 15, 86–117
Krypton Factor, The, 21

Lacey, Nick, 11, 12
Levi-Strauss, Claude, 93
Lewis, Bill, 3, 71
Lighting, 68–9
Liveness, and the quiz show, 62, 70
Logan, Brian, 100
Lovell, Alex, 88
Ludology, 58, 75–7; *see also*
   Huizinga; Caillois
Lury, Karen, 63, 68–9, 124, 125
Lusted, David, 3
Lythgoe, Nigel, 66, 112, 113

McCall, Davina, 88
McCarthyism, 97, 112
McCracken, Allison, 148, 159
Macdonald, Myra, 12, 86, 122, 127, 138
McEnroe, John, 66, 71, 127
McGregor, Tom, 67, 68, 126
McQuail, Denis, 151
Mahoney, Bridget, 109

Magnusson, Magnus, 65, 71, 91
Marr, Andrew, 94
Marshall, P. David, 143
Martell, Luke, 94, 100
Martindale, Wink, 91
Marx, Karl, 59, 81
Marxism, 59–62, 84, 103, 104, 107
Mastermind, 16, 18, 23, 29, 41, 52,
    58, 63–4, 68, 71, 79, 80, 92, 93,
    100, 123, 130, 132, 142, 145,
    147, 152, 159
Miles, Michael, 44
Mills, Adam, 5, 60
Mills, Sara, 90
Mint, The, 53, 146
Missen, James, 60
Mr and Mrs, 92
Mittell, Jason, 4, 6, 7, 22–3, 25, 35,
    37, 42, 43, 155, 162, 163
Mobile phone games, 143
Mole, The, 111
Monkhouse, Bob, 91
Moran, Albert, 17, 18, 20, 164
Morreale, Joanne, 103–4
Murnaghan, Dermot, 90

National Lottery Jet Set, The, 128
Neale, Steve, 11–12, 30
Newlywed Game, The, 92
Nightingale, Virginia, 147
No Win, No Fee, 32

1 vs 100, 68
Only Fools and Horses, 86
'Ordinary' people as television
    performers, 118–39, 163
    'authenticity' of, 124–7, 154–9
    ethnicity of, 132, 137–8
    'media/ ordinary' hierarchy,
        118–21, 156; see also Couldry
    female contestants, 131–3; see also
        gender

Parker, Ian, 118
Parsons, Nicholas, 87
Paxman, Jeremy, 71

Payday, 82–3, 103
People are Funny, 26, 45
People Versus, The, 88
People's Quiz, The, 28, 29, 30
Pfeffer, Wendy, 96
Philbin, Regis, 72, 88, 132
Pickles, Wilfred, 40, 52
Pierman, Rachel, 88
Pilkington Committee, The, 35
    attitude toward quiz/ game shows
        and ITV, 35, 108
Pimental, Nancy, 88
Play, 5, 16
    theories of, 75–83
    see also ludology
Play Your Cards Right, 24, 33, 95, 130
Pokerface, 21, 114, 116, 123, 128
Pop Idol, 21, 29, 120
Pop the Question, 39
Popstars, 21
Pot O' Gold, 37
Price is Right, The, 3, 4, 5, 9, 15, 16,
    32, 36, 50, 51, 66, 68, 69, 73,
    77–8, 88, 92, 94–5, 104, 123,
    124, 126, 130, 145–6, 147, 162
Prizes on quiz shows
    decline of commodities as prizes,
        104–5, 120
    early regulation of prizes the BBC,
        40–2, 45; see also BBC, 'ban' on
        prizes
    regulation by ITA, 50: IBA, 52; see
        also ITV
'Professional' quizzers, 150, 158
Professor Quiz, 42
Pullen, Kristen, 148
Puzzle Corner, 39, 40

Queen for a Day, 26
Quiz, origins of word, 34
Quizmania, 146
Quizzing.co.uk, 140, 147, 149, 150,
    151–2, 154, 156, 158

Ransome, Paul, 104, 106, 107, 115,
    116

Raworth, Sophie, 90
Reality TV
  comparison with quiz show,
    25–30, 115, 118, 120, 131, 157,
    153
  game structures in, 4
  'gamedocs', 25, 27
Rice, Phil, 5, 60
Rice-Oxley, Mark, 113
Rippon, Angela, 90
Robinson, Anne, 70, 88, 90, 91,
    127–8, 147
Robson, Miles, 106–7
Root, Jane, 119, 125, 138
Round Britain Quiz, 39, 43
Rupert, Janet M., 133, 134
Russian Roulette, 88

Sajak, Pat, 91, 147
Sale of the Century, 51, 59, 68, 69, 87,
    104, 105, 129
Scandal, American quiz shows,
    46–51, 126, 163
Scannell, Paddy, 35, 70, 128
Scott, Tom, 157
Selby, Keith, 33
Set design, 63–70, 72–5
Shafted, 68
Shattered, 4
Shopping Spree, 50
$64,000 Challenge, The, 130
$64,000 Question, The, 45, 46, 47, 95,
    97, 98, 132
64,000 Question, The, 45, 137
Skeggs, Bev, 106
Skovmand, Michael, 5, 58, 162, 164
Spelling Bee, 39
Steemers, Jeanette, 110
Stempel, Herbert, 47–8, 126
Stewart, William G., 29, 65
Sticky Moments with Julian Clary,
    136
Storey, John, 102
Strike it Lucky, 123
Strike it Rich, 26
Sturgis, Amy H., 134

*Sunday Night at the London
    Palladium*, 44
Supermarket, Sweep, 12, 36, 50,
    76–80, 92, 123, 145
Survivor, 14, 25
Sutcliffe, Thomas, 67, 68
Sykes, Melanie, 88
Syndicate, The, 32

Take it or Leave it, 46
Take Your Pick, 44, 45
Talkback Thames, 4
Tarrant, Chris, 70, 71, 72, 91, 101,
    106–7, 135, 136
Taylor, Celia, 4, 24
Terrorism, 112–13
Teurlings, Jan, 118, 121–2, 123, 126,
    129, 156, 158, 163
Thatcher, Margaret, 94, 95
Thatcherism, 94–5, 98
  and *The Price is Right*, 94–5
Theakston, Jamie, 29, 111
3–2–1, 21
Thynne, Jane, 32, 68, 100
Tic Tac Dough, 46
Time, in the quiz show, 62–3
To Buy or Not to Buy, 4
Todson, Bill, 24
Top of the Form, 39, 40, 43
Traitor, 111
Transatlantic Quiz, 39
Trinder, Tommy, 44
Trebek, Alex, 91
Trossett, Derek, 26, 27, 47, 121
Tucker, Ken, 90, 96
Tulloch, John, 59, 91
Turner, Graeme, 14, 17, 21, 22, 60,
    94
12 Yard Productions, 4, 89, 111, 124
Twenty-One, 32, 45, 46, 47–8, 95, 98,
    99, 126, 132
24 Hour Quiz, 28, 29, 30

UKGameshows.com, 24, 25, 74–5,
    111, 147
Unanimous, 27

Uncle Jim's Question Bee, 39
University Challenge, 41, 52, 70, 71, 74–5, 92, 100, 147, 152

Van Doren, Charles, 48, 98
Van Leuwen, Theo, 87
Vault, The, 32, 88
Venanzi, Katie, 47
Vieira, Meredith, 88, 90, 129
Vorderman, Carol, 89
Vox Pop, 39

Waisbord, Silvio, 20, 164
Waiting Game, The, 62, 88
Waldman, Ronald, 41
Walker, Cynthia W., 134
Walmsley, Andy, 67
Wax, Ruby, 88
Wayne, Mike, 33, 52–3, 60, 135
Weakest Link, The, 15, 18, 19, 21, 32, 52, 65, 68, 69, 70, 71, 82, 88, 96, 109–11, 116, 120, 127, 128, 130, 143, 145, 147
Whannel, Gary, 35, 65, 91, 95, 96, 98, 108, 122, 137, 138
What Do You Know?, 39, 41, 140
What's My Line?, 40
Wheel of Fortune, 5, 14, 32, 69, 88, 92, 108, 145, 153
White, Vanna, 147
Whitener, Rebecca, 133, 134

Wife Swap, 29, 120, 133
Wikipedia, 14, 15
Win Ben Stein's Money, 88
Win My Wage, 82–3
Winning Lines, 32
Winton, Dale, 79, 123
Who Wants to be a Millionaire, 4, 5, 6, 12, 16, 18, 20, 22, 24, 32, 33, 34, 52, 55, 63, 71, 81, 86, 88, 105, 108, 109, 111, 120, 121, 126–7, 130, 142, 147, 150, 152, 154, 163
  American version of, 33, 72, 129, 132, 145
  celebrity version, 130–1
  class and knowledge in, 99–102
  ethnic imbalance on (contestants), 132, 137
  gender on, 131–3, 135, 136–7
  international adaptation of, 20, 21, 101
  lighting in, 69
  PC game of, 143
  set design, 67–70, 73
Work, and the quiz/game show, 77, 83, 84, 106–8, 116
Wright, Bill, 63

X-Factor, The, 16, 29

Youtube, 129, 152, 153